CONTENTS

Printed in England by
G. Beard & Son
Brighton

ACKNOWLEDGEMENT

My thanks are due to General Motors Ltd for their unstinted co-operation and also for supplying data and illustrations.

I am also grateful to a considerable number of owners who have discussed their cars at length and many of whose suggestions have been included in this manual.

Ditchling
Kenneth Ball G I Mech E
Associate Member Guild of Motoring Writers

OPEL KADETT 1962–70 AUTOBOOK

Workshop Manual for all models of the Opel
Kadett, 993 cc, Kadett 'B', 1078 cc, with alternative
1492 cc, and 1897 cc engines, including
automatic transmission 1962–70

by

Kenneth Ball

G I Mech E

and the

Autopress team of Technical Writers

AUTOPRESS LTD

BENNETT ROAD BRIGHTON BN2 5JG ENGLAND

ISBN 0 85147 173 0

Books by the same author:

1100 MK 1 1962–67 AUTOBOOK
1100 MK 2, 1300, AMERICA 1968–69 AUTOBOOK
1800 AUTOBOOK
AUSTIN A30, A35, A40 AUTOBOOK
AUSTIN HEALEY 100/6, 3000 1956–68 AUTOBOOK
AUSTIN MAXI 1969 AUTOBOOK
BMC AUTOBOOK THREE
BMC AUTOBOOK FOUR
FIAT 500 1957–69 AUTOBOOK
FIAT 600, 600D 1955–69 AUTOBOOK
FIAT 850 1964–69 AUTOBOOK
FORD ANGLIA PREFECT 100E AUTOBOOK
FORD CAPRI 1968–69 AUTOBOOK
FORD CONSUL, ZEPHYR, ZODIAC 1, 2 1950–62 AUTOBOOK
FORD ESCORT 1967–69 AUTOBOOK
FORD ZEPHYR, ZODIAC MK 3 1962–66 AUTOBOOK
FORD ZEPHYR V4, V6 ZODIAC 1966–69 AUTOBOOK
HILLMAN MINX 1 to 5 1956–65 AUTOBOOK
HILLMAN MINX 1965–67 AUTOBOOK
HILLMAN SUPER MINX 1, 2, 3 1961–65 AUTOBOOK
JAGUAR XK120, 140, 150 MK 7, 8, 9 1948–61 AUTOBOOK
JAGUAR 2.4, 3.4, 3.8 MK 1, 2 1955–67 AUTOBOOK
MG TA–TF 1936–55 AUTOBOOK
MGA, MGB 1955–69 AUTOBOOK
MINI 1959–70 AUTOBOOK
MINI COOPER 1961–70 AUTOBOOK
MORRIS MINOR 1952–69 AUTOBOOK
RENAULT R8, R10, 1100 1962–69 AUTOBOOK
ROVER 60–110 1953–64 AUTOBOOK
ROVER 2000 1963–69 AUTOBOOK
ROVER 3 LITRE 1958–67 AUTOBOOK
SPRITE, MIDGET AUTOBOOK
SUNBEAM RAPIER ALPINE 1959–65 AUTOBOOK
TRIUMPH TR2, TR3, TR3A 1952–62 AUTOBOOK
TRIUMPH TR4, TR4A 1961–67 AUTOBOOK
VAUXHALL VELOX CRESTA 1957–69 AUTOBOOK
VAUXHALL VICTOR 1, 2, FB 1957–64 AUTOBOOK
VAUXHALL VICTOR 101 1964–67 AUTOBOOK
VAUXHALL VICTOR FD 1600, 2000 1967–69 AUTOBOOK
VAUXHALL VIVA HA 1964–66 AUTOBOOK
VAUXHALL VIVA HB 1966–69 AUTOBOOK
VOLKSWAGEN BEETLE 1964–67 AUTOBOOK

The AUTOBOOK series of Workshop Manuals covers the majority of British and Continental motor cars. For a full list see the back of this manual.

INTRODUCTION

This do-it-yourself Workshop Manual has been specially written for the owner who wishes to maintain his car in first class condition and to carry out his own servicing and repairs. Considerable savings on garage charges can be made, and one can drive in safety and confidence knowing the work has been done properly.

Comprehensive step-by-step instructions and illustrations are given on all dismantling, overhauling and assembling operations. Certain assemblies require the use of expensive special tools, the purchase of which would be unjustified. In these cases information is included but the reader is recommended to hand the unit to the agent for attention.

Throughout the Manual hints and tips are included which will be found invaluable, and there is an easy to follow fault diagnosis at the end of each chapter.

Whilst every care has been taken to ensure correctness of information it is obviously not possible to guarantee complete freedom from errors or to accept liability arising from such errors or omissions.

Instructions may refer to the righthand or lefthand sides of the vehicle or the components. These are the same as the righthand or lefthand of an observer standing behind the car and looking forward.

CHAPTER 1

THE ENGINE

1:1 Description

Engines fitted to Opel Kadett cars for the production period covered by this manual are of two basic types; the 1 litre engine, later with an increased cylinder bore measurement to bring the capacity to 1.1 litres; and secondly, the larger engine introduced with the 1968 range in 1.5 and 1.9 litre capacities. These engines are fitted as standard to some models and to others as an optional alternative. Details of engine types, capacities and differing power outputs are given in Technical Data at the end of this manual, together with extensive coverage of further technical information.

The 1 and 1.1 litre engines shown in **FIG 1:1** have a cast iron cylinder block integral with the crankcase. The forged steel crankshaft runs in three main bearings, axial thrust being accommodated at the centre bearing position. The crankshaft is fitted with renewable plain metal shell bearings. Similar bearings are fitted to the connecting rods. The pistons are of light alloy in which a steel expansion strip is integrally cast. This limits the thermal expansion of the piston to ensure an almost constant clearance in the cylinder at all operating temperatures.

Pushrod operated valves are set in line along the cylinder head. The camshaft runs in three plain bearings in the cylinder block and is driven by chain from the crankshaft.

An automatically adjusting chain tensioner is fitted which increases its pressure on the chain when engine oil pressure rises and this avoids unnecessary tension at low speed whilst preventing chain lash at high speed.

The distributor and oil pump are driven from the front of the crankshaft. The oil pump draws oil from the engine sump and delivers it under pressure to a fullflow oil filter. Through drilled passages the oil then passes to the main, big-end and camshaft bearings, and to the timing chain tensioner.

The cast iron cylinder head has the exhaust manifold fitted to the side and the inlet manifold on the top. Part of the hot exhaust gas is routed through a passage cast into the inlet manifold to heat the incoming fuel/air mixture.

FIG 1:2 shows the construction of the 1.5 and 1.9 litre engines and the details of the lubrication system. These engines have a cast iron cylinder block integral with the crankcase. The forged steel crankshaft runs in five main bearings, axial thrust being accommodated at the rear main bearing position. The crankshaft is fitted with renewable plain metal bearings. Similar bearings are fitted to the connecting rods. The light alloy pistons have two horizontal slots in the oil control ring groove which partly separates the piston head and skirt to minimize thermal expansion effects at all engine operating temperatures.

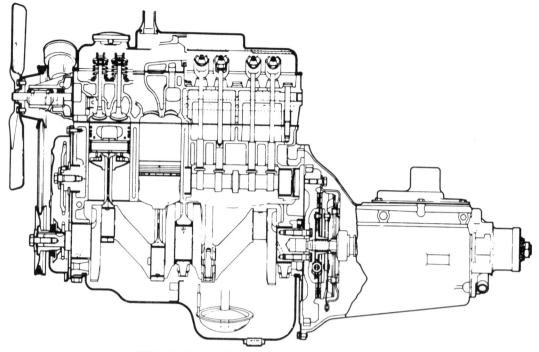

FIG 1:1 Longitudinal section, 1 and 1.1 litre engines

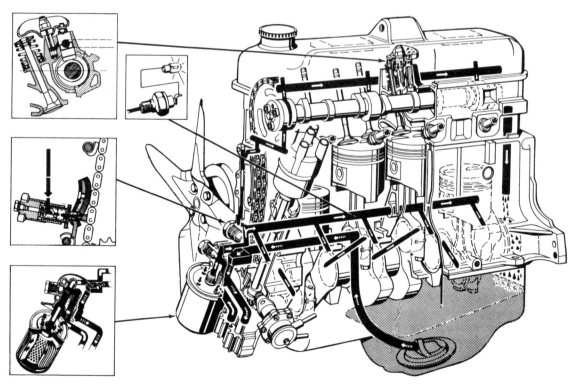

FIG 1:2 Longitudinal section, 1.5 and 1.9 litre engines, showing engine lubrication system

Valves operated by short lifters are set in line along the cylinder head. The camshaft is also in the cylinder head and runs in three plain bearings. The camshaft is driven by chain from the crankshaft. An automatically adjusting chain tensioner is fitted which increases its pressure on the chain when oil pressure rises and this avoids unnecessary tension at low speed whilst preventing chain lash at high speed.

The distributor and oil pump are driven from the front of the crankshaft. The oil pump draws oil from the engine sump and delivers it under pressure to a fullflow oil filter. Through drilled passages the oil then passes to the main, big-end and camshaft bearings, and to the timing chain tensioner.

The cast iron cylinder head has the inlet and exhaust manifolds mounted together on one side. Hot exhaust gases heat a plate cast into the inlet manifold to heat the incoming fuel/air mixture.

1:2 Removing the engine

The normal operations of decarbonizing and servicing the cylinder head can be carried out without removing the engine (refer to **Sections 1:3** and **1:4**), and on 1.5 and 1.9 litre the camshaft can be removed in this manner as it is mounted in the cylinder head (refer to **Section 1:6**).

Big-ends can be worked on and pistons removed with the engine in the car (refer to **Section 1:10**). A major overhaul however can only be carried out with the engine removed from the car. If the operator is not a skilled automobile engineer it is suggested that he will find much useful information in 'Hints on Maintenance and Overhaul' at the end of this manual, and that he should read it before starting work. Engine removal procedure requires that the car be supported clear of the ground on floor stands. Also suitable lifting equipment will be needed to raise and lower the engine. It must be stressed that all supports must be firmly based and not likely to collapse during the operation.

1 and 1.1 litre engines can be removed without removing the gearbox. 1.1 litre SR (GT) engines and all 1.5 and 1.9 litre engines must be removed as a unit with the gearbox. 1 and 1.1 litre engines are removed by lifting from the car, 1.5 and 1.9 litre engines must be lowered from the car and removed from below.

1 and 1.1 litre engines:

1 Raise the bonnet and mark the position of the hinge plates to facilitate their alignment on reassembly. Remove the hinge bolts and washers and remove the bonnet.
2 Disconnect both battery leads.
3 Drain and remove the radiator as described in **Chapter 4.**
4 Remove the gearlever as described in **Chapter 6.**
5 Remove air cleaner(s). Remove throttle rod from carburetter and rear support. Remove the fuel feed pipe.
6 Detach the control cables from the carburetter and heater. Remove the heater hoses and disconnect the cable connections to the starter, generator and distributor. Disconnect the leads from the reversing light switch at the transmission.

7 Remove the three star-bolts and remove the oil filter housing assembly. Release the exhaust pipe from the manifold.
8 Jack up the front and rear of the car, supporting the car on floor stands in a safe manner. Refer to **Chapter 8** and remove the propeller shaft.
9 Place a jack under the gearbox to support it. Attach the lifting equipment to the engine.
10 Remove the bolts attaching the gearbox to the engine and the gearbox mounting bolts. Remove the engine mounting bolts, two on each side. Check that all cables and pipes connecting the unit to the car frame have been detached and that the gearbox is safely supported by the jack. Take the weight of the engine and move it forward to clear the transmission. Lift the engine from the car.

1.1 litre SR (GT):

Refer to the previous section for the removal of 1 and 1.1 litre engines and carry out operations 1 to 8 then proceed as follows: Disconnect the clutch cable from the clutch release fork. Attach the lifting equipment to the engine and gearbox assembly. Disconnect the speedometer from the gearbox. Remove the crossmember supporting the gearbox from the gearbox and frame. Remove the crossmember supporting the engine from the engine and frame. Pull the engine towards the front as far as possible and carefully lift the engine and gearbox assembly from the car.

1.5 and 1.9 litre engines:

On these models the engine is mounted on the front suspension crossmember. As the engine must be removed from below the car the front suspension must be removed as well. The most practical way to carry out this operation is to remove the engine and front suspension as a unit then separate the engine and suspension with the unit on the ground. This is the method described:

1 Disconnect the battery and remove the air cleaner.
2 Drain the radiator as instructed in **Chapter 4** and remove the upper and lower radiator hoses. There is no need to remove the radiator.
3 Disconnect all electrical connections to the engine from the coil, alternator or generator, starter solenoid and oil pressure switch.
4 Remove vacuum hoses from the T-bracket on the inlet manifold and remove the T-bracket to avoid interference during engine lowering. Remove the cables from the choke and the heater control valve. Remove the throttle linkage. Remove the heater hoses from the heater and the water valve bracket from the manifold.
5 Refer to **Chapter 6** and remove the gearlever.
6 Raise the car both front and rear, supporting the front of the car on floor stands under the jacking brackets, in a safe manner.
7 From beneath the car remove the fuel pipe from fuel pump and plug, making sure it is clear of all mounting clips. Disconnect the speedometer cable from the gearbox and the clutch cable from the clutch release fork. Refer to **Chapter 8** and remove the propeller shaft.
8 Disconnect the exhaust pipe from the manifold without completely removing the two bolts from the slotted holes on the inboard side, as this will facilitate

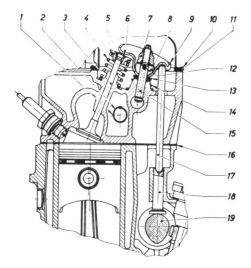

FIG 1 : 3   Valve mechanism, 1 and 1.1 litre engines

Key to Fig 1 : 3 1 Calibrated bore in water line
2 Water line   3 Valve   4 Valve spring   5 Valve cap
6 Valve cotter   7 Adjusting nut   8 Ball seat
9 Rocker arm   10 Rocker arm cover
11 Rocker arm cover gasket   12 Lubrication hole
13 Spacer   14 Detent spring   15 Rocker arm stud
16 Cylinder head gasket   17 Pushrod   18 Tappet
19 Camshaft

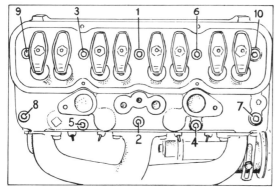

FIG 1 : 4   Slacken or tighten the cylinder head bolts in this order, 1 and 1.1 litre engines

reassembly. Remove the silencer and tailpipe hangers. Detach the engine earthing strap from the side rail.

9 Remove the flexible hoses from the brake pipes as instructed in **Chapter 11**. Remove the steering shaft clamp pinch bolt, marking the position of the shaft to the flange. From the steering mast cover bracket remove the guide sleeve stop bolt as instructed in **Chapter 10**. Pull out the steering column until it clears the mast flange.

10 Attach suitable lifting equipment to the engine and gearbox assembly making sure that the suspension is supported to prevent the assembly tilting during removal. Disconnect upper shock absorber mounting bolts. Remove suspension to car body fixings and remove the gearbox support bracket bolts. Check that

all cables and pipes connecting the unit to the car frame have been detached and carefully lower the engine, gearbox and suspension unit from the car.

11 With the assembly on the ground, remove the gearbox to bellhousing bolts and remove the gearbox. Remove the starter and solenoid and then remove the bellhousing. Attach the lifting gear to the engine, remove engine mounting bolts and lift the engine from the front suspension unit.

The brakes must be bled in accordance with the instructions in **Chapter 11** after engine and suspension reassembly.

1.9 litre S (GT):

GT engines do not rest on the front suspension crossmember as in the Kadett but on a separate crossmember, so the front suspension need not be detached. Refer to the previous section for the removal of 1.5 and 1.9 litre Kadett engines and carry out operations 1 to 8 then proceed as follows: Refer to **Chapter 2** and remove the water heated choke housing and the carburetter. Attach the lifting equipment to the engine and raise it to relieve the weight on the front engine mounts. Detach the gearbox crossmember from gearbox and frame. Detach the engine crossmember from engine and frame and carefully lower the engine and gearbox and remove from beneath the car. Remove the gearbox to bellhousing bolts and remove the gearbox. Remove starter and solenoid and then remove the bellhousing.

1 : 3 Removing and refitting the head

Later model cars for the US market are fitted with Opel exhaust emission control systems. The removal and maintenance of these systems are described in **Section 1 : 15** and for cars fitted with these systems reference should be made to that section before commencing work on the cylinder head.

1 and 1.1 litre engines:

1 Drain the cooling system as described in **Chapter 4**. Loosen drain plug located on the right side of the engine to drain the cylinder block. Disconnect the battery cables. Remove air cleaners and remove throttle rod from carburetter and rear support.

2 Detach fuel pipe, control cables and vacuum lines from the carburetter(s), and heater hose and control cable from heater temperature control valve. Slacken the generator mounting bolts and swing it towards the engine to slacken the fan belt. Remove the fan belt.

3 Refer to **Chapter 2** and remove the carburetter(s) and linkage. Remove the star-bolts from the intake manifold, one of which is inside the manifold and accessible after carburetter removal. Remove the intake manifold. Disconnect the exhaust pipe and remove the exhaust manifold. Remove temperature switch and heater inlet hose. Disconnect spark plug leads.

4 Refer to **FIG 1 : 3** and remove rocker arm cover 10 and gasket 11. Remove self-locking nuts 7, rocker arms 9, ball seats 8, spacers 13 and pushrods 17. Store all of these parts in the correct order for replacement.

5 Using a star wrench (service tool J.21737) remove the cylinder head bolts, loosening them a turn at a time in the order shown in **FIG 1 : 4**. Lift off the head and

remove and discard the head gasket. Remove the sparking plugs to prevent damage during work.

When refitting the head, clean the faces of the head and block. Coat a new gasket on both sides with graphite grease and install it with the word 'OBEN' uppermost. Do up the head bolts finger tight and replace the pushrods and rocker assemblies, making sure that the top and bottom of the pushrods are properly located. Tighten the head nuts a part of a turn at a time in the order shown in **FIG 1:4**, and finally to a torque of 35 lb ft. Refit the manifolds with new gaskets and carburetters with new O-ring seals.

After head removal and replacement check and adjust valve clearances as described in **Section 1:13**. After the engine has been run for some time, the head bolts must be retightened and the clearance checked again. Replace all other parts in the reverse order of dismantling and refill the cooling system.

1.5 and 1.9 litre engines:

1 Drain the cooling system as described in **Chapter 4**. Loosen drain plug located on the right side of engine to drain the cylinder block. Disconnect the battery. Remove the air cleaner and disconnect the throttle linkage from the carburetter.

2 Remove the vacuum hose and fuel pipe from carburetter, and breather valve from rocker cover. Remove water hoses from automatic choke and plug. Disconnect the exhaust pipe.

3 Remove the six bolts from the manifold, loosening them a little at a time in the order shown in **FIG 1:5**, and remove the manifold and carburetter as an assembly. Note that for routine decarbonizing or head gasket replacement the manifold and carburetter assembly need not be removed from the cylinder head, but care must be taken to prevent damage during work if the assembly is not removed.

4 Remove the sparking plug leads and the bolt holding them away from the cylinder head. Remove the rocker cover.

5 Using a star wrench (service tool J.22915) remove the cylinder head bolts, loosening them a turn at a time in the order shown in **FIG 1:6**. Remove the three bolts

FIG 1:5   Slacken or tighten the manifold bolts in this order, 1.5 and 1.9 litre engines

FIG 1:6   Slacken or tighten the cylinder head bolts in this order, 1.5 and 1.9 litre engines

FIG 1:7   Camshaft sprocket details, 1.5 and 1.9 litre engines

Key to Fig 1:7   1 Timing chain   2 Camshaft sprocket
3 Sprocket timing mark   4 Timing case
5 Support timing mark   6 Support   7 Cylinder block
8 Rubber gasket ring

from the plate at the front of the cylinder head, and remove the plate. Remove plastic screw from front of camshaft. Remove three bolts attaching camshaft sprocket to cylinder head.

6 Slide the sprocket off the camshaft, keeping the sprocket teeth firmly engaged in the chain and the

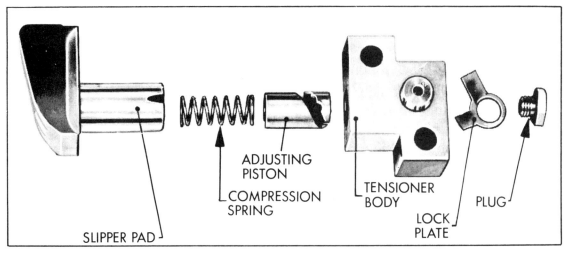

FIG 1:8 Timing chain tensioner components

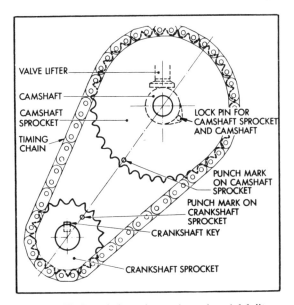

FIG 1:9 Timing chain and sprockets, 1 and 1.1 litre engines

chain tight, supporting the assembly as shown in **FIG 1:7. If the chain is allowed to slip on the sprockets the engine will have to be further dismantled and retimed according to Section 1:7.**

7 Remove the cylinder head, collecting the rubber gasket ring (8 in **FIG 1:7**).

When the valves are fully open they protrude below the level of the cylinder head joint face and the cylinder head should therefore be supported on the bench by a block of wood at each end.

When refitting the head, clean the faces of the head and block and use a new gasket. Replace the head squarely over its guide pins ensuring that the rubber gasket is properly positioned in the timing case. Rotate the camshaft until the recesses are vertical to allow head bolt installation. Do up the head bolts finger tight then tighten them a part of a turn at a time in the order given in **FIG 1:6,** and finally to a torque of 72 lb ft. Slide camshaft sprocket and chain onto camshaft and guide pin and bolt in place. Close front access plate. Check camshaft end float (see **Section 1:6**).

1:4 Servicing head and valves

Remove the head as in the previous sections. If decarbonizing is intended, plug all the waterways in the top face of the cylinder block with pieces of rag. Scrape the carbon from the combustion chambers before removing the valves to avoid damage to the seats. When decarbonizing 1.5 and 1.9 litre engines avoid scratching the alumetized surface of the combustion chambers. It is not necessary to remove the rockers on 1.5 and 1.9 engines, just loosen the adjusting nuts and swing the rockers off the lifters. Remove the lifters and store them in the correct order for reassembly. Valve lifter guides with pitting marks can be smoothed with fine emerycloth, making sure that all particles of metal are cleaned off afterwards.

Use a spring compressor to remove the valves. With the spring compressed remove the split taper collets, release the compressor and lift off the cap and spring. Remove the valve after marking it for correct reassembly. Clean the ports and examine the valve seats and stems.

Valves must be replaced if the stems have any signs of wear or if they are bent. If the valve seats show signs of pitting too deep for removal with grinding paste, have the seats reground at a garage. Fit new valves if the seat is too far gone or has been burnt. In order not to damage the alumetized surface, new inlet valves for 1.5 and 1.9 litre engines should not be refaced with grinding paste, instead the seats in the head should be recut at a garage.

To grind-in valves put a light spring under the valve head and use medium grade carborundum paste unless the seats are in very good condition, when fine grade paste can be used at once. Use a suction cup tool and grind with a semi-rotary movement, letting the valve rise off its seat occasionally by pressure of the spring under the head. Use paste sparingly. When both seats have a smooth matt grey finish clean away every trace of grinding paste from port and valve.

If, on inspection the valve guides are found to be worn they can be reamed to accept oversize valves. See Technical Data for details of valve oversizes. Check the rockers and ball seats and renew any parts worn or damaged. Finish decarbonizing by cleaning carbon from the piston crowns.

Reassemble the valve and rocker assemblies in the reverse order of dismantling, noting that the valve springs must be fitted with the closely wound coils toward the cylinder head. Lubricate the valve stems with engine oil before reassembly.

Refit the cylinder head as instructed in **Section 1:3** and adjust valve clearances as described in **Section 1:13**.

1:5 Overhauling valve timing gear

1 and 1.1 litre engines:

1 Slacken generator bolts and swing generator towards engine to slacken the fan belt. Remove the fan belt. Remove the crankshaft pulley attaching bolt. Remove the pulley, tapping it with a soft-faced hammer if necessary.
2 Remove the timing chain cover and oil deflector from the front of the engine. Remove the timing chain tensioner, which is spring-loaded. Hold the tensioner by slipper pad and body to avoid loss of parts (see **FIG 1:8**). If the timing chain is to be re-used it must be replaced the same way round so mark the front of the chain for this reason. If the chain is worn, both chain and sprockets have to be replaced as a set.
3 Refer to **FIG 1:9**. Remove camshaft sprocket retaining bolt and special washer. Pull off camshaft sprocket and crankshaft sprocket together with timing chain. Note

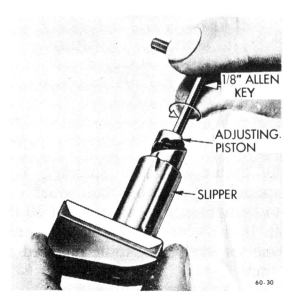

FIG 1:10   Turning chain tensioner adjusting screw

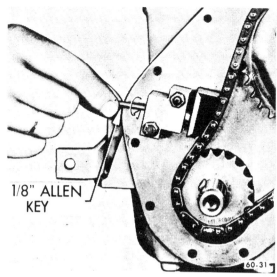

FIG 1:11   Releasing tensioner adjusting piston

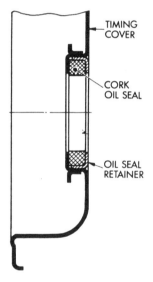

FIG 1:12   Timing case oil seal, 1 and 1.1 litre engines

the Woodruff key on the crankshaft shown in the diagram. Check all parts of the chain tensioner for wear before reassembly. If any parts are defective the complete assembly must be replaced.

Reassembly:

1 Refer to **FIG 1:9** and install crankshaft sprocket onto crankshaft with the punch mark facing forwards and push it over the Woodruff key up to its stop. Install camshaft sprocket onto camshaft and lockpin so that the punch mark faces forward.
2 Turn crankshaft and camshaft until the punch marks are opposite each other. Remove the sprockets without turning them and fit the timing chain around them,

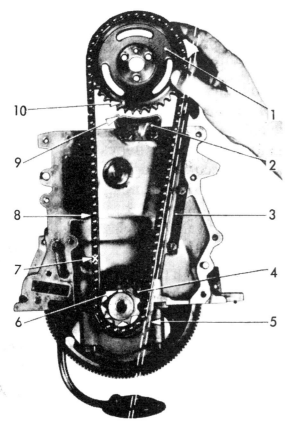

10
9
8
7
6
1
2
3
4
5

FIG 1 :13 Timing chain and sprocket details, 1.5 and 1.9 litre engines

Key to Fig 1 :13
1 Camshaft sprocket
2 Camshaft sprocket support 3 Long damper block
4 Crankshaft sprocket   5 Chain and damper block in parallel
6 Crankshaft key   7 Paint mark on front of chain
8 Timing chain   9 Mark on camshaft sprocket support
10 Mark on camshaft sprocket

making sure that the punch marks on the sprockets are correctly lined up. If the chain is re-used, note the mark made at the removal stage for correct fitting.

3 Replace sprockets and chain complete. Secure camshaft sprocket with its bolt and washer.

4 Fit the chain tensioner compression spring into slipper pad and adjusting piston so that the helical slot in the piston engages the guide pin in slipper pad sleeve. Refer to **FIG 1 :10**. Use $\frac{1}{8}$ inch Allen key to turn the adjusting piston clockwise until the guide pin reaches the top of the helical slot. This will hold the piston in position for installation. Coat all tensioner parts with engine oil and slide slipper assembly into tensioner body. Bolt the tensioner to the engine front plate. Remove the end plug and release the adjusting piston as shown in **FIG 1 :11**. Replace end plug.

5 Refit oil deflector to crankshaft so it engages on the Woodruff key. Fit a new gasket to the timing chain cover and replace the cover, tightening the bolts alternatively to avoid distortion of the cover. Replace the crankshaft pulley and fan belt, finally adjusting the fan belt and tightening the generator bolts.

Replacing timing case oil seal:

With timing chain cover suitably supported on the bench, drive cork seal and outer seal retainer out of cover as shown in **FIG 1 :12. The inner seal retainer must not be removed.** Fit a new oil seal into retainer and drive in through the front of the cover.

1.5 and 1.9 litre engines:

1 If the engine is not removed from the car it must be supported in position using service tool J.23098 for the Kadett or J.23375 for GT models. See **Chapter 9** for the correct fitting of these tools. Drain the cooling system and remove the radiator as instructed in **Chapter 4.**

2 Refer to the instructions in **Section 1 :3** and remove the cylinder head.

3 Slacken generator bolts and swing generator inwards to slacken and remove the fan belt. Remove generator bracket and the fuel pump. Refer to **Chapter 3** and remove the distributor.

4 Remove the timing chain tensioner assembly from the timing cover. Undo the bolt and remove the crankshaft pulley. Remove the water pump and the engine sump.

5 Remove timing cover bolts, noting that one bolt is hidden behind the water pump cover. Pull off sprockets and chain complete, marking the chain for reassembly if it is not to be renewed.

Clean all parts and inspect them, renewing any that are worn or damaged. Timing chains are supplied either separately or complete with sprockets, it not being permissible to renew sprockets alone. If the timing chain tensioner is worn it must be replaced as a unit.

Reassembly is a reversal of the removal procedure, carrying out the following instructions to obtain correct valve timing.

1 Refer to **FIG 1 :13** and turn crankshaft until key 6 is vertical. Fit timing chain around camshaft sprocket, then fit chain around the crankshaft sprocket already installed. Make sure the chain is replaced the right way round, using the mark made during removal.

2 Keeping the crankshaft sprocket in the correct position, align the camshaft sprocket mark 10 with the mark 9 on the support ensuring that the chain and damper block are parallel during this operation. Rest the camshaft sprocket on the support 9.

3 Replace the cylinder head as instructed in **Section 1 :3**. Close front access plate. Check camshaft end float as instructed in **Section 1 :6**.

Replacing timing case oil seal:

With the timing cover removed, drive out the seal with a drift, working from the back of the case. Coat circumference of a new seal with gasket cement and press it into position, keeping it square.

To remove the seal without the removal of the timing case service tool J.22924 will be required. Remove the fan belt and the crankshaft pulley. Using a screwdriver, lever out the seal carefully, avoiding damage to the timing case. Coat the circumference of a new seal with gasket cement and fit it in the service tool. Put the tool and seal onto the crankshaft and replace the pulley bolt and washer. Tighten the pulley bolt to push the seal home.

Remove the tool and replace the crankshaft pulley. Replace and adjust the fan belt.

1:6 Removing and replacing camshaft

1 and 1.1 litre engines:

1 Remove the engine from the car as instructed in **Section 1:2**.
2 Refer to **Section 1:3** and remove the rocker cover, rocker arms, ball seats and pushrods.
3 Remove crankshaft pulley, timing chain cover and timing chain as described in **Section 1:5**. Refer to **Chapter 3** and remove the distributor.
4 Invert the engine and remove the camshaft thrust plate (see **FIG 1:14**). The camshaft and engine front plate can now be removed, but if the tappets are to be removed as well, the engine sump must be taken off to provide the necessary access. See **FIG 1:3** for tappet details and **Section 1:8** for removal and replacement of the sump.

Check all parts and renew any that are worn or damaged. Replacement camshaft bearings are available .020 inch undersize, but as the installation of camshaft bearings requires the use of special in-line reaming equipment the work should be carried out by a properly equipped Opel main dealer.

Reassembly is a reversal of the dismantling procedure, with reference to the following points:

1 Replace the tappets and engine sump if they were removed.
2 Coat camshaft and bearing with engine oil before reinstallation.
3 Install camshaft thrust plate into the guide groove of camshaft so that the closed side of the plate is facing the crankshaft, as in **FIG 1:14**. The thrust plate controls camshaft end float.
4 When reassembly is complete, replenish engine oil to the correct level and adjust valve clearances as described in **Section 1:13**.

1.5 and 1.9 litre engines:

1 Refer to **Section 1:3**, and remove the cylinder head and the valve lifters.
2 Remove covers from access holes on the left side and at the rear of the cylinder head.
3 Remove the camshaft towards the front, supporting it with one hand through the side access hole as shown in **FIG 1:15**.

Check all parts and renew any that are worn or damaged. New camshaft bearings must be fitted by a properly equipped Opel main dealer as installation requires the use of special in-line reaming equipment.

Reassembly is a reversal of the dismantling procedure, with reference to the following points:

1 Coat the camshaft and bearing with engine oil before reinstallation.
2 Using a feeler gauge, check camshaft end float clearance between the plastic screw and the cover. Clearance should be between .004 and .008 inch. Excess clearance can be eliminated by carefully readjusting the cover with a suitable drift.
3 When reassembly is complete, replenish engine oil to the correct level and adjust valve clearances as described in **Section 1:13**.

1:7 Valve timing

Valve timing on all models is set by the correct assembly

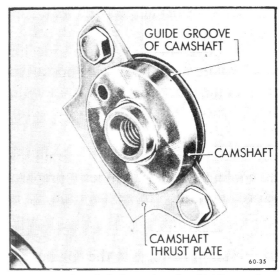

FIG 1:14   Camshaft thrust plate, 1 and 1.1 litre engines

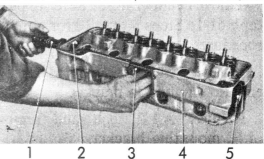

FIG 1:15   Camshaft removal, 1.5 and 1.9 litre engines
Key to Fig 1:15   1 Camshaft   2 Front access hole
3 Lateral access hole   4 Cylinder head   5 Rear access hole

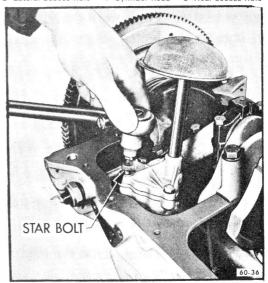

FIG 1:16   Oil strainer and pump removal, 1 and 1.1 litre engines

FIG 1:17 Oil strainer assembly, 1.5 and 1.9 litre engines

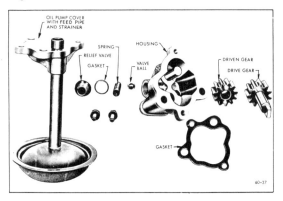

FIG 1:18 Oil pump components, 1 and 1.1 litre engines

of the timing chain and sprockets. Sprockets are provided with positive location at both the camshaft and crankshaft, timing marks being provided on both sprockets to ensure correct alignment.

If incorrect valve timing is suspected, reference should be made to **Section 1:5** for removal of the timing chain cover. If, on inspection, the timing chain and sprockets are seen to be wrongly installed, they must be removed and correctly reinstalled according to the instructions.

1:8 Sump and oil strainer

Pressed steel sumps are fitted to all models. A gauze strainer, through which the oil pump suction tube fits, is located in the bottom of the sump. Access to the strainer is by removal of the sump and, on every third or fourth oil change, the strainer should be removed and cleaned. Fluffy rags should not be used for cleaning the oil strainer, due to the possibility of small fibres clogging the gauze or finding their way into the oil pump. Wash the oil strainer in clean petrol and allow it to dry off before replacing.

Removal:

1 and 1.1 litre engines:

To remove the sump, on Kadett models, the front suspension must be lowered first as instructed in **Chapter 9**. GT models must have the front engine support cross-member removed before the sump can be taken off. Remove the fixing bolts and detach the sump. **FIG 1:16** shows the oil strainer in position. As removal of the oil strainer is together with the lower oil pump housing, reference should be made to **Section 1:9** for the correct procedures. Use new gaskets when replacing the sump, first fitting the flange gasket with tabs in slots of front and rear main bearing caps, then fitting the small strips in the grooves in the bearing caps. Note that flat washers are used on the sump fixing bolts that are adjacent to the rear main bearings.

1.5 and 1.9 litre engines:

On GT and Kadett models the engine must be supported in the car and Kadett front suspension lowered, as instructed in **Chapter 9**. Remove the fixing bolts and detach the sump. Refer to **FIG 1:17** for oil strainer details, and remove the two flange bolts to release the assembly. Discard the old gasket. Make sure that the flange joint is clean on both surfaces before reassembly and use a new flange gasket. Also fit a new gasket to the sump before bolting it into place. Lastly, refit the suspension and lower the engine.

1:9 The oil pump

1 and 1.1 litre engines:

A gear-type oil pump is fitted in the lower part of the crankcase, access to the pump is by removing the sump as described in **Section 1:8**. A relief valve is contained in the pump body which feeds surplus oil back to the sump when the correct oil pressure is exceeded. Oil pump components are shown in **FIG 1:18**. To remove the oil pump refer to **FIG 1:16** and remove the two star-bolts, oil pump assembly and gasket. Remove the oil pump cover and strainer assembly, and slide out the pump gears. Remove the pressure relief valve plug, gasket, spring and ball.

Wash all parts in petrol and inspect them carefully, replacing any parts that are worn or damaged. See that the relief valve spring is in good condition. Replace the internal parts and check the clearance between the meshing gear teeth with a feeler gauge. Clearance should be between .004 and .008 inch. Using a straightedge, check that the gears do not protrude above the housing more than .004 inch. Refit all parts in the reverse order of dismantling, using new gaskets throughout. Lubricate the gears and housing with engine oil before refitting the cover.

1.5 and 1.9 litre engines:

A gear-type oil pump is fitted at the front of the engine, the pump body forming part of the timing case. A passage cast in the cylinder block connects the pump to the oil strainer assembly in the sump, and an oil filter bypass valve is located in the timing case. The oil pump componets are shown in **FIG 1:19**.

To remove the pump assembly take out the screws fixing the oil pump cover to the timing case. Remove the

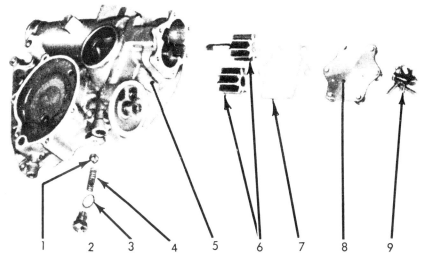

FIG 1:19   Oil pump components, 1.5 and 1.9 litre engines

Key to Fig 1:19   1 Bypass valve ball   2 Bypass valve plug   3 Gasket   4 Spring   5 Timing case   6 Oil pump gears
7 Cover gasket   8 Cover   9 Cover attaching screws

cover assembly and slide out the gears. Wash the internal parts in petrol and inspect for wear or scoring. Replace any parts that are not serviceable.

Some production models are fitted with oversize gears which must be replaced with gears of the same size. Pump housings that contain oversize gears are marked '0.2' on the lefthand side. Renew pump covers scored by gear action. If pump housing or distributor drive shaft bushing are worn the entire timing case and pump assembly must be renewed.

Replace the gears and check the clearance between meshing teeth with a feeler gauge. Clearance should be between .004 and .008 inch. If new gears are installed their end clearance in the housing should be checked with a straightedge. Gears must not protrude more than .004 inch. Check the relief valve ball and seat for free action, and carefully clean them. On reassembly, lightly tap the ball onto its seat to seat it properly, using a brass drift.

Reassemble all parts in the reverse order of dismantling, using new gaskets throughout. Lubricate the gears and housing with engine oil before refitting the cover.

1:10 Pistons and rods

On all models the pistons and rods can be removed with the engine in the car. The pistons, however, will not pass the crankshaft and it is therefore necessary to remove the cylinder head and withdraw the pistons and rods up through the top of the cylinder bores.

Removal:

Jack up the car and remove the sump as described in **Section 1:8,** and the dipstick. If all the pistons and rods are to be removed, it will be found easier to deal with them in pairs, and, by turning the crankshaft, to work on the pair which are at BDC. The piston and rod assembly for 1 and 1.1 litre engines is shown in **FIG 1:20,** and for 1.5 and 1.9 litre engines in **FIG 1:21.** Pistons, rods and caps

1. NOTCH IN PISTON HEAD FOR VALVES
2. RUBBER STAMPED ARROW POINTING TOWARD THE <u>FRONT</u>
3. NOTCH IN CONNECTING ROD CAP POINTING TOWARD THE <u>REAR</u>

FIG 1:20   Piston and connecting rod, 1 and 1.1 litre engines

should be marked so that they will be reinstalled the right way round, and to the correct cylinder. It is suggested that the cylinder number be marked on the forward side of the components. Starting from the front of the crankcase, the cylinders are numbered 1—2—3—4.

Big-end bearings can be examined and changed without removing the pistons and rods, and therefore, without the need to remove the cylinder head. With that exception, proceed as described but, when the connecting rod cap has been removed, lift the connecting rod off the crankpin

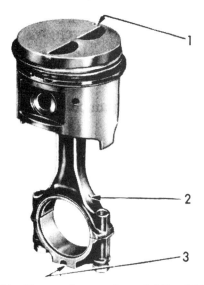

FIG 1:21 Piston and connecting rod, 1.5 and 1.9 litre engines

Key to Fig 1:21   1 Notch in piston head pointing towards the front   2 Oil hole in connecting rod pointing towards the right (manifold side)   3 Notch in connecting rod cap pointing toward the rear

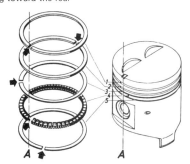

FIG 1:22 Location of piston ring gaps, 1.5 and 1.9 litre engines

Key to Fig 1:22   1 First compression ring
2 Second compression ring   3 Upper oil control ring
4 Centre oil control ring   5 Lower oil control ring
'A' Vertical line to show ring gap positions

and detach the bearing shells. If there has been a big-end bearing failure, the crankpin must be examined for damage, and for the transfer of metal to its surface. The oilway in the crankshaft must be checked to ensure there is no obstruction. Crankpins should not be more than .002 inch out of round. If the crankpins are worn or damaged, they must be reground to accept suitable under-size bearings. Big-end bearing clearance can be checked by the use of Plastigage, as described in Hints on Maintenance and Overhaul at the end of this manual. If the bearing clearance is more than .003 inch or the shell is scored or damaged, a new bearing of the correct size should be selected and fitted. Under no circumstances should the rod, cap or bearing be filed to take up wear.

When bearing shells are fitted they extend slightly beyond the joint face of the bearing to ensure positive seating when the cap bolts are tightened.

The connecting rods and pistons are fitted through the cylinder bores to the same cylinders from which they were removed. Use the marks made on disassembly, and the information in FIG 1:20 or 1:21 to ensure that pistons, rods and caps are fitted correctly. Lubricate all parts with engine oil, and use a piston ring clamp when entering the pistons and rings into the bores.

Make sure that the ring gaps are offset 90 degrees to each other for 1 and 1.1 litre engines, and are as shown in FIG 1:22 for 1.5 and 1.9 litre engines.

Pistons and rings:

Pistons for 1 and 1.1 litre engines are fitted with three rings. The upper ring is chrome-plated, and can be installed either way up. The second ring must be fitted the correct way up, and is marked 'TOP' for this purpose. The oil control ring at the bottom can be fitted either way up.

For 1.5 and 1.9 litre engines five rings are fitted to the pistons, and these must be fitted as shown in FIG 1:23. Pistons are cam-ground to a slightly oval shape, so care must be exercised to ensure they are refitted correctly.

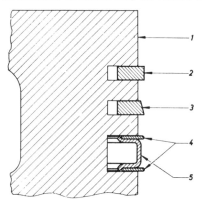

FIG 1:23 Piston ring details, 1.5 and 1.9 litre engines

Key to Fig 1:23   1 Piston   2 First compression ring
3 Second compression ring   4/5 Oil control rings

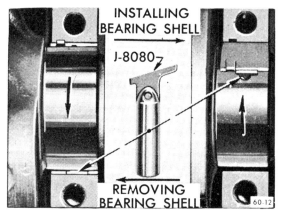

FIG 1:24 Removing and installing main bearing shell, 1.5 and 1.9 litre engines

Gudgeon pins:

Gudgeon pins are a tight press-fit in the pistons and connecting rods, which makes removal a specialist operation, requiring the use of special tools and hydraulic press equipment to ensure correct removal and assembly, so the work, if necessary, should be carried out by an Opel main dealer. Gudgeon pin removal, however, would not apply to the majority of pre-1970 models, as the pistons and connecting rods for these models are only renewable as an assembled unit. Check this point with the supplier before ordering parts. New pistons are supplied complete with gudgeon pins, and neither is available separately.

Overhaul:

Check the cylinder for score marks, and remove glaze and carbon deposits. Badly scored surfaces will necessitate a rebore. Examine the pistons for rough or scored bearing surfaces, and for chipped ring grooves. Clean the carbon from the top of the piston, and remove any glaze from the skirt. Clean carbon from the ring grooves. A length broken from an old piston ring will prove an excellent tool for this purpose.

New pistons must be carefully measured, and the bore honed to receive them, noting that cylinder bores may be different sizes in the same crankcase. For these reasons the work should be referred to a properly equipped Opel main dealer.

Check the piston ring fitted gap in the cylinder bore from which it was removed. Push the piston well down the bore and press the ring down on top of it. Measure the ring gap with a feeler gauge. The gap should not be more than .016 inch for 1 and 1.1 litre engines, or .021 inch for 1.5 and 1.9 litre engines. If the ring gap is larger than the measurements quoted, a new ring must be fitted.

Oil the bearing surfaces and reassemble all components in the reverse order of dismantling, ensuring that all oil holes are clear.

1:11 Crankshaft, main bearings and flywheel

The crankshaft runs in three main bearings on 1 and 1.1 litre engines, and in five main bearings in 1.5 and 1.9 litre engines. On all models, the crankshaft bearings can be checked and removed without the need for engine removal. Crankshaft removal requires, in addition, the removal of the gearbox, clutch and flywheel. If the engine is being dismantled for main bearing inspection, the operator would be well advised to check the big-end bearings at the same time, as both types of bearing require the same dismantling procedures for access to them (see **Section 1:10**).

A crankshaft bearing consists of two halves or shells. The ends of the shells extend slightly beyond the joint face of the bearing, and shells or caps must never be filed to take up wear. If there has been a main bearing failure, the crankshaft must be examined for damage, and for the transfer of metal to its surface. The oilway must be checked to ensure there is no obstruction.

Removal:

1 and 1.1 litre engines:

Jack up the car and remove the sump as described in **Section 1:8,** and remove the dipstick. Remove and

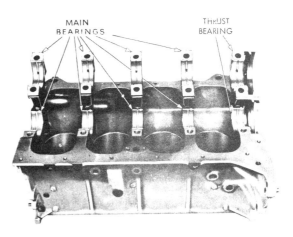

FIG 1:25   Main bearings, 1.5 and 1.9 litre engines

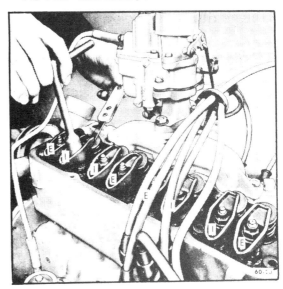

FIG 1:26   Adjusting valve clearance

FIG 1:27   Timing chain oil deflector

O KAD

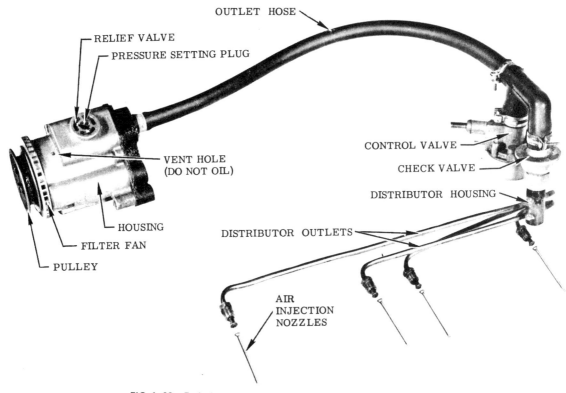

FIG 1:28 Emission control system components (earlier type)

replace one bearing at a time, so that the crankshaft will be supported by the other bearings while it is being worked on.

Main bearing clearance can be checked by the use of Plastigage, as described in Hints on Maintenance and Overhaul at the end of this manual. If the clearance is more than .003 inch, or if the shell is scored or damaged, a new bearing of the correct size should be selected and fitted. If the journals are worn or damaged, the crankshaft should be reground to accept suitable undersize bearings. Crankshaft runout at the centre main bearing position should not exceed .001 inch.

Coat all bearings with engine oil, and replace components in the reverse order of dismantling. Correct torque for main bearing cap bolts is 45 lb ft.

1.5 and 1.9 litre engines:

Jack up the car and remove the sump as described in **Section 1:8**, and remove the dipstick and oil strainer assembly. Remove and replace one bearing at a time, so that the crankshaft will be supported by the other bearings while it is being worked on.

Check the condition of the bearings and crankshaft, and the main bearing clearance, as described in the previous section. Crankshaft runout at the centre main bearing position should not exceed .0012 inch.

Main bearing shells should be fitted into place using a rotary movement, starting one end of the shell squarely into the bearing and sliding it round the bearing into place.

If the crankshaft has not been removed, the upper bearing shells must be removed with the use of service tool J.8080 shown in **FIG 1:24**, in the following manner:

Loosen all crankshaft bearing cap bolts half a turn, and remove the cap from the bearing to be removed or replaced. Fit the tool into the oil hole in the crankshaft, then slowly turn the crankshaft so that the tool rotates the shell out of place by pushing against the plain end of the shell. When replacing shells, start the shell into its bearing by hand, then push it fully home with the tool, in the manner described. Replace each lower bearing and shell after removing the upper shell, so that the crankshaft is always supported by four bearing caps. When turning the crankshaft with the rear main bearing cap removed, hold the oil seal to prevent it moving out of place. **FIG 1:25** shows the bearing positions in the crankcase.

When a rear main bearing shell has been replaced, its thrust surfaces must be lined up before the cap bolts are tightened. To do this, install the cap bolts finger tight and move the crankshaft backwards and forwards several times. Make the last movement in the forward direction, and tighten the cap bolts.

Coat all bearings with engine oil and replace components in the reverse order of dismantling. Correct torque for main bearing cap bolts is 72 lb ft.

Renewing rear main bearing oil seal:

If the engine has not been removed from the car, refer to the appropriate Chapters and remove the gearbox, clutch and flywheel.

Punch a small hole into the oil seal and screw in a self-tapping screw. Holding the head of the screw with pliers, pull out the oil seal. Grease a new seal and, using the fingers, fit the seal into position in the crankcase, making sure that the lips of the seal are correctly entered. Drive home the seal, keeping it square.

Flywheel:

The flywheel is a steel forging, and the starter ring-gear teeth are integral with it. The flywheel and clutch are balanced as a unit, so their relative positions must be marked during removal as described in **Chapter 5,** before dismantling. The flywheel must be removed if the engine is to be completely dismantled and the crankshaft removed.

Removal:

Remove the gearbox as described in **Chapter 6** and the clutch as described in **Chapter 5**. Remove the bolts attaching the flywheel to the crankshaft and remove the flywheel.

Reassembly is a reversal of the dismantling procedures, using new bolts when refitting the flywheel to the crankshaft, tightening them to a torque of 25 lb ft for 1 and 1.1 litre engines, 43 lb ft for 1.5 and 1.9 litre engines.

1 : 12 External oil filter

The oil filter is of the fullflow type and pressure oil is fed to it direct from the oil pump. A pressure relief valve is incorporated in parallel with the filter system so that, in the event of the filter becoming clogged, or the oil becoming too thick to pass through the filter element, the valve will open and allow pressure oil to bypass the filter and pass directly to the lubrication points in the engine.

The oil filter housing is located at the front of the crankcase. Remove the element by unscrewing the canister and lifting it out. Renew the element every 3000 miles. Thoroughly clean the canister before inserting the new element.

1 : 13 Valve clearance adjustment

Final adjustment of valve clearances must be carried out with the engine at normal operating temperature, and running at a slow-idle. If the rocker assembly has been removed and replaced, however, the clearance should first be adjusted in the following manner, in order that the engine can be started and tuned.

Remove the rocker cover. Work on one pair of valves at a time, and, with the piston at the top of the cylinder on the compression stroke (both valves closed), adjust the valves as shown in **FIG 1 : 26**. Using a feeler gauge between the rocker and the valve stem, adjust the clearance to these figures:

1 and 1.1 litre engines: Inlet .008 inch, Exhaust .012 inch
1.5 and 1.9 litre engines: Inlet .012 inch, Exhaust .012 inch.

Turn the adjusting nut clockwise to reduce the clearance, or anticlockwise to increase the clearance. The adjusting nut is self-locking. This adjustment is only a temporary measure, and final adjustment must be carried out as follows:

Run the engine to warm it up to normal operating temperature. Stop the engine and remove the rocker cover. On 1.5 and 1.9 litre engines an oil deflector such as service tool J.22933 must be fitted over the timing chain as shown in **FIG 1 : 27**, to prevent oil splashing from the chain into the engine compartment.

Start the engine and leave it running at a slow-idle. Insert the feeler gauge as previously described, and turn the adjusting nut until the clearance is correct, then remove the spanner and recheck. Leave the feeler gauge between the rocker and valve stem while the rocker is operating, and, during the short period that the valve is closed check that the feeler moves in the gap with a slight drag, being neither tight nor loose. Correct final running clearances are:

1 and 1.1 litre engines: Inlet .006 inch, Exhaust .010 inch
1.5 and 1.9 litre engines: Inlet .012 inch, Exhaust .012 inch.

Replace the rocker cover. If the head has been off and a new gasket fitted, run the engine for about 100 miles and then tighten the head bolts and check the valve clearance again. Every time the head bolts are tightened it will affect the clearance, so always check it.

1 : 14 Reassembling the engine

Reassembling the engine and installing it into the car is the reverse of the procedure given in **Section 1 : 2** and reference should be made to that section and to the various chapter and section numbers quoted in it. Always fit new gaskets, and renew any hoses which show signs of deterioration. Cars on which the front suspension was removed will need the brake system bled as described in **Chapter 11**. Torque wrench settings for all important fixings are given in the text.

When installing the engine do up the fixings for the crossmembers, engine and gearbox mountings and exhaust pipe finger tight only, then rock the engine sideways to seat the mountings. Uniformly tighten all fixings, starting from the front. This will ensure freedom from resonance and stress. Refer to the appropriate sections and adjust the valve clearances, and, if the gearbox was removed, the clutch cable free play. Fill the engine with the correct grade of oil, and the cooling system as described in **Chapter 4**.

If new parts such as pistons, rings or crankshaft bearings have been installed, avoid high speeds until a reasonable time has been allowed for bedding-down, so that over-heating and scuffing of new parts is avoided.

1 : 15 Exhaust emission control systems

The purpose of an emission control system is to reduce to a very low level the amount of carbon monoxide and hydrocarbons entering the atmosphere from the vehicle exhaust system. **It does not reduce the danger of inhaling carbon monoxide in a confined space.**

Basically, excessive exhaust emissions are caused by incomplete combustion of the fuel/air mixture in the engine cylinders, and emission control systems are designed to reduce the amount of unburned mixture to a minimum. In the early emission control system this is achieved by injecting metered quantities of air into the exhaust manifold to continue the burning process, and in the later system by a combination of special carburetter and ignition tuning, and a heated air intake. The early

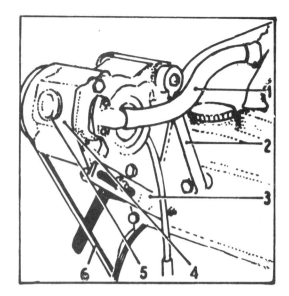

FIG 1:29   Air pump installation, 1.1 litre engine

Key to Fig 1:29   1 Air hose   2 Pump support bracket
3 Fan belt adjuster rail   4 Air pump   5 Pressure relief valve
6 Air pump drive belt

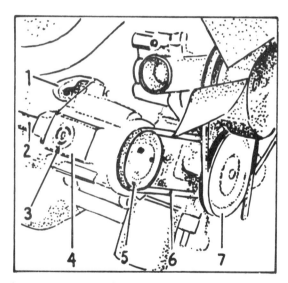

FIG 1:30   Air pump installation, 1.5 and 1.9 litre engines

Key to Fig 1:30   1 Air pump support bracket
2 Air hose   3 Pressure relief valve   4 Air pump
5 Air pump pulley and filter fan   6 Air pump drive belt
7 Twin-pulley on crankshaft

system is shown in **FIG 1:28** and the later system in
FIGS 1:33 and **1:34**.

Emission control systems will not function correctly
if the ignition timing and carburetters are not properly
adjusted, so reference should be made to the appropriate
Chapters before checking the emission control system, to
ensure that the engine is properly tuned. All the separate

components of the emission control systems are factory-
sealed units, and must be replaced complete if defective.
The following instructions will cover the removal of the
emission control systems, and details of testing and fault-
finding procedures.

Removal (earlier models):
Drive belt:

Remove the fan belt on 1.5 and 1.9 litre engines.
Loosen pump mounting bolts and push the pump towards
the engine to slacken the drive belt. Remove the drive belt.

Outlet hoses:

Refer to **FIG 1:31** for 1.1 litre engines, or **FIG 1:32**
for 1.5 and 1.9 litre engines. Remove hoses by loosening
the clamps and twisting the hose off pump, control valve
and check valve.

Control valve:

Remove air cleaner and rubber hose connector, and the
air bleeder and vacuum lines. Remove three fixing bolts,
then remove the control valve from the bracket.

Check valve:

Remove the air cleaner on 1.5 and 1.9 litre engines.
Remove the rubber hose and unscrew the valve from the
air distributor housing, holding the air distributor assembly
with suitable pliers to avoid damage to the air pipes.

Air distributor assembly:

Disconnect the battery and remove the air cleaner.
Disconnect the fuel and vacuum hoses from the carburetter,

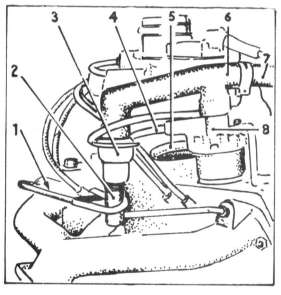

FIG 1:31   Valve and air distributor assembly, 1.1 litre
engine

Key to Fig 1:31   1 Air distributor pipes
2 Air distributor housing   3 Check valve   4 Air bleeder line
5 Vacuum line   6 Rubber hose connector
7 Air pump hose   8 Control valve

and the vacuum hose from the inlet manifold. Remove the radiator cap to release pressure from the cooling system and remove the water hose from heater outlet to inlet manifold. On 1.5 and 1.9 litre engines, disconnect and plug the two hoses from the automatic choke. Remove vent hose from inlet manifold.

Disconnect the throttle linkage and remove the carburetter(s). Detach the hose connector from check valve. Remove the bolts fixing the inlet manifold to exhaust manifold and cylinder head. Remove the inlet manifold. Unscrew the four air distributor pipe fittings from the exhaust manifold, and lift off the air distributor assembly. Use new gaskets when refitting the manifolds.

Air injection nozzles:

Remove the air distributor assembly as just described, and remove the exhaust manifold. Drive out the nozzles from the inside of the manifold, using a drift.

Air pump:

Disconnect the hose at the pump. Remove the drive belt as previously described. Undo the fixing bolts and remove the pump.

Reassembly of all components is a reversal of the removal procedure.

Removal (late models):

Vacuum motor:

Refer to **FIGS 1:33** and **1:34.** Remove the vacuum motor retaining spring. Remove the vacuum motor, turning it to one side to unhook the motor linkage at the control door.

Air cleaner sensor:

Remove the air cleaner. Spring off the sensor retaining clips and pull off the sensor vacuum hoses. Note carefully

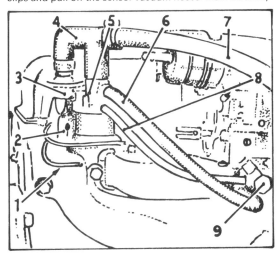

FIG 1:32   Valve and air distributor assembly, 1.5 and 1.9 litre engines

Key to Fig 1:32   1 Air distributor pipes
2 Air distributor housing   3 Check valve
4 Rubber hose connector 5 Control valve 6 Air bleeder line
7 Air pump line 8 Vacuum line 9 Vacuum control connector

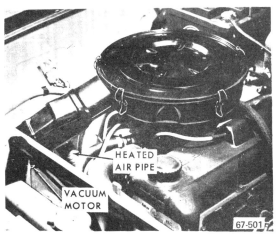

FIG 1:33   Heated air system (1.9 litre shown)

FIG 1:34   Sensor unit (1.1 litre shown)

the position of the sensor for correct replacement, then remove it. Replace the sensor with care, to avoid damage to the temperature sensing spring.

Reassemble all components in the reverse order of dismantling.

Checking and testing procedures:

Earlier models:

The air injection system is not noiseless in operation. If, however, there is excessive noise from the air pump, remove the drive belt and check if the pump is binding or is seized. If the pump is damaged or the bearings have failed, the pump must be renewed. Replace the drive belt, and swing the pump away from the engine to tighten the drive belt, then tighten the pump fixing bolts.

Check that the pump is delivering air by removing an air exhaust pipe and feeling for air pressure. If the pump is not delivering air while the engine is running, or if air leaks from the relief valve while the engine is idling, the pump must be renewed. Check that all connections are secure and that the hoses are not touching any other part of the car. Check that the pump mounting bracket is secure. With the pump running, check the entire system for air leaks in the hoses and around the clamps. The pump operates with the engine idling, so air leaks can be located by feeling for air blowing from any holes.

To test the control valve:

Remove the air cleaner and the hose from the top of the control valve. Start the engine and leave it idling. Use a lamp so that the white valve can be seen inside the control valve. Locate the hose on the control valve that leads to the manifold. Pull off the hose and wait 5 seconds before replacing it. The white valve should move upwards for 1 to 3 seconds. If the white valve stays up for more than 5 seconds, or will not move at all, it is defective; and the control valve assembly must be renewed.

Later models:

To test the thermo air cleaner operation:

Inspect all hoses for kinks, obstructions or damage. With the engine switched off, observe the damper door position through the end of the snorkel, using a mirror if necessary. In this condition the damper door should be in a position to close the heat stove passage and open the snorkel passage. If not, check the linkage for free movement.

To test the diaphragm unit:

Apply a vacuum to the diaphragm unit through the hose disconnected from the sensor unit. This can be done by mouth. The damper door should then completely close the snorkel passage. If not, check for a leak in the vacuum hose, and check the linkage. Again apply the vacuum to the diaphragm unit, and bend or clamp the hose to trap the vacuum in the diaphragm assembly. If the damper door does not remain in position under these conditions there is a vacuum leak in the diaphragm, and the unit must be renewed.

To test the sensor unit:

With the engine cold, check that the damper door is fully opened, using the method already described. Start the engine and leave it idling. Immediately after starting the engine the damper door should close. As the engine warms up, the damper door should start to open and the air cleaner should become warm to the hand. If, during this test the damper door does not operate as described, the sensor unit is defective and must be renewed.

1:16 Fault diagnosis

(a) Engine will not start

1 Defective coil
2 Faulty distributor capacitor (condenser)
3 Dirty, pitted or incorrectly set contact breaker points
4 Ignition wires loose or insulation faulty
5 Water on spark plug leads
6 Battery discharged, corrosion of terminals
7 Faulty or jammed starter
8 Sparking plug leads wrongly connected
9 Vapour lock in fuel pipes
10 Defective fuel pump
11 Overchoking or underchoking
12 Blocked petrol filter or carburetter jet(s)

13 Leaking valves
14 Sticking valves
15 Valve timing incorrect
16 Ignition timing incorrect

(b) Engine stalls

1 Check 1, 2, 3, 4, 5, 10, 11, 12, 13 and 14 in (a)
2 Sparking plugs defective or gaps incorrect
3 Retarded ignition
4 Mixture too weak
5 Water in fuel system
6 Petrol tank vent blocked
7 Incorrect valve clearances

(c) Engine idles badly

1 Check 2 and 7 in (b)
2 Air leak at manifold joints
3 Carburetter adjustment wrong
4 Air leak in carburetter
5 Over-rich mixture
6 Worn piston rings
7 Worn valve stems or guides
8 Weak exhaust valve springs

(d) Engine misfires

1 Check 1, 2, 3, 4, 5, 8, 10, 12, 13, 14, 15 and 16 in (a); 2, 3, 4 and 7 in (b)
2 Weak or broken valve springs

(e) Engine overheats (see Chapter 4)

(f) Compression low

1 Check 13 and 14 in (a); 6 and 7 in (c); and 2 in (d)
2 Worn piston ring grooves
3 Scored or worn cylinder bores

(g) Engine lacks power

1 Check 3, 10, 11, 12, 13, 14, 15 and 16 in (a); 2, 3, 4 and 7 in (b); 6 and 7 in (c); and 2 in (d). Also check (e) and (f)
2 Leaking joint washers
3 Fouled sparking plugs
4 Automatic advance not working

(h) Burnt valves or seats

1 Check 13 and 14 in (a); 7 in (b); and 2 in (d). Also check (e)
2 Excessive carbon around valves and seats

(j) Sticking valves

1 Check 2 in (d)
2 Bent valve stem
3 Scored valve stem or valve guide
4 Incorrect valve clearance

(k) Excessive cylinder wear

1 Check 11 in (a)
2 Lack of oil
3 Dirty oil
4 Piston rings gummed up or broken
5 Badly fitting piston rings
6 Connecting rod bent

(l) Excessive oil consumption

1 Check 6 and 7 in (c) and check (k)
2 Ring gaps too wide
3 Oil return holes in piston choked with carbon
4 Scored cylinders
5 Oil level too high
6 External oil leaks

(m) Crankshaft and connecting rod bearing failure

1 Check 2 in (k)
2 Restricted oilways
3 Worn journals or crankpins
4 Loose bearing caps
5 Extremely low oil pressure
6 Bent connecting rod

(n) Internal water leakage (see Chapter 4)

(o) Poor water circulation (see Chapter 4)

(p) Corrosion (see Chapter 4)

(q) High fuel consumption (see Chapter 2)

(r) Engine vibration

1 Loose generator bolts
2 Mounting rubbers loose or ineffective
3 Engine installed without relieving mounting stresses
   (see **Section 1:14**)
4 Fan blades out of balance
5 Misfiring due to mixture, ignition or mechanical faults
6 Exhaust pipe mountings too tight

CHAPTER 2

THE FUEL SYSTEM

2:1 Description

All models are fitted with mechanically operated fuel pumps. **FIG 2:1** shows the type of fuel pump fitted to 1 and 1.1 litre models, operation being via an eccentric on the camshaft which actuates the pump diaphragm by means of a rocker arm. On 1.5 and 1.9 litre models pump operation is via an eccentric on the distributor drive shaft, the diaphragm being pushrod operated (see **FIG 2:4**).

Three variants of carburetters are fitted to the models covered by this manual. 1 litre models are fitted with a single Opel carburetter, 1.1 litre models with single or twin Solex carburetters. 1.5 and 1.9 litre models use a dual-barrel Solex carburetter, that of the 1.9 litre engine being fitted with an automatic choke operated by a thermostatic switch actuated by water temperature.

Three types of air cleaner are fitted to the models covered by this manual and they are described in **Section 2:18.**

For cars fitted with Emission Control systems reference should be made to **Chapter 1, Section 1:15** for removal and maintenance of these systems. Carburetter adjustments for cars fitted with Emission Control systems are described in **Section 2:17.**

2:2 Routine maintenance

The fuel pump filter and sediment bowl should be cleaned at intervals of about 6000 miles. Remove the fuel inlet pipe and plug it to prevent loss of fuel, as the level of the pump is below that of the fuel tank. Remove the fuel pump cap, gasket and plastic filter. Wash the filter and sediment bowl with petrol. If the filter cannot be cleaned successfully or is damaged, it must be renewed. Upon reassembly, position the filter with the projections upwards and use a new gasket. Ensure the sealing ring is on the fixing screw. Do not use cloth to clean the filter as particles of lint will contaminate the fine mesh. Occasionally, lubricate the carburetter throttle linkage and inspect for wear.

At intervals determined by the type of cleaner and the conditions of operation, service the air cleaner as described in **Section 2:18**

2:3 Pump removal and dismantling

1 and 1.1 litre engines:

Remove the bolts fixing the pump to the engine crankcase and remove the pump. Refer to **FIG 2:1**. Mark the

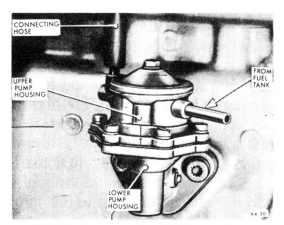

FIG 2:1 Fuel pump, 1 and 1.1 litre models

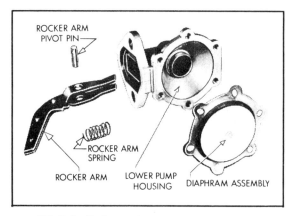

FIG 2:2 Fuel pump lower housing assembly

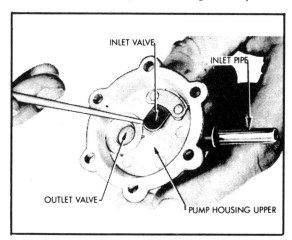

FIG 2:3 Fuel pump upper housing assembly

upper and lower pump housings to ensure correct reassembly. Remove the filter cap and plastic filter. Undo the six fixing screws and remove the upper from the lower housing. Refer to FIG 2:2 and remove the rocker arm

spring and the circlip from the pivot pin. Drive out the pivot pin and remove the rocker arm and the diaphragm assembly. Work the rubber oil seal off the diaphragm operating rod and slide off the seal retainer and spring.

1.5 and 1.9 litre engines:

Remove the bolts fixing the pump to the engine crankcase and remove the pump, collecting the asbestos spacer. Refer to FIG 2:4. Mark the upper and lower pump housings to ensure correct reassembly. Remove the filter cap and plastic filter. Undo the six fixing screws and remove the upper from the lower housing. Remove the circlip 7, spring seat 8 and spring 9. Press the pushrod into the pump body to remove the diaphragm and pushrod assembly, collecting the spring 11.

2:4 Examination of the pump

The following points apply to both types of pump.

Wash all parts in clean petrol and inspect them for wear, renewing any part found defective. If fuel starvation has been traced to the pump, suspect a leaking diaphragm or valves. Two holes in the lower housing serve to ventilate the space below the diaphragm. If fuel has been leaking from these holes, the diaphragm is defective and must be renewed.

2:5 Reassembling the pump

Reassembly is a reversal of the dismantling procedure, making sure that the diaphragm and springs are fitted correctly. Use the marks made on removal to ensure correct reassembly of the upper and lower housings. Use new gaskets throughout. When refitting the pushrod type pump, make sure the asbestos spacer is in place with a gasket on each side as shown in FIG 2:5.

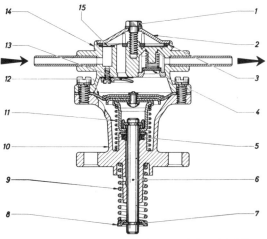

FIG 2:4 Section through fuel pump, 1.5 and 1.9 litre models

Key to Fig 2:4 1 Pump cover attaching screw with seal ring
2 Pump cover   3 Gasket   4 Outlet valve   5 Oil seal
6 Pushrod   7 Circlip   8 Spring seat   9 Pushrod spring
10 Lower housing   11 Diaphragm spring   12 Diaphragm
13 Leaf spring (inlet valve)   14 Upper housing   15 Filter

2:6 Testing pump

Before testing the pump ensure that the fuel tank vent pipe is not blocked. If it is suspected that fuel is not reaching the carburetter, remove the carburetter feed pipe from the fuel pump. Turn the engine over several times with the starter and watch for fuel squirting from the fuel pump and, if so, check the carburetter needle valves are not stuck.

Reduced flow can be caused by blocked fuel pipes or a clogged filter. Check the pump filter as described in **Section 2:2**. If an obstructed pipeline is suspected, it may be cleared with compressed air. Disconnect the pipeline at the pump and carburetter. **Do not pass compressed air through the pump or the valves will be damaged.** If there is an obstruction between the pump and the tank, remove the tank filler cap before blowing the pipe through from the pump end.

If the pump delivers insufficient fuel, suspect an air leak between the pump and the fuel tank, dirt under the valves or faulty valve seatings. If fuel leaks from the vent holes in the underside of the pump, the diaphragm is faulty and must be renewed.

FIG 2:5 Fitting the fuel pump, 1.5 and 1.9 litre models

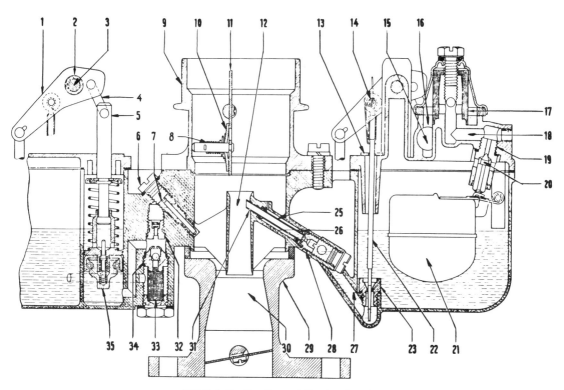

FIG 2:6 Section through Opel carburetter

Key to Fig 2:6 1 Accelerator pump lever   2 Bush   3 Pin   4 Accelerator pump link   5 Pump plunger   6 Pump passage plug   7 Pump discharge jet   8 Choke valve spring   9 Air intake   10 Choke valve   11 Choke butterfly   12 Venturi   13 Dust washer   14 Metering rod retaining spring   15 Fuel inlet   16 Sediment bowl   17 Filter   18 Fuel passage   19 Needle valve seat   20 Needle   21 Float   22 Metering rod   23 Main jet   25 Nozzle channel   26 Nozzle   27 Fuel passage   28 Nozzle jet   29 Throttle body   30 Throttle venturi   31 Bleed hole   32 Outlet check valve   33 Filter   34 Inlet check valve   35 Accelerator pump plunger

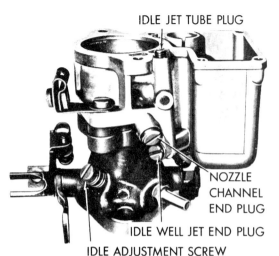

IDLE JET TUBE PLUG

NOZZLE CHANNEL END PLUG

IDLE WELL JET END PLUG

IDLE ADJUSTMENT SCREW

FIG 2:7   Opel carburetter idle system

2:7 Opel carburetters

The Opel carburetter fitted to 1 litre models has a non-variable choke and a metering rod which controls the flow of fuel through the main jet. The metering rod has several steps of reducing diameter, the lower step controlling full throttle operation when the rod is raised to its highest position in the main jet. When the throttle is closed the metering rod cuts off the fuel supply through the main jet, and engine idle is controlled by an independant idling system. An accelerator pump operates from the throttle linkage and delivers fuel through a jet into the main venturi.

2:8 Removing, servicing Opel carburetters

Removing:

Remove the air cleaner and disconnect the throttle rod from the carburetter. Detach the fuel and vacuum lines and the control cables from the carburetter. Remove the bolt holding the support bracket and the two nuts fixing the carburetter to the inlet manifold. Remove the carburetter, collecting the O-ring seal from between the flange and the manifold.

Refitting:

Reverse the removal instructions, using a new O-ring seal in the carburetter flange groove. Remember to refit the sparking plug lead support under the outer carburetter fixing nut.

Dismantling:

Refer to FIG 2:6. Remove the bolts attaching the air intake 9 to the carburetter body. Lift off the air intake and choke assembly and disconnect the fast-idle operating rod. Remove the filter cover and filter 17. Unhook the spring 14 then turn the metering rod 22 a quarter of a turn and lift it from the carburetter, collecting the washer 13. Detach the accelerator pump plunger link 4. Remove the fixing screws, then lift and rotate the float chamber cover. Slide off accelerator pump lever 1 and remove the float chamber cover assembly. Remove float 21, needle 20, seat 19 and the gasket.

Remove the accelerator pump operating rod and withdraw the pump plunger. Refer to FIG 2:7 and remove idle well jet end plug, jet tube plug and the jet. Remove the main metering jet, which is 23 in FIG 2:6. Take out passage plug 6 and jet 7. Remove the check valve plug and the filter 33, inlet valve 34 and outlet valve 32. Refer to FIG 2:7 and remove the nozzle channel end plug and nozzle jet, and the idle adjustment screw. Remove the throttle body and plastic spacer from the float chamber.

Servicing:

Clean and inspect all parts carefully, renewing any found worn or damaged. Clean all sediment from the float chamber and examine the float needle 20. If there is a noticeable ridge on the tapered seat, the assembly must be renewed. Check for correct float level by inverting the float chamber cover and fitting the float and needle valve assembly into it, so that the float rests against the needle. In this condition, a straightedge 12 mm (.47 inch) thick should just clear the float when placed across the joint face of the float chamber. If this is not the case, adjust the float level by bending the flange that contacts the needle, being careful not to damage the float.

The metering rod position can be checked by installing service tool J.21685 in its place. The square shoulder of the tool should just fit under the metering rod pin on the actuating lever, with the throttle fully closed. If not, use pliers to carefully bend the actuating lever linkage rod to obtain the correct adjustment.

Reassemble the carburetter in the reverse order of dismantling, noting that there are no retainers fitted to the plunger link 4. Fit the link from the air intake side. **The idle well jet and plug must be installed before the idle jet tube (see FIG 2:7).** Use new gaskets throughout, noting that no gasket is fitted between the air intake assembly and the carburetter. Do up the idle adjustment screw fully, then unscrew it three quarters of a turn. This will suffice until final adjustments to the slow-running can be made with the engine at operating temperature.

2:9 Adjustment of Opel carburetters

Adjustment of the carburetter must be carried out with the engine at operating temperature, and will only be effective if the ignition timing, sparking plugs and contact breaker points are in order.

Turn the throttle stop screw to obtain a reasonable idle, then adjust the idle adjustment screw to obtain the fastest idle possible under these conditions. Finally, reduce to a slow-idle with the throttle stop screw.

2:10 Solex single-barrel carburetters

The Solex carburetters fitted to 1.1 litre engines have non-variable chokes and fixed jets. A power valve operated by vacuum from the inlet manifold richens the mixture when the engine operates under conditions of heavy load or high speed. The accelerator pump jet, in addition to its normal function, supplements the main jet at full throttle conditions, permitting the use of an economical main jet size for cruising conditions. Full details of jet sizes are given in Technical Data.

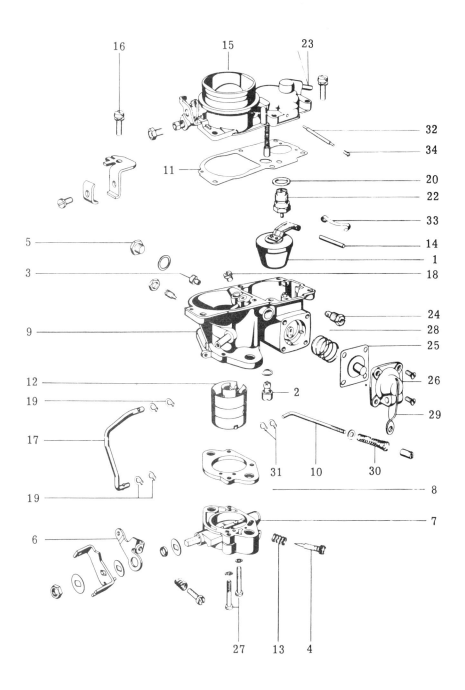

FIG 2:8 Components of a Solex single-barrel carburetter

Key to Fig 2:8   1 Float   2 Power valve   3 Main jet   4 Idle mixture screw   5 Main jet plug   6 Throttle lever
7 Throttle body   8 Insulating flange gasket   9 Float chamber   10 Pump rod   11 Gasket   12 Choke tube   13 Spring
14 Float pivot   15 Float chamber cover   16 Cover fixing screw   17 Throttle rod   18 High speed bleeder jet   19 Circlip
20 Seal ring   22 Needle valve assembly   23 Fuel inlet   24 Idle jet   25 Diaphragm   26 Pump cover   27 Screws
28 Diaphragm spring   29 Pump lever   30 Duration spring   31 Circlips   32 Filler pin   33 Leaf spring   34 Plug

O KAD

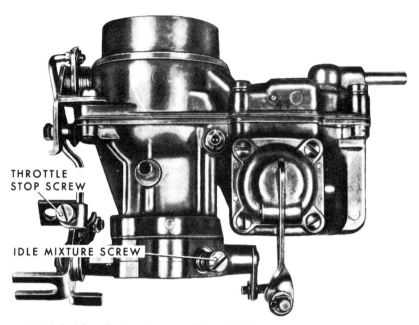

FIG 2:9   Idle adjustment screws, Solex single-barrel carburetter

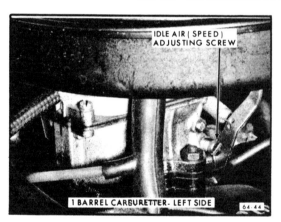

FIG 2:10   Idle air adjusting screw, 1968 onwards

2:11 Removing, servicing Solex carburetters

Removing:

Remove the air cleaner(s) and pull the vacuum and fuel hoses off the carburetter fittings. Loosen the clamp and setscrew to disconnect the choke cable. Unhook the throttle linkage by removing the cotterpin and two washers. Remove the carburetter from the inlet manifold by removing the two fixing nuts and lockwashers collecting the rubber seal ring from the groove in the inlet manifold joint face.

Refitting:

Reverse the removal instructions, fitting a new rubber seal ring into the inlet manifold groove, unless the original seal is in good condition. When attaching the choke cable, ensure that the choke butterfly valve is fully open when the control on the instrument panel is pushed in. Adjust the carburetter as described in **Section 2:12**, referring to **Section 2:16** if twin carburetters are fitted.

Dismantling:

Refer to **FIG 2:8** and remove clips 19 and throttle rod 17. Remove the float chamber cover 15 and the gasket 11, collecting the cable clamp mounted on the cover. Remove the needle valve assembly 22, noting the position of copper ring 20 for reassembly. Remove the plug from the accelerator pump passage in the float chamber cover. **The accelerator pump nozzle is not removable.**

Remove the float 1 with pivot 14 and spring 33 from the float chamber. Remove the outer clip 31 from the pump rod 10 at the throttle body, then remove the throttle body from the float chamber by taking out the two fixing screws, and remove the insulating flange gasket 8. Remove the idle adjustment screw 4 and spring 13.

Remove the accelerator pump cover 26 by taking out the four fixing screws and tapping the cover gently with a screwdriver handle to free it. Separate the cover from the diaphragm and remove cover, diaphragm and spring. Loosen the locknut on the screw attaching the choke tube 12 to the float chamber, then remove the screw and pull out the choke tube. Unscrew the idle jet 24. Remove the high-speed bleeder 18 from inside the carburetter. Remove the plug 5, seal ring and main jet 3. Remove the plug screw from the bypass passage in the diaphragm housing.

The carburetter will now be dismantled as far as possible . Do not remove any additional parts.

Servicing:

Clean and inspect all parts carefully, renewing any found worn or damaged. Clean out all sediment from the float chamber, jets and passages. Use compressed air,

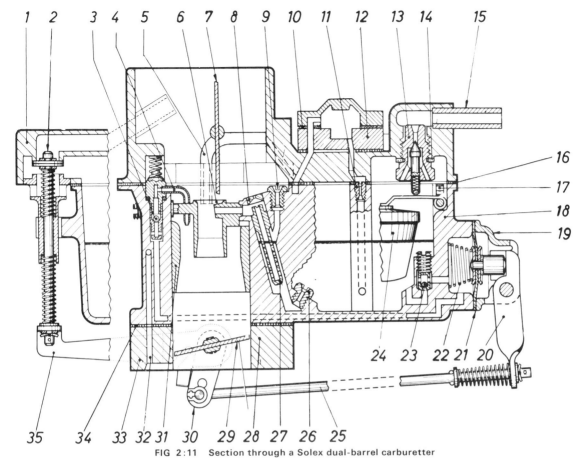

FIG 2:11 Section through a Solex dual-barrel carburetter

Key to Fig 2:11   1 Carburetter cover   2 Vent valve   3 Ball valve, pump outlet   4 Injection tube   5 Enrichment tube
6 Primary venturi   7 Choke valve   8 Main nozzle bleed   9 High-speed air jet   10 Seal ring   11 Enrichment jet
12 Enrichment housing   13 Needle valve   14 Seal ring   15 Fuel line fitting   16 Cover gasket   17 Leaf spring
18 Float chamber   19 Pump cover   20 Pump lever   21 Diaphragm   22 Diaphragm spring   23 Ball valve, pump inlet
24 Float   25 Pump connecting rod   26 Main jet   27 Emulsion tube   28 Throttle valve body   29 Throttle valve
30 Intermediate lever   31 Main venturi   32 Vacuum passage for automatic choke   33 Throttle valve body   34 Gasket
35 Vent valve lever

clean petrol and a small stiff brush. Do not use cloth or a wire probe. Check the needle valve assembly 22. If there is a noticeable ridge on the tapered seat of the needle, the assembly must be renewed. Inspect the float for leaks and check that its mounting flange is not bent. The float must be renewed if it is defective in any way.

Check the radial play of the throttle valve shaft in the throttle body 7. Too much play will allow the entry of air which will impair starting and slow-running, so if there is excessive play in the shaft bearings the throttle body should be renewed.

Reassemble the carburetter in the reverse order of dismantling. Be sure to fit the copper washer 20 properly when refitting the needle valve assembly, or the float level will be incorrect. Install the choke tube so that the lugs rest in the cut-outs in the float chamber, and do not overtighten the fixing screw and locknut to avoid distorting the choke tube. Do up the idle adjustment screw fully, then unscrew it one turn, final idle adjustment being made

when the engine is at operating temperature, as described in the next Section.

2:12 Adjustments to Solex carburetters

The engine must be at operating temperature and the air cleaner fitted before idle adjustments are made to the carburetter. The following instructions are for single carburetter engines. For twin carburetter installations reference should be made to **Section 2:16,** and for engines fitted with later type Emission Control systems to **Section 2:17.** Carburetter adjustments will only be effective if the ignition timing, sparking plugs and contact breaker points are in order. Carburetters fitted from 1968 onwards differ slightly in methods of adjustment from earlier models, due to the inclusion of an idle air adjusting screw.

An accurate engine tachometer will be necessary for adjusting carburetters on models from 1968 onwards, due to the need for accurate measurement of engine rev/min.

O KAD

35

FIG 2:12 Removing enrichment system cover

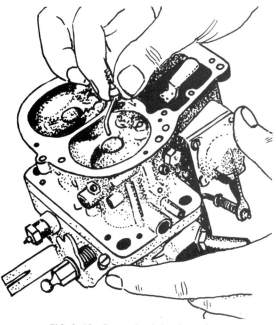

FIG 2:13 Removing injection tube

Connect the tachometer between the distributor side of the coil and an earth point on the car.

1966–67 models:

Refer to **FIG 2:9**. Adjust the throttle stop screw to obtain an idling speed of approximately 800 rev/min, then adjust the idle mixture screw to obtain the fastest possible idle under these conditions. If the idling speed is then too high, reduce it with the throttle stop screw, then adjust the idle mixture screw to obtain a smooth idle.

1968 models:

Refer to **FIG 2:10** and fully close the idle air adjusting screw by turning it in until seated. By adjusting the throttle stop screw to alter the engine speed, and the idle mixture screw to obtain the smoothest possible running, set the engine at an idle of 650 to 700 rev/min. This will set the throttle valve in the best possible position for low-speed running, and all further changes to the idling speed will be made with the idle air adjusting screw.

Raise the engine idling speed to 850 to 900 rev/min by turning the idle air adjusting screw. If the idle is not smooth and even, make a final adjustment with the idle mixture screw to correct it.

1969–70 models:

On these models the throttle stop screw is positioned and locked by the Manufacturer for best economy and performance and must not be moved. Adjust the air idle adjusting screw to obtain an engine idling speed of 850 to 900 rev/min. Adjust the idle mixture screw to obtain the fastest possible idle under these conditions. If the speed then exceeds 900 rev/min, reduce it with the idle air adjusting screw. If the idle is not smooth and even, make a final adjustment with the idle mixture screw to correct it.

2:13 Solex dual-barrel carburetters

These carburetters are fitted to 1.5 and 1.9 litre engines and have two barrels of 1.25 inch diameter each, the 1.5 litre model having a manually operated choke and the 1.9 litre model an automatic choke. The secondary valve is operated by a linkage from the primary valve for 1.5 litre models, and by a vacuum diaphragm assembly for 1.9 litre models. A diaphragm operated accelerator pump is fitted to both models.

FIG 2:14 Removing idle and air jets

Key to Fig 2:14
A2 Secondary idle jet   A1 Primary idle jet
B2 Secondary high-speed air jet   B1 Primary high-speed air jet

2:14 Removing, servicing dual-barrel carburetters

Removing:

Remove the air cleaner. Pull the fuel and vacuum hoses from the carburetter fittings. Disconnect the choke on 1.5 litre engines by loosening the cable clamp and set-screw. On 1.9 litre engines disconnect the two hoses from the automatic choke and plug them to prevent loss of coolant. Disconnect throttle linkage by removing the ball from the socket on the end of the throttle shaft. Remove the carburetter by removing the four fixing nuts and lock-washers.

Refitting:

Reverse the removal instructions, using a new gasket at the carburetter to intake manifold joint. Make sure that the automatic choke housing is set on the index and that the choke valve is nearly closed at room temperature. Check the choke valve is free in all positions. Adjust the engine idle as described in **Section 2:15.**

Dismantling, 1.5 litre models:

When dismantling the carburetter note the positions of parts removed. Be careful not to mix the parts of the primary and secondary barrels. Details of jet sizes are given in Technical Data.

1 Refer to **FIG 2:11.** Take out the fixing screws and remove the carburetter cover 1. Remove the needle valve assembly 13 and the copper sealing washer.
2 Remove the enrichment system cover (see **FIG 2:12**). Pull accelerator pump injection tube assembly from float chamber (see **FIG 2:13**). Remove the float, float spindle and leaf spring.
3 Refer to **FIG 2:14** and remove primary and secondary idle jets and primary and secondary high-speed air jets,

FIG 2:16 Removing accelerator pump

FIG 2:17 Removing vacuum case lever

marking them to ensure they are fitted to the correct barrel on reassembly.
4 Refer to **FIG 2:15** and remove primary and secondary main jets, and the enrichment jet. Remove accelerator pump valve assembly. Remove the circlip from the connecting rod and remove the accelerator pump (see **FIG 2:16**).
5 Remove the idle mixture screw from the throttle valve body and the idle air adjusting screw from the float chamber (see **FIG 2:24**).

Dismantling, 1.9 litre models:

1 Remove the circlip from the lower end of the throttle lever to choke link. Lever off the vacuum case connect-

FIG 2:15 Removing main jets

Key to Fig 2:15
A2 Secondary main jet
C Enrichment jet
A1 Primary main jet
B Accelerator pump inlet valve

FIG 2:18   Removing vent valve cotterpin

5 Pull accelerator pump injection tube assembly from float chamber (see **FIG 2:13**). Remove the float, float spindle and leaf spring.

6 Refer to the previous instructions for dismantling carburetters on 1.5 litre models and carry out operations 3, 4 and 5.

Servicing, all models:

Clean and inspect all parts carefully, renewing any found worn or damaged. Clean out all sediment from the float chamber, jets and passages. Use compressed air, clean petrol and a small stiff brush. Do not use cloth or a wire probe. Check the needle valve assembly. If there is a noticeable ridge on the tapered seat of the needle, the assembly must be renewed. Inspect the float for leaks and check that its mounting flange is not bent. The float must be renewed if it is defective in any way. Reassembly is a reversal of the dismantling procedure, using new gaskets throughout. Install automatic choke cover so that the catch of the bi-metal spring is positioned onto the intermediate lever as shown in **FIG 2:20**. Align the cover on the index as shown in **FIG 2:21**, then tighten the fixing

FIG 2:19   Removing vacuum diaphragm cover

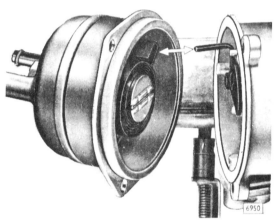

FIG 2:20   Positioning automatic choke cover

FIG 2:21   Automatic choke housing on index

ing lever as shown in **FIG 2:17**. Refer to **FIG 2:18** and remove the vent valve cotterpin. Remove the circlip, two flat washers and thrust spring.

2 Take out the fixing screws and remove the carburetter cover and the needle valve assembly and copper sealing washer (see **FIG 2:11**).

3 Unscrew vacuum diaphragm cover from choke housing (see **FIG 2:19**). Remove the enrichment system cover (see **FIG 2:12**).

4 Remove the retaining ring from the automatic choke body and take off the cover. Unscrew vacuum diaphragm case from the carburetter cover and remove the reduction jet from the case.

screws. The choke valve should be nearly closed at room temperature.

Refer to **FIG 2:22** and adjust the throttle valve of the secondary barrel by releasing and turning the adjusting screw as shown. A small gap of .002 inch must exist at the point shown by the arrow to avoid jamming of the throttle valve. Check the compression of the vent valve lower spring as shown in **FIG 2:23**. It should be compressed $\frac{1}{4}$ inch with the throttle valve fully closed. If not, correct the adjustment by carefully bending the valve operating lever, using pliers.

Screw in the idle mixture screw fully, then unscrew it two and a half turns, final adjustment being made when the engine is at operating temperature, as described in the next Section.

2:15 Adjustment to dual-barrel carburetters

An accurate tachometer will be needed for adjusting these carburetters, due to the need for accurate measurement of engine rev/min. Connect the tachometer between the distributor side of the coil and an earth point on the car.

1968 models:

Refer to **FIG 2:24** and fully close the idle air adjusting screw by turning it in until seated. By adjusting the throttle stop screw to alter the engine speed, and the idle mixture screw to obtain the smoothest possible running, set the engine at an idling of 650 to 700 rev/min. This will set the throttle valve in the best possible position for low-speed running, and all further changes to the idling speed will be made with the idle air adjusting screw.

Raise the engine idling speed to 750 to 800 rev/min by turning the idle air adjusting screw. If the idle is not smooth and even, make a final adjustment with the idle mixture screw to correct it.

1969–70 models:

On these models the throttle stop screw is positioned and locked by the Manufacturers for best economy and performance and must not be moved. Adjust the air idle adjusting screw to obtain an engine idling speed of 750 to 800 rev/min. Adjust the idle mixture screw to obtain the fastest possible idle under these conditions. If the speed then exceeds 800 rev/min, reduce it with the idle air adjusting screw. If the idle is not smooth and even, make a final adjustment with the idle mixture screw to correct it.

Fast-idle speed adjustments

These adjustments concern models equipped with automatic chokes.

With the engine at operating temperature and switched off, set the carburetter to the cold starting position in the following manner: Actuate the linkage with one hand so that the throttle valve is approximately half open. With the other hand, completely close the choke valve, then release the linkage and choke valve.

Now start the engine, but do not touch the accelerator pedal or linkage as the slightest touch will return the throttle valve to the hot idle position, necessitating a fresh start. With the throttle valve set as just described the engine should run at 2700 rev/min. To adjust to this figure, refer to **FIG 2:25** and turn the nuts on the throttle

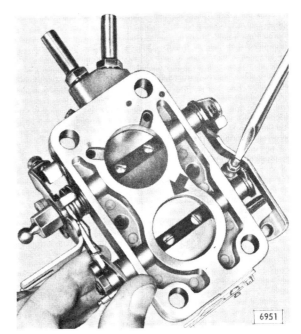

FIG 2:22 Adjusting secondary throttle valve gap

FIG 2:23 Checking vent valve adjustment

link as shown to increase engine speed, or in the opposite direction to decrease engine speed.

2:16 Twin carburetters

Twin carburetters are fitted to 1.1 litre engines such as the 1966–67 Rallye models, and high performance models in the 1969–70 ranges. Correct idle adjustment requires the carburetters to be synchronized as follows:

1966–67 models:

Remove the air cleaners. Check that both choke valves are correctly adjusted at the linkage to obtain fully opened and fully closed positions when the linkage is moved.

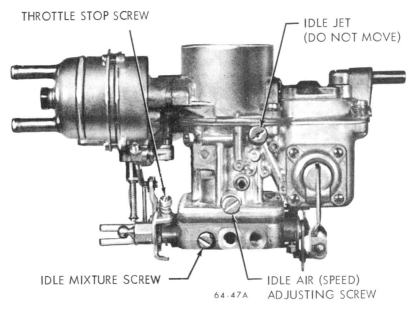

FIG 2:24   Idle adjusting screws, dual-barrel carburetters (1.9 litre model shown)

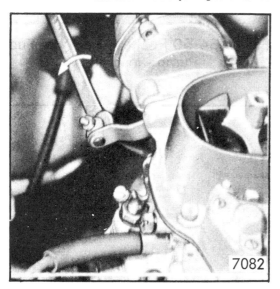

FIG 2:25   Increasing fast-idle speed (automatic choke)

Refer to **FIG 2:26.** Loosen the coupling screw to provide clearance between the screw and its lever. Close both idle mixture screws by turning them in. On the rear carburetter only, open the idle mixture screw three quarters of a turn. On the front carburetter, make sure the throttle valve is completely closed by slackening the idle speed screw right off.

Start the engine on the rear carburetter and adjust the idle speed screw to obtain an engine idling speed of 700 rev/min, using the idle mixture screw to obtain smooth running. Stop the engine and screw in the idle mixture screw on the rear carburetter, counting the number of turns. Slacken the idle speed screw on the rear carburetter right off and open the idle mixture screw on the front carburetter three quarters of a turn. Adjust the front carburetter in the manner just described for an engine idling speed of 700 rev/min.

With the engine idling at 700 rev/min on the front carburetter, open the rear idle mixture screw by the number of turns previously counted. Now raise the engine idling speed to 1000 rev/min with the rear idle speed screw. The carburetters should now be synchronized to the correct idling speed. If the idle is not smooth and even, however, a minor finish balance may be necessary as follows:

Slacken the idle speed screw on the front carburetter and check the idling speed. Tighten the screw again to obtain an idling speed of 1000 rev/min and repeat the operation on the rear carburetter. With either carburetter operating the idling speed of the engine should be nearly the same. If there is a difference of more than 100 rev/min, half the difference must be added to the lower reading carburetter by adjusting the idle speed screw, i.e., for a difference of 100 rev/min, run the engine on the low reading carburetter and add 50 rev/min with its adjusting screw. Then raise the idle to 1000 rev/min with the adjusting screw on the other carburetter.

Finally, lock the coupling between the carburetters by tightening the coupling screw, allowing a clearance of .006 inch between the screw and its operating lever. Refit the air cleaners.

1969–70 models:

On these models the throttle stop screws and idle mixture screws are positioned and locked by the Manufacturers, so idle adjustment is preset and should need no attention. If for any reason the screws mentioned are disturbed and carburetter adjustment becomes necessary,

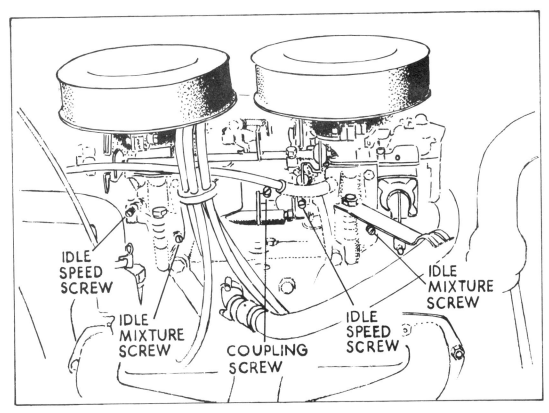

FIG 2:26 Twin carburetters, 1966–67 Rallye models

the work should be referred to an Opel main dealer equipped with the appropriate tuning apparatus.

2:17 Carburetter adjustments with Emission Control systems

Cars fitted with Emission Control systems should have the carburetter adjustments set for a slightly leaner mixture than standard to enable the cars to pass the US Federal requirements. In addition, these adjustments reduce the tendency for the engines of cars equipped with Emission Control to speed up momentarily when the foot is removed from the accelerator pedal. The adjustment is carried out as follows:

Refer to the appropriate previous Section for the type of carburetter fitted and carry out the instructions for setting the engine idling speed correctly. Having done so, turn the idle mixture screw inwards slightly to reduce the engine idling speed by 20 rev/min for 1.1 litre engines, or by 30 rev/min for 1.5 and 1.9 litre engines.

2:18 Air cleaners

Oil bath type:

The earlier 1 litre cars are fitted with oil bath type air cleaners which should be serviced every 6000 miles under normal conditions and more frequently in dusty conditions. Remove the air cleaner cover and lift out the filter element.

Servicing consists of discarding the oil from the container, cleaning it of accumulated sludge and swilling the element in paraffin to clean it. Fill the container to the correct level with engine oil. Ensure that all paraffin has drained from the element and refit it.

Paper element type:

If this type of element is fitted it should be removed from the air cleaner every 6000 miles and cleaned by gently tapping it to remove dirt and grit. The element should be renewed every 12,000 miles. Clean or renew the element at shorter intervals if the vehicle is operated under dusty conditions.

Wiremesh type:

Wiremesh type air filters should be serviced every 6000 miles, or more frequently if operational conditions are very dusty. Servicing consists of removing the element from the air cleaner and washing it in petrol or paraffin. Allow the element to dry, then coat it with engine oil, shaking off surplus oil before refitting it to the air cleaner.

2:19 Fault diagnosis

(a) Leakage or insufficient fuel delivered

1 Air vent to tank restricted
2 Fuel pipes blocked

3 Air leaks at pipe connections
4 Pump or carburetter filters blocked
5 Pump gaskets faulty
6 Pump diaphragm defective
7 Pump valves sticking or seating badly
8 Fuel vaporizing in pipelines due to heat

(b) Excessive fuel consumption

1 Carburetter(s) need adjusting
2 Fuel leakage
3 Sticking throttle or choke controls
4 Dirty air cleaner(s)
5 Thermo control fault (Emission Control System)
6 Excessive engine temperature
7 Brakes binding
8 Tyres under-inflated
9 Idling speed too high
10 Car overloaded

(c) Idling speed too high

1 Rich fuel mixture
2 Carburetter controls sticking
3 Incorrect slow-running adjustment
4 Worn throttle valve

(d) Noisy fuel pump

1 Loose mountings
2 Air leaks on suction side or at diaphragm
3 Obstruction in fuel pipe
4 Clogged pump filter

(e) No fuel delivery

1 Float needle stuck
2 Tank vent blocked
3 Pipeline obstructed
4 Pump diaphragm stiff or damaged
5 Pump inlet valve stuck open
6 Bad air leak on suction side of pump

CHAPTER 3

THE IGNITION SYSTEM

3:1 Description

All the cars covered by this manual use Bosch ignition components. The distributor incorporates automatic timing control by centrifugal mechanism and a vacuum operated unit. As engine speed increases, the centrifugal action of rotating weights pivoting against the tension of small springs moves the contact breaker cam relative to the distributor drive shaft, and progressively advances the ignition. The vacuum control unit is connected by small bore pipe to a fitting on the carburetter. At high degrees of vacuum the unit advances the ignition, but under load, at reduced vacuum, the unit progressively retards the ignition. **FIG 3:1** shows the distributor fitted in 1 and 1.1 litre engines and **FIG 3:2** shows distributor installation in 1.5 and 1.9 litre engines.

3:2 Routine maintenance

Pull off the two spring clips and remove the distributor cap. Pull the rotor off the cam spindle. Refer to **FIG 3:3** which shows the distributor with cap and rotor removed. Apply a few drops of oil to the moving parts of the contact breaker plate at points 'B' and oil the felt in the cam at 'C'. Then apply a thin smear of grease to the cam at 'A'. When lubricating the internal parts of the distributor take great care to avoid letting oil or grease get onto the contact breaker points.

Adjusting the contact breaker points:

Turn the engine until one of the cams has opened the points to the fullest extent, then check the gap between the points with a feeler gauge. The correct gap is .015 inch for 1 litre engines, and .018 inch for 1.1, 1.5 and 1.9 litre engines. To adjust the gap, loosen the contact point clamp screw and move the fixed contact breaker point until the gap is correct. Tighten the clamp screw and recheck the gap.

Cleaning the contact points:

Use a fine carborundum stone to polish the contact points if they are dirty or pitted, taking care to keep the faces flat and square. Afterwards, wipe away all dust with a cloth moistened in petrol. The contact points may be dismantled to assist cleaning by referring to **Section 3:4.**

3:3 Ignition faults

If the engine runs unevenly, set it to idle at about 1000 rev/min and, taking care not to touch any metal part of the sparking plug leads, remove and replace each lead from its plug in turn. Doing this to a plug which is firing properly will accentuate the uneven running but will make no difference if the plug is not firing.

Having located the faulty cylinder, stop the engine and remove the plug lead. Start the engine and hold the lead

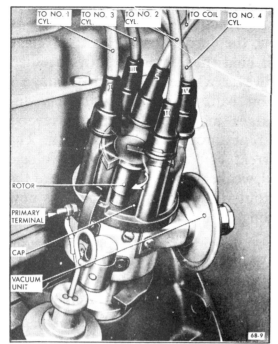

FIG 3:1 Distributor installation, 1 and 1.1 litre engines

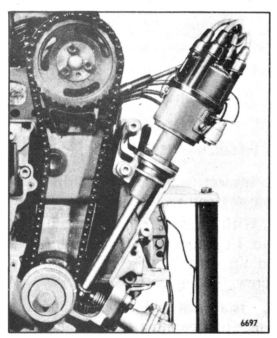

FIG 3:2 Distributor installation, 1.5 and 1.9 litre engines

carefully to avoid shocks so that the metal end is about $\frac{1}{8}$ inch away from the cylinder head. A strong, regular spark confirms that the fault lies with the sparking plug which should be cleaned as described in **Section 3:6** or renewed if defective.

If the spark is weak and irregular, check the condition of the lead, and, if it is perished or cracked, renew it and repeat the test. If no improvement results, check that the inside of the distributor cap is clean and dry, that the carbon brush at its centre can be moved freely against its internal spring and that there is no 'tracking', which can be seen as a thin black line between the electrodes or to some metal part in contact with the cap. 'Tracking' can only be rectified by fitting a new cap.

Testing the low-tension circuit:

Check that the contact breaker points are clean and correctly set, then proceed as follows:

Disconnect the thin wire from the coil that connects to the distributor. Connect a test lamp between these terminals, turn on the ignition and turn the engine slowly. If, when the contacts close, the lamp lights and goes out when they open the circuit is in order. If the lamp fails to light, there is a fault in the low-tension circuit. Remove the test lamp and reconnect the cable to the coil and distributor.

If the fault lies in the low-tension circuit, use the test lamp to carry out the following tests with the ignition switched on.

Remove the wire from the ignition switch side of the coil and connect the lamp between the end of this wire and earth. If the lamp fails to light it indicates a fault in the wiring or connections between the battery and the coil, or in the ignition switch. Reconnect the wire if the lamp lights.

Disconnect the wire from the coil that connects to the distributor. Connect the lamp between the coil terminal and earth. If the lamp fails to light it indicates a fault in the primary winding and a new coil must be fitted. Reconnect the wire if the lamp lights, and disconnect its other end from the distributor. If the test lamp does not light when connected between the end of the wire and earth it indicates a fault in that section of wire.

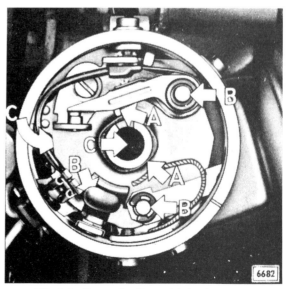

FIG 3:3 Upper distributor lubrication points

Capacitor:

The best method of testing a capacitor (condenser) is by substitution. Disconnect the original capacitor and connect a new one between the low-tension terminal on the side of the distributor and earth for test purposes. If a new capacitor is proved to be required, it may then be properly fitted. The capacitor is of .23 to .32 microfarad capacity.

3:4 Removing and dismantling distributor

1 and 1.1 litre engines:

1 Remove the distributor cap.
2 Turn the engine until No. 1 cylinder is in the firing position by aligning the notch on the rotor tip with the notch on the distributor housing as shown in **FIG 3:4,** and the raised mark on the crankshaft pulley with the raised mark on the timing chain cover as shown in **FIG 3:5.**
3 Remove the vacuum line from the vacuum advance unit and the primary wire from the terminal on the distributor.
4 Refer to **FIG 3:6** and remove the distributor clamp bolt and clamp, then remove the distributor.

Refitting:

1 Inspect the gasket on the distributor housing and renew it if necessary.
2 With the crankshaft in the firing position for No. 1 cylinder as shown in **FIG 3:5,** turn the rotor to align the mark on the rotor tip with the centre of the contact breaker clamp screw as shown in **FIG 3:7.** Install the distributor with the vacuum advance unit pointing rearwards and parallel with the engine. The rotor will turn as the distributor is installed and the mark on the rotor tip should align with the mark on the case as the distributor seats.
3 Install the clamp with its fixing bolt finger tight, then align the rotor with the mark on the case as shown in **FIG 3:4** before finally tightening the clamp bolt. Reconnect primary wire and vacuum line.

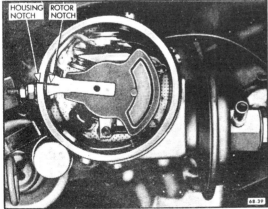

FIG 3:4 Rotor position for firing No. 1 cylinder, 1 and 1.1 litre engines

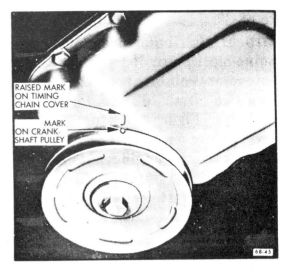

FIG 3:5 Timing marks on crankshaft pulley and timing chain case, 1 and 1.1 litre engines

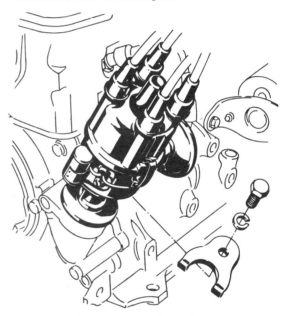

FIG 3:6 Removing distributor clamp

1.5 and 1.9 litre engines:

1 Refer to **Chapter 2, Section 2:3** and remove the fuel pump. This is necessary because the fuel pump blocks the distributor drive gear, preventing removal of the distributor (see **FIG 3:2**).
2 Turn the engine until No. 1 cylinder is in the firing position by aligning the centre of the shaft cut-out with the mark on the distributor casing as shown in **FIG 3:8,** and the ball imbedded in the engine flywheel with the pointer in the housing as shown in **FIG 3:9.**
3 Remove the vacuum advance lines from the vacuum advance units and the primary wire from the terminal on the distributor.

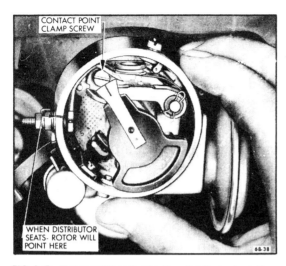

FIG 3:7 Rotor position for starting distributor installation, 1 and 1.1 litre engines

FIG 3:8 Distributor shaft position for firing No. 1 cylinder, 1.5 and 1.9 litre engines

4 Refer to **FIG 3:6** and remove the distributor clamp bolt and clamp, then remove the distributor, noting its position for correct reassembly. To ensure easy refitting of the distributor, do not rotate the crankshaft or oil pump while it is removed.

Refitting:

1 Inspect the gasket on the distributor housing and renew it if necessary.
2 Make sure the oil pump slot is in the correct position to receive the distributor shaft drive dog as shown in **FIG**

3:10. Install the distributor correctly as noted during removal and with the shaft cut-out in the position shown in **FIG 3:11**. The shaft will turn as the distributor is installed and the mark on the rotor tip should align with the mark on the case when the distributor is seated.

3 Install the clamp with its fixing bolt finger tight, then align the rotor with the mark on the case before finally tightening the clamp bolt. Connect the primary wire and the vacuum hoses. Refit the fuel pump.

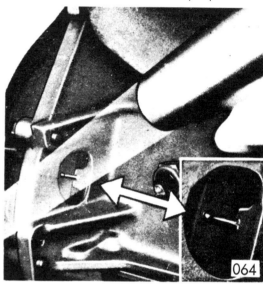

FIG 3:9 Timing marks on flywheel and housing, 1.5 and 1.9 litre engines

FIG 3:10 Oil pump drive position for correct location of distributor drive dog, 1.5 and 1.9 litre engines

Dismantling:

1 Unscrew and remove both cap retaining spring clips. Disconnect the capacitor wire. Remove vacuum control units and the capacitor.
2 Remove the retaining ring from the groove in the distributor shaft and push the shaft upwards. Undo clamp screw and remove the contact breaker assembly, then remove the contacts from the mounting plate.

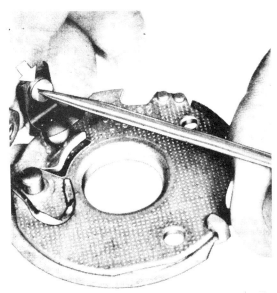

FIG 3:13   Dismantling contact breaker plate

FIG 3:11   Distributor shaft position for starting distributor installation, 1.5 and 1.9 litre engines

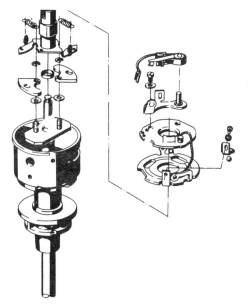

FIG 3:12   Removing contact breaker assembly

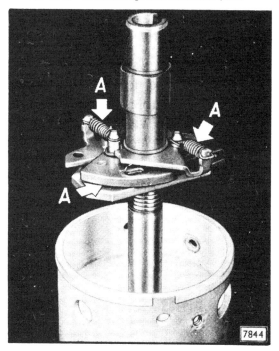

FIG 3:14   Centrifugal advance mechanism lubrication points

FIG 3:12 shows the components of the contact breaker and centrifugal advance assemblies.

3 Dismantle the contact breaker plate by unscrewing the ball thrust spring screw as shown in FIG 3:13. For cleaning, pull the distributor shaft together with the centrifugal advance mechanism partly out of the

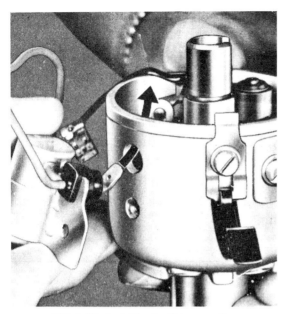

FIG 3:15   Installing ignition capacitor

distributor housing. Do not dismantle the advance mechanism.

Clean and inspect all parts, renewing any found worn or defective. Reassembly is a reversal of the dismantling procedure but note the following points:

Coat the moving parts of the centrifugal advance mechanism with grease at the points shown at 'A' in **FIG 3:14**. Lubricate the contact breaker assembly as described in **Section 3:2**. Be sure to correctly position the contact spring insulating washer in its support. Refit the capacitor as shown in **FIG 3:15** and reconnect the capacitor wire. Refit the distributor assembly to the engine as described previously. If the crankshaft has been turned resulting in lost timing, refer to the next Section.

3:5   Timing the ignition

1 Remove the distributor and the rocker cover. Remove the sparking plugs, engage top gear and move the car until No. 1 cylinder is in the firing position, which is when both timing marks coincide and the valves in the No. 1 cylinder are both closed. Correct alignment of the timing marks is shown in **FIG 3:5** for 1 and 1.1 litre engines or **FIG 3:9** for 1.5 and 1.9 litre engines.

2 Install the distributor in the engine so that the vacuum advance unit is in the original position and the mark on the rotor aligned with the mark on the case. If the distributor does not seat in the engine block, turn the distributor shaft until it is positioned as shown in **FIG 3:7** for 1 and 1.1 litre engines or **FIG 3:11** for 1.5 and 1.9 litre engines, then press down lightly on the distributor while turning the engine with the starter. When the drive mechanism engages and the distributor seats, start timing again from step 1, leaving the distributor installed.

3 Refit the distributor clamp and bolt, leaving the bolt just loose enough to permit movement of the dis-

tributor. Reconnect the primary wire to the distributor terminal.

Electrical setting of timing

Use this method to obtain an accurate setting. Ensure that the contact breaker points are fully closed, turning the distributor clockwise to do so. Switch on the ignition and connect a test lamp of the same voltage as the battery in parallel with the points. One lead will go to the terminal on the side of the distributor and one to earth. Slowly rotate the distributor anticlockwise until the lamp lights up, which indicates the points are just opening. Tighten the clamp bolt and fit the vacuum line.

Stroboscopic timing:

With this method of timing do not let the engine exceed 500 rev/min for 1 and 1.1 litre engines or 700 rev/min for 1.5 and 1.9 litre engines or the centrifugal advance mechanism will start to operate. Disconnect and plug the vacuum lines or the ignition will be retarded.

3:6   Sparking plugs

Inspect, clean and adjust sparking plugs regularly. When removing sparking plugs, ensure that their recesses are clean and dry so that nothing can fall into the cylinders. Plug gaskets can be re-used provided they are not less than half their original thickness. Have sparking plugs cleaned on an abrasive-blasting machine and tested under pressure with the electrode gaps correctly set at .030 inch. The electrodes should be filed until they are bright and parallel. The gaps must always be adjusted by setting the earth electrode. **Do not try to bend the centre electrode.**

Before refitting the plugs, clean the threads with a wire brush. Clean the threads in the cylinder head with a tap if the plugs cannot be screwed in by hand. Failing a tap, use an old sparking plug with crosscuts down the threads. Plugs should be tightened to a torque of 30 lb ft but, in the absence of a torque wrench, tighten with a normal box spanner through half a turn.

Inspection of the deposits on the electrodes can be helpful when tuning. Normally, from mixed periods of high and low-speed driving, the deposit should be powdery and range in colour from brown to greyish tan. There will also be slight wear of the electrodes. Long periods of constant speed driving or low-speed city driving will give white or yellowish deposits. Dry, black, fluffy deposits are due to incomplete combustion and indicate running with a rich mixture, excessive idling and possibly defective ignition. Overheated plugs have a white, blistered look about the centre electrode and the side electrode may be badly eroded. This may be caused by poor cooling, incorrect ignition or sustained high speeds with heavy loads.

Black, wet deposits result from oil in the combustion chamber from worn pistons, rings, valve stems or guides. Sparking plugs which run hotter may alleviate the problem but the cure is an engine overhaul.

Sparking plug leads:

Renew high-tension leads if they are defective in any way. Inspect for broken, swollen or deteriorated insulation which can be the cause of 'tracking', especially in wet weather conditions. Check the condition of the rubber covers on the terminal nuts, and renew if perished. Thread the new lead through the rubber covers and the knurled terminal nuts before refitting the lead end connections.

3:7 The distributor drive shaft

The distributor drive shaft is removed together with the distributor assembly in 1.5 and 1.9 litre engines as described in **Section 3:4**. The drive shaft in 1 and 1.1 litre engines is part of the oil pump drive gear and removal is covered in **Chapter 1, Section 1:9**.

3:8 Fault diagnosis

(a) Engine will not fire

1 Battery discharged
2 Distributor contact points dirty, pitted or maladjusted
3 Distributor cap dirty, cracked or 'tracking'
4 Carbon brush inside distributor cap not touching rotor
5 Faulty cable or loose connection in low-tension circuit
6 Distributor rotor arm cracked
7 Faulty coil
8 Broken contact breaker spring
9 Contact points stuck open

(b) Engine misfires

1 Check 2, 3, 5 and 7 in (a)
2 Weak contact breaker spring
3 High-tension plug and coil leads cracked or perished
4 Sparking plug(s) loose
5 Sparking plug insulation cracked
6 Sparking plug gap incorrectly set
7 Ignition timing too far advanced

CHAPTER 4

THE COOLING SYSTEM

4:1 Description

The cooling system is pressurized and thermostatically controlled. The water circulation is assisted by a centrifugal pump which is mounted at the front of the cylinder block and the cooling fan, which draws air through the radiator, is fitted to the same shaft as the pump impeller. The pump and fan and the generator are driven from a pulley on the crankshaft by a common belt. The tension of this belt is adjustable at the generator mounting.

The pump takes coolant from the bottom of the radiator and delivers it to the cylinder block from which it rises to the cylinder head. At normal operating temperatures the thermostat is open and the coolant returns from the head to the top of the radiator. At lower temperature, the valve is closed and the coolant bypasses the radiator and returns to the pump inlet to provide a rapid warm-up.

4:2 Maintenance

The pump bearing is a permanently sealed and lubricated assembly and requires no maintenance.

The cooling system should be filled with an inhibited, year-round ethylene glycol coolant solution, formulated to withstand two years of normal operation without draining. **Alcohol base coolants or plain water must not be used in the cooling system.** If for any reason water only is used as a coolant in an emergency, the system must be drained and refilled with the correct solution as soon as possible. The cooling system should be completely drained and refilled with the recommended coolant every two years.

Draining:

Refer to **FIG 4:1**. Some Opel radiators are not fitted with drain taps, in which case it will be necessary to remove the bottom hose from the radiator to drain the coolant. With that exception proceed as follows. Remove the filler cap 3 and open the drain tap 15. Loosen the drain plug on the right of the cylinder block and set the heater control in the HOT position. Have a clean container ready to catch the coolant if it is to be re-used.

Flushing:

Close the drain tap or reconnect the hose. Tighten the drain plug. Fill the system with clean water and run the engine for long enough to open the thermostat for complete circulation, then completely drain the system before the sediment has a chance to settle.

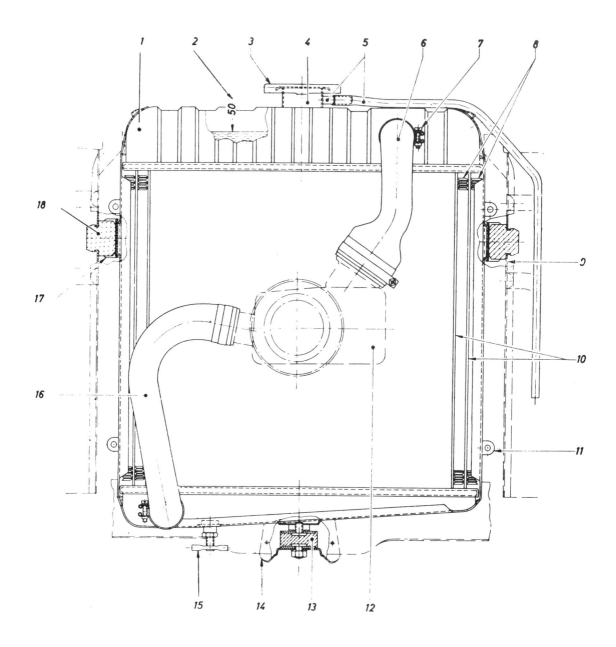

FIG 4:1 Radiator details

Key to Fig 4:1 1 Radiator   2 Coolant level   3 Filler cap   4 Filler neck   5 Overflow pipe   6 Top hose   7 Hose clamp
8 Cooling fins   9 Radiator side support   10 Coolant pipes   11 Lugs for radiator blind   12 Water pump
13 Lower rubber mounting   14 Lower radiator support   15 Drain tap   16 Bottom hose   17 Rubber mounting guide
18 Rubber mounting

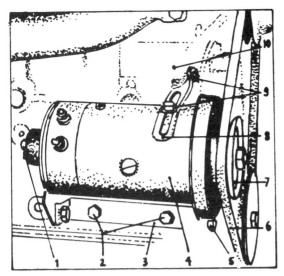

FIG 4:2 Generator and fan belt details

Key to Fig 4:2   1 Commutator end bracket
2 Bracket securing bolts   3 Mounting bracket
4 Generator   5 Generator securing bolts   6 Fan belt
7 Generator pulley   8 Tensioning bracket   9 Securing bolts
10 Cylinder block

Filling:

Check all hose connections, including those for the heater system, to ensure that leaks will not develop in the system. Close the radiator tap and the cylinder block drain plug. Leave the heater control in the HOT position. Fill the cooling system to a level about two inches from the filler neck. Check the coolant level after running the engine and top up if necessary.

4:3 Removing the radiator

Removal:

Drain the radiator as described in **Section 4:2.** Refer to **FIG 4:1** and remove the top and bottom hoses. Remove the nut from the lower rubber mounting 13 and lift the radiator out of the side support panels.

Refitting:

Refitting is a reversal of the removal procedure, but check the condition of the rubber mounting pad and renew it if necessary.

4:4 Adjusting fan belt

A tight fan belt will cause rapid wear of the generator and water pump bearings, a loose belt will slip and wear excessively with the consequent possibility of engine overheating, reduced generator output and a squealing noise. The tension is correct when the belt can be manually flexed by approximately $\frac{1}{2}$ inch midway between the generator pulley and the fan pulley. To adjust the fan belt tension refer to **FIG 4:2** and loosen the three bolts securing the generator to its mounting brackets. Swing the generator away from the engine until the belt tension is correct, then tighten the bolts. To remove the fan belt

loosen the generator mounting bolts as just described and push the generator towards the engine until the belt can be removed from the crankshaft and generator pulleys then withdrawn over the fan.

4:5 The water pump

The water pump bearing outer race is shrunk fitted into the water pump cover and for this reason the cover, shaft bearing and hub cannot be repaired, so a defective water pump must be renewed as an assembly.

Removal:

Drain the cooling system as described in **Section 4:2** and remove the fan belt as described in **Section 4:4.** Refer to **FIG 4:3** and disconnect the top and bottom hoses from the water pump. Remove the fixing bolts and lift off the water pump, being careful not to damage the radiator matrix. Check the pump shaft bearing for end play or roughness in operation. If the bearings are not in a serviceable condition the water pump assembly must be renewed.

Refitting:

Refitting is a reversal of the removal procedure, noting the following points. Make sure the joint faces on the pump and cylinder head are clean. Use a new water pump gasket and tighten the pump fixing bolts evenly.

4:6 The thermostat

The thermostat is located in the upper elbow of the water pump as shown in **FIG 4:4.**

Removal:

Drain sufficient coolant so that the level is below the thermostat and disconnect the top hose from the water

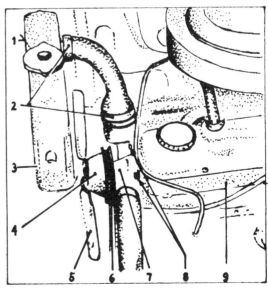

FIG 4:3 Water pump in position

Key to Fig 4:3   1 Overflow pipe   2 Hose clamps
3 Radiator   4 Water pump pulley   5 Fan   6 Fan belt
7 Water pump   8 Mounting bolts   9 Cylinder head

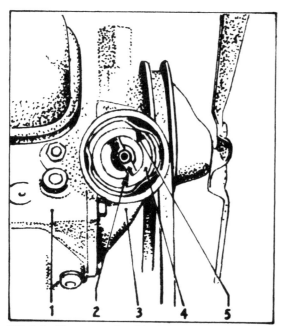

FIG 4:4 Thermostat fitted in the water pump housing

Key to Fig 4:4
2 Arrow facing toward the top
4 Thermostat   5 Retaining spring
1 Cylinder head
3 Water pump

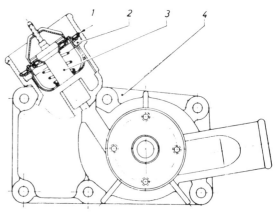

FIG 4:5   Section through thermostat housing

Key to Fig 4:5   1 Retaining spring
2 Rubber sealing ring   3 Thermostat   4 Water pump housing

pump. Refer to **FIG 4:5** and prise the retaining spring from the groove in the water pump elbow and lift out the thermostat.

Testing:

Clean the thermostat and immerse it in a container of cold water together with a zero to 100°C thermometer. Heat the water, keeping it stirred and observe the operation of the valve. As the temperature rises the valve should begin to open at 87°C. Around 95°C it should be open .178 inch (4.5 mm). Total opening takes place with the thermostat installed and the cooling system under pressure, at 102°C. If the thermostat does not operate correctly it must be renewed.

Refitting:

Renew the rubber sealing ring if it is not in good condition. Make sure that the thermostat is seating correctly after inserting the retaining spring. The arrow on the thermostat must face towards the top as shown in **FIG 4:4**.

4:7 Frost precautions

With the correct coolant solution installed as described in **Section 4:2**, no additional frost precautions should be necessary. However, it is advisable to test the solution at intervals during the winter to make certain that it has not been weakened. An hydrometer calibrated to read both specific gravity and temperature for the type of coolant in the system must be used.

4:8 Fault diagnosis

(a) Internal coolant leakage

1 Cracked cylinder wall
2 Loose cylinder head bolts
3 Cracked cylinder head
4 Faulty head gasket

(b) Poor circulation

1 Radiator matrix blocked
2 Engine coolant passages restricted
3 Low coolant level
4 Loose fan belt
5 Defective thermostat
6 Perished or collapsed radiator hoses

(c) Corrosion

1 Impurities in the coolant
2 Too infrequent draining and flushing

(d) Overheating

1 Check (b)
2 Sludge in crankcase
3 Faulty ignition timing
4 Low oil level in sump
5 Tight engine
6 Choked exhaust system
7 Binding brakes
8 Slipping clutch
9 Incorrect valve timing
10 Retarded ignition
11 Mixture too weak

CHAPTER 5

THE CLUTCH

5:1 Description

The clutch is a $6\frac{3}{4}$ inch diameter single plate dry disc operating on the inner face of the flywheel. The clutch obtains its operational pressure from a radially slotted diaphragm spring pivoting on two steel wire rings which is attached to the clutch cover by eight rivets. **FIG 5:1** shows the layout of the clutch assembly and the operating mechanism. When the clutch is fully engaged, the driven plate which is splined to the gearbox first motion shaft is nipped between the pressure plate and the flywheel, causing it to rotate with the flywheel and transmit torque to the gearbox. The clutch is disengaged when the pressure plate is withdrawn from the driven plate by pressure transmitted through the operating cable to the clutch release lever and release bearing. The driven plate then ceases to transmit torque. The clutch assembly is enclosed in a bellhousing which is integral with the gearbox on 1 and 1.1 litre engines, the bellhousing on 1.5 and 1.9 litre engines being a separate casting.

5:2 Removing and dismantling clutch

1 and 1.1 litre engines:

Remove the gearbox as described in **Chapter 6.** Check for assembly alignment marks at clutch cover flange and flywheel rim and if none are visible, punch or scribe mark both parts so they will be reassembled in their original positions relative to each other.

Remove the four clutch cover retaining bolts by loosening alternately and evenly to prevent distortion. Remove the pressure plate and driven disc, ensuring that the driven disc faces are kept clean.

1.5 and 1.9 litre engines:

1 Remove the gearbox as described in **Chapter 6.** Remove the exhaust pipes from the exhaust manifold. Disconnect the clutch return spring and the clutch control cable from the release lever.
2 Refer to **FIG 5:2** and remove the first motion shaft oil seal from the clutch release bearing sleeve 6. Remove clutch support to flywheel housing attaching bolts, loosen clutch support to cylinder block attaching bolts and swing clutch support downwards.
3 Remove flywheel housing lower cover then remove the flywheel housing from the engine.
4 To remove the release bearing refer to **FIGS 5:2** and **5:3** and slide the release lever off the ball stud against spring action. Remove the ball stud locknut and remove ball stud from the housing.

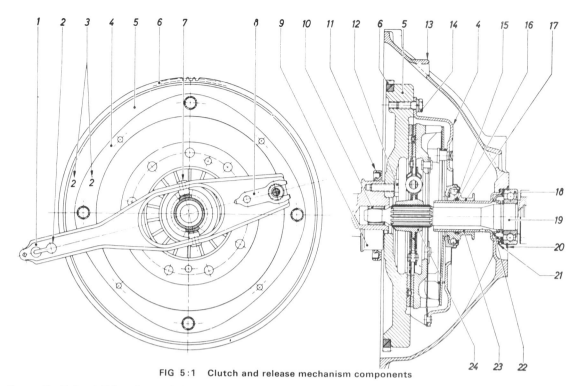

FIG 5:1 Clutch and release mechanism components

Key to Fig 5:1   1 Release lever   2 Control cable slot   3 Assembly marks   4 Clutch assembly   5 Flywheel   6 Ring gear
7 Thrust pin   8 Retaining spring   9 Crankshaft   10 Pilot bearing   11 Oil seal   12 Flywheel bolt   13 Clutch housing
14 Clutch assembly bolt and lockwasher   15 Release bearing lubricant   16 Felt ring   17 Release bearing   18 Bearing
19 Clutch shaft   20 Circlip   21 Gasket   22 Oil seal   23 Release bearing sleeve   24 Driven plate hub

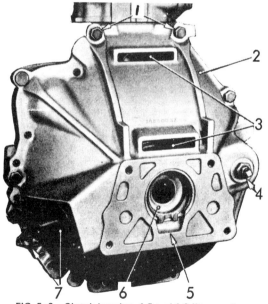

FIG 5:2   Clutch housing, 1.5 and 1.9 litre engines

Key to Fig 5:2
2 Housing   3 Vent holes
5 Recess in housing
7 Release lever and rubber boot
1 Upper attaching bolts
4 Ball stud
6 Release bearing sleeve

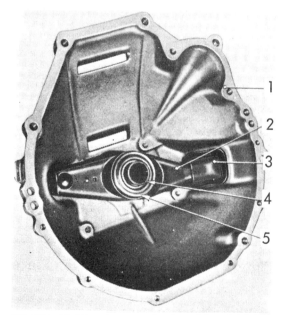

FIG 5:3   Clutch release mechanism, 1.5 and 1.9 litre engines

Key to Fig 5:3   1 Clutch housing   2 Release lever
3 Boot   4 Release bearing sleeve   5 Release bearing

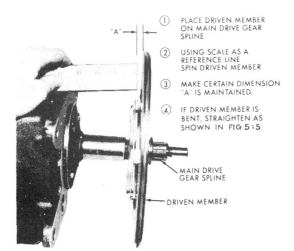

① PLACE DRIVEN MEMBER ON MAIN DRIVE GEAR SPLINE

② USING SCALE AS A REFERENCE LINE SPIN DRIVEN MEMBER

③ MAKE CERTAIN DIMENSION "A" IS MAINTAINED.

④ IF DRIVEN MEMBER IS BENT, STRAIGHTEN AS SHOWN IN FIG 5:5

MAIN DRIVE GEAR SPLINE

DRIVEN MEMBER

FIG 5:4 Checking driven plate runout

5 Check for assembly alignment marks at clutch cover flange and flywheel rim and if none are visible, punch or scribe mark both parts so they will be reassembled in their original positions relative to each other. Remove the four clutch cover retaining bolts by loosening alternately and evenly to prevent distortion. Remove the pressure plate and driven disc, ensuring that the driven disc faces are kept clean.

Servicing:

Clutch cover, spring and pressure plate assembly must not be dismantled. If any part is faulty the assembly must be renewed.

Clean all metal parts of the clutch except the release bearing and driven plate in petrol or paraffin to remove dirt and grease. Solvents must not be used to clean the release bearing as they will destroy the internal lubricant.

Inspect the flywheel and pressure plate friction surfaces for scoring or roughness. Slight roughness may be smoothed with fine emerycloth, but if the surface is deeply scored the part should be renewed. Check the driven plate for loose rivets and broken or very loose torsional springs. The friction linings should be well proud of the rivets and have a light colour, with a polished glaze through which the grain of the material is clearly visible. A dark, glazed deposit indicates oil on the facings and, as this condition cannot be rectified, a new plate will be required. Any signs of oil in the clutch will call for examination of the pilot bearing and the rear main bearing for oil leaks. The renewal of the rear main bearing oil seal is described in **Chapter 1.** Check the driven plate hub for a smooth sliding fit on the first motion shaft. Excessive wear, which results from faulty alignment, will dictate renewal of the plate. Regardless of whether the original or a new driven plate is to be fitted, it must be checked for runout as shown in **FIG 5:4** and straightened as shown in **FIG 5:5** if necessary. Lateral runout should not exceed .016 inch at the outer diameter. Renew the release bearing if it feels rough when the front race is pressed and turned slowly. If the clutch cover or spring are faulty, or if the pressure plate surface is badly scored, the assembly

must be replaced and, as it will be necessary to rebalance the pressure plate and flywheel as a unit, the work should be left to a fully equipped agent.

5:3 Assembling and refitting clutch

Reassembly is a reversal of the dismantling instructions. The hub of the driven plate must be centralized with the hub of the flywheel during reassembly, using service tool J.21714 for 1 and 1.1 litre engines, or J.22934 for 1.5 and 1.9 litre engines. When refitting the driven plate note that for 1 and 1.1 litre engines the long end of the splined hub faces rearward, for 1.5 and 1.9 litre engines the long end of the splined hub faces forward.

Place the driven plate correctly on the pressure plate and insert the service tool through both as shown in **FIG 5:6.** Hold the complete assembly against the flywheel

⑤ STRAIGHTEN DRIVEN MEMBER

⑥ RECHECK FOR STRAIGHTNESS

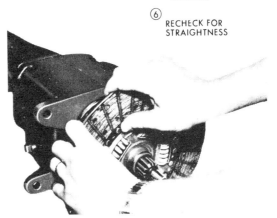

FIG 5:5 Straightening driven plate

FIG 5:6 Clutch installation and alignment

Key to Fig 5:6 1 Flywheel 2 Clutch assembly 3 Assembly marks 4 Clutch aligning tool

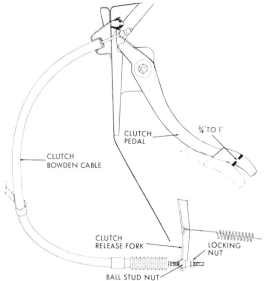

FIG 5:7 Clutch operating cable, 1 and 1.1 litre engines

while inserting the end of the tool into the pilot bearing in the crankshaft. Index the alignment marks noted during the dismantling procedure and install the clutch cover to flywheel attaching bolts finger tight. Complete tightening the bolts alternately and evenly to a final torque of 15 lb ft, then remove the service tool. After reassembly, adjust the clutch cable free play as described in **Section 5:4**.

5:4 Adjusting operating cable

1 and 1.1 litre engines:

Refer to **FIG 5:7**. Hold the hexagon on the cable with a 7 mm spanner to prevent the cable from twisting. Loosen the locking nut and adjust the ball stud nut to obtain a free play of between $\frac{3}{4}$ and 1 inch at the clutch pedal, then tighten the locking nut.

1.5 and 1.9 litre engines:

Adjust the ball stud shown in **FIG 5:2** so that the outer end protrudes approximately $\frac{3}{4}$ inch out of the clutch housing, then make further adjustments until the release lever is approximately $4\frac{1}{4}$ inch away from the clutch housing, measured from the point where the clutch cable enters the housing. Hold the inner and outer parts of the cable in their positions in the release lever and clutch housing and place the E-ring two grooves ahead of the washer on the rubber grommet, as shown in **FIG 5:8**. The clutch pedal free travel will then be adjusted to between $\frac{3}{4}$ and 1 inch with the release bearing contacting the diaphragm spring.

5:5 Removing operating cable

1 and 1.1 litre engines:

Refer to **FIG 5:7** and remove the locking nut and ball stud nut from the end of the cable, then detach the cable from the clutch release lever. Pull off the rubber bellows and pull the cable out of its attaching clip. Slide the cable out of the guide hole in the clutch housing. Prise the rubber grommet off the clutch pedal and remove the cable. Refitting is a reversal of the removal procedure.

1.5 and 1.9 litre engines:

Refer to **FIG 5:8** and disconnect the return spring 13. Disconnect the cable from the release lever 14 and slide it out of the clutch housing. Using a screwdriver, remove the E-ring 1 from the groove in the cable. Disconnect the cable from the clutch pedal. Pull the cable out of the retainer on the dash panel and remove the washers and rubber grommet. Refitting is a reversal of the removal procedure.

5:6 Fault diagnosis

(a) Drag or spin

1 Oil or grease on driven plate linings
2 Misalignment between engine and splined shaft
3 Driven plate hub binding on splined shaft
4 Distorted driven plate
5 Warped or damaged pressure plate or clutch cover
6 Broken driven plate linings
7 Dirt or foreign matter in clutch
8 Incorrect clutch pedal free travel

(b) Fierceness or snatch

1 Check 1, 2 and 3 in (a)
2 Worn driven plate linings

(c) Slip

1 Check 1, 2 and 8 in (a)
2 Check 2 in (b)
3 Weak diaphragm spring
4 Seized clutch cable

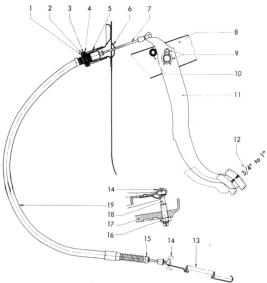

FIG 5:8 Clutch operating cable, 1.5 and 1.9 litre engines

Key to Fig 5:8   1 E-ring   2 Washer   3 Grommet
4 Washer   5 Sleeve   6 Dash panel   7 Cable   8 Bracket
9 Washer and clip   10 Rubber stop   11 Clutch pedal
12 Clutch free play   13 Return spring   14 Release lever
15 Bellows   16 Locknut   17 Housing   18 Ball stud
19 Cable

(d) Judder

1 Check 1 and 2 in (a)
2 Pressure plate not parallel with flywheel face
3 Contact area of driven plate linings not evenly distributed
4 Bent or worn splined shaft
5 Badly worn splines in driven plate hub
6 Buckled driven plate
7 Faulty engine or gearbox mountings

(e) Rattle

1 Check 3 in (c)
2 Check 4 and 5 in (d)
3 Broken springs in driven plate

4 Worn release mechanism
5 Excessive backlash in transmission
6 Wear in transmission bearings
7 Release bearing loose on fork

(f) Tick or knock

1 Check 4 and 5 in (d)
2 Release plate out of line
3 Loose flywheel

(g) Driven plate fracture

1 Check 2 in (a)
2 Drag and distortion due to hanging gearbox in driven plate hub

CHAPTER 6

THE GEARBOX

PART 1, 1 AND 1.1 LITRE ENGINES

6:1 Description

The gearbox fitted to 1 and 1.1 litre engines has synchromesh on all four forward gears, selection of the gears being by means of a floor mounted gearlever. This type of gearbox is shown in **FIG 6:1**. Coupé, Rallye and GT models are fitted with a remote control gearchange assembly as shown in **FIG 6:2**. The gearlever is in two parts joined by flexible rubber mountings which absorb shocks and vibration. On cars produced after August 1965 the gearbox extension housing has been altered slightly so that the damper plate gearbox mounting also serves as a rear mounting for the engine. Gearbox oil level should be maintained at the level of the filler plug on the side of the gearbox. Details of gear ratios for all models are given in Technical Data in the Appendix.

6:2 Removing and refitting the gearbox

1 Remove the air cleaner and disconnect the throttle rod from the carburetter and rear support. Place the gearlever in neutral. Remove the gearlever on standard cars by pulling up the rubber boot and, using service tool J.21709, press down on the lock cap and turn it anticlockwise until it unlocks as shown in **FIG 6:3**. On cars fitted with remote control gearchange assemblies remove the gearlever by pulling up the rubber boot and removing the circlip as shown in **FIG 6:4**. Raise the front or rear of the car safely onto floor stands.

2 Remove the locknut and adjusting nut from the clutch cable and disengage the cable from the gearbox case. Loosen the front exhaust pipe to manifold flange joint. Disconnect the wires from the reversing light switch. Unscrew the coverplate between the sump and the gearbox and disconnect the speedometer drive cable.

3 Unhook the handbrake cable return spring and remove cable equalizing assembly as described in **Chapter 11**. Remove the two bolts attaching the gearbox mounting to the underbody. Disconnect and remove the propeller shaft from the central joint as described in **Chapter 8**. **At no time during removal or refitting of the gearbox must the weight of the gearbox be be allowed to rest on the first motion shaft, or the clutch driven plate will be damaged.** To avoid the possibility of clutch damage the use of two

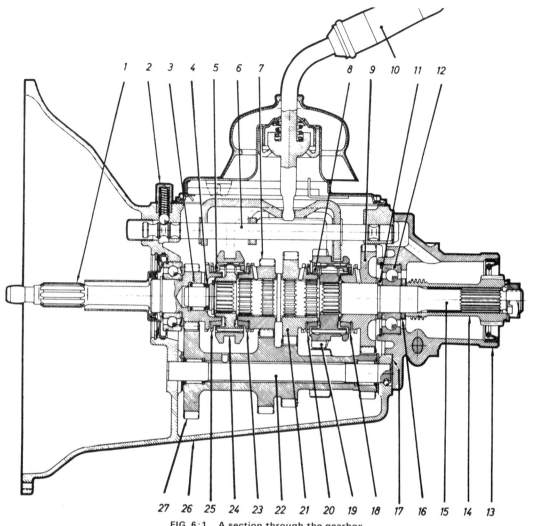

FIG 6:1 A section through the gearbox

Key to Fig 6:1   1 First motion shaft   2 Lock ball and spring plug   3 Needle bearing   4 Thrust ring   5 Synchronizer key
6 Selector shaft   7 Third-speed gear   8 Synchronizer key   9 First-speed gear   10 Gearlever   11 Spacer   12 Ballbearing
13 Speedometer drive housing   14 Third motion sleeve   15 Third motion shaft   16 Spacer
17 Gasket   18 First-speed baulk ring   19 First and second-speed sliding gear   20 Second-speed baulk ring   21 Second-speed gear
22 Layshaft   23 Third-speed baulk ring   24 Third and fourth-speed synchronizer sleeve   25 Fourth-speed baulk ring
26 Gearbox case   27 Laygear

guide pins, service tool J.21722, is strongly recommended. Remove the lower gearbox to crankcase bolt from each side and insert the guide pins in their place, as shown in **FIG 6:5**.

4 Place a jack under the lower front generator to engine block bracket. Remove the right engine mount to crossmember bracket bolts. Raise the engine, thereby lowering the gearbox so that enough clearance is provided for its removal. Remove the remaining gearbox to crankcase bolts and slide the gearbox back off the guide pins and clutch spline, noting that it may be necessary to rotate the gearbox slightly to do this.

Refitting is a reversal of the removal procedure, noting the following points:

Make sure the first motion shaft splines are clean and dry and that the gearbox is in neutral so that the splines may be turned if necessary to facilitate refitting. If the clutch has been disturbed, align the driven plate as described in **Chapter 5**. Refill the gearbox with the correct lubricant. Adjust the clutch pedal free play as described in **Chapter 5**.

6:3 Dismantling and reassembling the gearbox

Dismantling:

1 Remove the six cover screws and remove the gearbox cover and gasket. Invert the gearbox to drain the oil. Using pliers, remove the reverse speed stop spring from the cover.

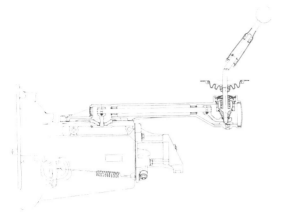

FIG 6:2 Remote control gearchange assembly

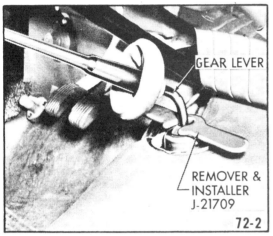

FIG 6:3 Removing standard gearlever

2 Refer to **FIG 6:6** and prise the end cover 3 from the speedometer housing 2. Withdraw the driven gear 4 from the top of the housing. Examine the seal 1 which must be renewed if faulty.

3 Refer to **FIG 6:7** and remove the six circlips shown from the selector shafts. Using pliers, remove the spring plugs from the top of the gearbox and remove the lockballs and springs. Remove the lower speedometer drive housing bolt and rotate the housing until the rear of the first and second-speed shaft is exposed. This is the centre shaft. Drive out the shaft towards the front of the case. Drive out the third and fourth-speed shaft and the reverse speed shaft in the same manner, collecting the shaft end plugs and spring washers. Lift out the selector forks, selector head and reverse lever.

Mainshaft assembly:

1 **FIG 6:8** shows the components of the third motion shaft assembly. Before removal, mark the relative positions of the third and fourth-speed operating sleeve and first and second-speed sliding gear, as well as the corresponding baulk rings and synchronizing hubs to ensure the same tooth or spline contact on

reassembly. Turn the speedometer drive housing to expose the end of the layshaft. Drive the layshaft out of the gearbox towards the rear, paying careful attention to the lockball on the shaft. Withdraw the third motion shaft out of the gearbox together with the speedometer drive housing.

2 Refer to **FIG 6:8**. Slide the third and fourth-speed operating sleeve 27 off the synchronizer hub 5 and remove keys 26 and spring 4. Clamp the third motion shaft assembly in a vice and remove the third motion shaft nut, using a vice with soft jaws or padding the third motion shaft assembly to avoid damage to it.

3 Using press plate J.21684 or a similar support, press off the ballbearing and speedometer drive housing, together with the two spacers, the third motion shaft sleeve and the first-speed gear from the third motion shaft, as shown in **FIG 6:9**. Slide the first and second-speed sliding gear (22 in **FIG 6:8**), from the hub and remove the keys 21 and the rear retaining spring 11. Keep the baulk rings with their respective gears for reassembly.

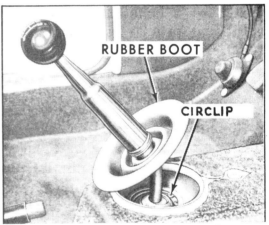

FIG 6:4 Removing remote control gearlever

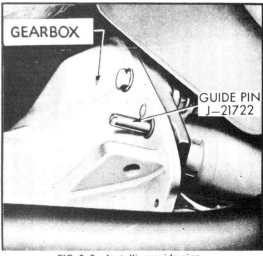

FIG 6:5 Installing guide pins

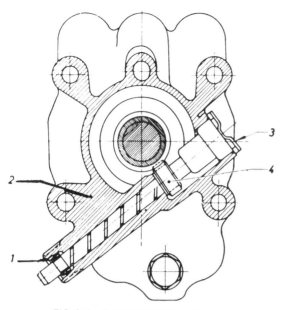

FIG 6:6   Speedometer drive housing

Key to Fig 6:6   1 Seal   2 Housing   3 Cover
4 Driven gear

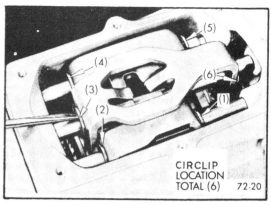

CIRCLIP
LOCATION
TOTAL (6)   72·20

FIG 6:7   Removing selector shaft circlips

4 Remove the retaining ring from the speedometer drive housing and, with a hammer handle, drive out the ballbearing. Remove the oil seal from the housing. Remove the retaining ring 12 and press off the second-speed gear 8, the hub 10 and the baulk ring 23 as shown in **FIG 6:10**. Remove the retaining ring from the third motion shaft and press the synchronizer hub for third and fourth-speed and the third-speed gear off the third motion shaft as shown in **FIG 6:11**.

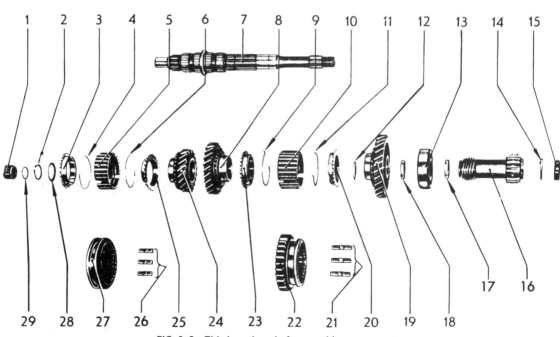

FIG 6:8   Third motion shaft assembly components

Key to Fig 6:8   1 Needle bearing   2 Circlip   3 Fourth-speed baulk ring   4 Key spring
5 Third and fourth-speed synchronizer hub   6 Key spring   7 Third motion shaft   8 Second-speed gear   9 Key spring
10 First and second-speed synchronizer hub   11 Key spring   12 Circlip   13 Ballbearing   14 Tabwasher   15 Nut
16 Third motion shaft sleeve   17 Spacer   18 Spacer   19 First-speed gear   20 First-speed baulk ring   21 Keys
22 First and second-speed sliding gear   23 Second-speed baulk ring   24 Third-speed gear   25 Third-speed baulk ring
26 Keys   27 Third and fourth-speed operating sleeve   28 Spring washer   29 Thrust ring

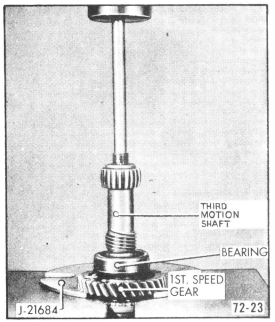

FIG 6:9 Pressing third motion shaft sleeve, first-speed gear and ballbearing off shaft

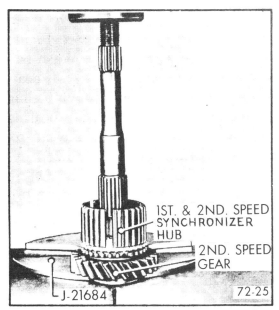

FIG 6:10 Pressing hub and second-speed gear off third motion shaft

The first motion shaft:

Remove the clutch lever together with the release bearing from the first motion shaft. Refer to **FIG 6:12** and remove the circlip and washer and slide the release bearing sleeve and seal assembly off the front of the shaft. Withdraw the first motion shaft and bearing assembly from the gearbox, collecting the O-ring seal from the groove in the front of the case. Remove the retaining ring and press off the ballbearing.

Layshaft gear unit:

The layshaft has been removed during removal of the third motion shaft, so the layshaft cluster has only to be removed from the bottom of the gearbox case, removing the thrust washers. The needle bearings can be removed from the bores in the laygear assembly.

Reverse idler gear:

Refer to **FIG 6:13**. Drive the reverse idler gear shaft to the rear of the gearbox and collect the lockball imbedded in the shaft. Remove the idler gear and selector lever.

Reassembly:

Thoroughly clean all parts before reassembly, including the gearbox case. Check all parts for abnormal wear, nicks or scoring and bearings for roughness or binding. Use SAE.90 gear oil to lubricate parts during reassembly.

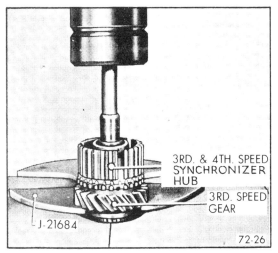

FIG 6:11 Pressing hub and third-speed gear off third motion shaft

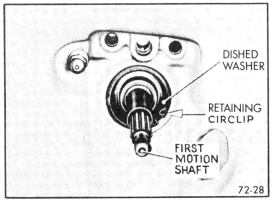

FIG 6:12 First motion shaft

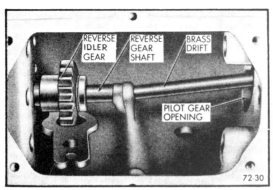

FIG 6:13 Removing reverse idler gear shaft

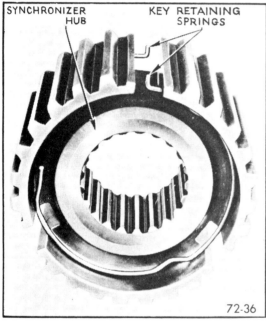

FIG 6:14 Both key springs installed

Reverse idler gear:

Oil and replace reverse idler gear with the long bearing hub to the rear. Install the shaft together with the lockball and drive the shaft in until the end is flush with the case.

Layshaft gear unit:

On all models except the Kadett A series, service tool J.22414 laygear bearing loader must be used to retain the positions of the needle bearings during assembly.

1 Coat new thrust washers with grease and fit them into the gearbox case so that the lugs on the washers engage the recesses provided.
2 Fit service tool J.22414 to the laygear assembly and install the needle bearings into the counterbores. Position the laygear assembly, with the loading tool installed, into the bottom of the gearbox with the large end facing forward, using care to avoid disturbing the thrust washers or needle bearings **Do not install the laygear shaft until the first and third motion shafts have been fitted.**

3 Place spring washer over the reverse selector lever guide pin and install the lever as shown in **FIG 6:13.**

The first motion shaft:

1 Lubricate and install a new O-ring into the groove in the gearbox case. Press the ballbearing onto the first motion shaft with the groove in the bearing toward the front and fit the bearing retaining ring.
2 Fit the first motion shaft into the gearbox. Lubricate and fit a new oil seal to the release bearing sleeve, pressing the seal in until it touches the bearing. Slide the sleeve over the shaft and fit the dished washer and retaining ring, pushing the retaining ring firmly into its groove.

Third motion assembly:

Renew the keys and retaining springs when reassembling the third motion shaft.

1 Slide the third-speed gearwheel onto the shaft from the front, checking that it turns freely. Fit the baulk ring for third-speed over the cone face of the gearwheel.
2 Fit the retaining spring to the third and fourth-speed synchronizer hub so that the hook rests in one of the slots. Index the marks made when dismantling and press the synchronizer hub onto the shaft and fit the retaining ring.
3 Slide second-speed gear (8 in **FIG 6:8**), onto the shaft from the rear and check that it turns freely. Fit the second-speed baulk ring 23 onto the cone face of the gearwheel.
4 Fit both key retaining springs to the synchronizer hub 10 for first and second-speeds so that the hooks on both springs engage the same hub slot and the other spring ends are opposite each other, as shown in **FIG 6:14.** Index the marks made when dismantling and press the synchronizer hub onto the shaft. Fit the keys into the first and second-speed synchronizer hub and install first and second-speed sliding gear 22 onto the hub, observing the alignment marks made when dismantling. Fit the retaining ring.
5 Note the alignment marks on the parts and fit the first-speed baulk ring 20 onto the shaft and slide on the first-speed gearwheel 19 and spacer 18.

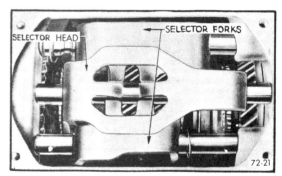

FIG 6:15 Selector head and forks

6 Lubricate the speedometer drive housing oil seal and drive it into the housing to its stop then press in the bearing and fit the securing ring, noting the following. If the bearing has been renewed, a new retaining ring must be fitted to correctly match the outer race width of the bearing. New bearing boxes marked 'A' use a silver retaining ring, 'B' a blue ring and 'C' a black ring.

7 Slide the third motion shaft assembly through the bearing onto the speedometer drive housing and fit the spacer 17 and the shaft sleeve 16 onto the shaft. Press all the parts onto the shaft. Fit the retaining spring into the synchronizer hub for the third and fourth-speed so that the hook on the spring engages in the same slot as the spring on the reverse side. Insert the keys and fit the operating sleeve 27, observing the alignment marks made when dismantling.

8 Place a new gasket onto the speedometer drive housing and fit the fourth-speed baulk ring to the shaft. Insert the shaft into the gearbox case and index the alignment marks on the fourth-speed baulk ring and the third and fourth-speed operating sleeve made when dismantling.

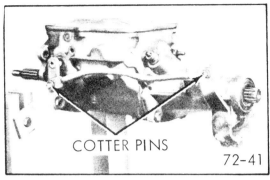

FIG 6:17 Cotterpins on gearchange control rod

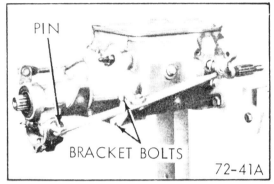

FIG 6:18 Pin and bracket securing selector lever to intermediate shaft and speedometer drive housing

9 Line up the laygear assembly and its thrust washers with the shaft holes in the front and rear of the gearbox case. Install the layshaft into position, pushing out the loading tool previously installed in the laygear. Make sure the locating ball is in place and enters the groove in the case. Tap in the shaft until it is flush with the case.

10 Position the speedometer drive housing, install the lower attaching bolt and tighten to a torque of 25 lb ft. Use service tool J.22399 on the third motion shaft sleeve or engage two gears to lock the shaft then fit the tabwasher and shaft nut and tighten to a torque of 18 lb ft, securing the nut with the tabwasher.

Selector shafts:

1 Fit one lockpin in the hole so that it is located between the reverse speed selector shaft and the first and second-speed shaft, then fit the second pin between the selector shafts for first and second and third and fourth-speeds. Make sure the gearbox is in neutral and fit the selector shafts and head into position as shown in FIG 6:15. From the front of the gearbox insert the reverse speed selector shaft, place the shaft through the reverse idler fork, fit the spring washer and feed the shaft through the selector head. In the same manner, fit the first and second-speed selector shaft, fitting the spring washer and feeding the shaft through the fork and head, then finally the third and fourth-speed selector shaft.

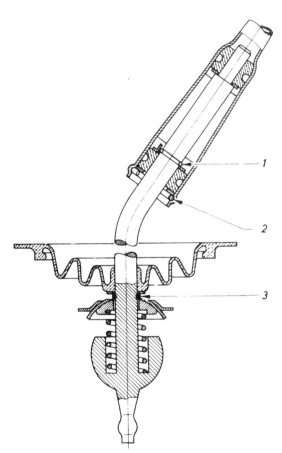

FIG 6:16 Section through the gearlever

Key to Fig 6:16 1 Upper circlip on gearlever lower part 2 Circlip on gearlever upper part 3 Lower circlip on gearlever lower part

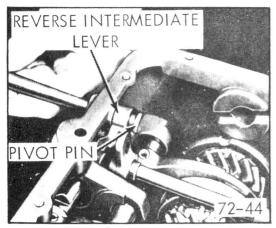

FIG 6:19 Reverse intermediate lever pin

2 Fit six new circlips into the grooves in the selector shafts, noting that the spring washers are located between the selector forks or head and the circlips. Fit the selector shaft bore caps. Lubricate the lockballs and springs, refit them and drive in the plugs.

3 Refer to **FIG 6:6** and insert the speedometer driven gear into the drive housing and drive the cover fully home. Fit the seal into the groove.

6:4 Dismantling and reassembling gearlever

Remove the gearlever as described in **Section 6:2**. Refer to **FIG 6:16**. Remove the circlip 2 and pull the gearlever upper part from the lower part. Remove circlips 1 and 3 from the gearlever and remove all the loose parts. Check all parts and renew any found worn or damaged. Reassembly is a reversal of the dismantling procedure.

6:5 Fault diagnosis

Fault diagnosis for all gearboxes will be found in **Section 6:12**. Refer to this part of the Chapter for maintenance instructions for gearboxes fitted to 1 and 1.1 litre cars after using **Section 6:12**.

PART 2, 1.5 AND 1.9 LITRE ENGINES

6:6 Description

The gearbox fitted to 1.5 and 1.9 litre engines has synchromesh on all four forward gears, selection of the gears being by means of a floor-mounted gearlever operating external linkage connected to a selector shaft mounted within the gearbox case. The gearbox is fitted to the clutch bellhousing which, being a separate casting, does not have to be removed with the gearbox. Gearbox oil level should be maintained at the level of the filler plug on the side of the gearbox. Details of gear ratios for all models are given in Technical Data in the Appendix.

6:7 Removing and refitting the gearbox

1 Remove the air cleaner and disconnect the throttle rod from the carburetter and rear support. Loosen the exhaust pipe to manifold flange. Place the gearlever into neutral. Remove the three gearlever coverplate screws, pull the rubber boot upwards, unhook the spring and remove the gearlever finger bolt. Remove the gearlever from the housing.

2 From under the car, remove the clutch cable lock and adjuster nuts and withdraw the cable from the gearbox. Disconnect both wires from the reversing light switch. Disconnect the speedometer cable from the speedometer drive housing.

3 Refer to **Chapter 11** and remove the handbrake return spring and equalizer assembly. Disconnect and remove the propeller shaft as described in **Chapter 8**. Remove the two bolts attaching the rear engine mount to the underbody. Remove the gearbox to clutch housing attaching bolts and carefully slide the gearbox rearward to remove it.

Refitting is a reversal of the removal procedure, noting the following points:

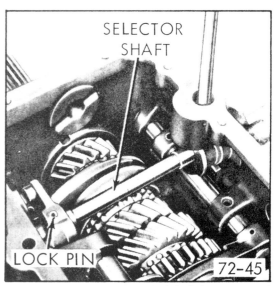

FIG 6:20 Selector shaft lockpins

FIG 6:21 Selector fork lockpins

Make sure the first motion shaft splines are clean and dry and that the gearbox is in neutral so that the splines may be turned if necessary to facilitate refitting. If the clutch has been disturbed the bellhousing will have to be removed and the driven plate re-aligned as described in **Chapter 5**. Refill the gearbox with the correct lubricant. Adjust the clutch pedal free play as described in **Chapter 5**.

6:8 Dismantling and reassembling gearbox

Dismantling:

Make sure the relative positions of all mating parts are retained by marking the parts with paint to ensure correct reassembly.

1 Refer to **FIG 6:17** and remove the cotterpins that retain the control rod, then remove the rod. Remove the

FIG 6:22 Removing reverse idler gearshaft

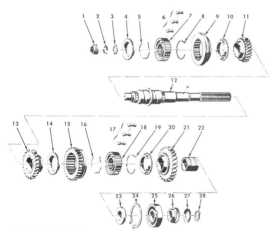

FIG 6:23 Third motion shaft assembly components

Key to Fig 6:23   1 Needle bearing   2 Thrust ring
3 Circlips   4 Fourth-speed baulk ring   5 Key spring
6 Keys   7 Third and fourth-speed synchronizer hub
8 Key spring   9 Third and fourth-speed synchronizer sleeve
10 Third-speed baulk ring   11 Third-speed gear
12 Third motion shaft   13 Second-speed gear
14 Second-speed baulk ring   15 Synchronizer sleeve
16 Key spring   17 Keys   18 First and second-speed
synchronizer hub   19 Key spring
20 First-speed baulk ring   21 First-speed gear
22 Needle bearing   23 Spacer   24 Gearbox case
extension retaining ring   25 Ballbearing
26 Speedometer drive gear   27 Dished washer   28 Circlip

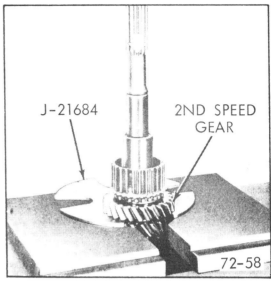

FIG 6:24 Pressing off hub and needle bearing sleeve

pin securing the selector lever to the intermediate shaft and the two bolts from the speedometer drive housing which secure the selector lever bracket, as shown in **FIG 6:18**. Remove the selector lever. Remove the locknut and selector ring.

2 Remove the gearbox cover bolts, gasket and cover, then invert the gearbox to drain the oil.

Laygear assembly:

Turn the speedometer drive housing to expose the laygear shaft. Using service tool J.22911, drive out the layshaft from the front of the gearbox, collecting the lockball. With the service tool inserted take out the laygear assembly and remove both thrust washers.

Selector shaft and intermediate levers:

Use a $\frac{1}{8}$ inch punch to remove all pins.

1 Refer to **FIG 6:19** and drive out reverse intermediate lever pivot pin and remove the lever. Turn the selector shaft so that the lockpins are vertical and drive out the pin from the third and fourth-speed intermediate lever, then drive out the pin from the first and second-speed lever, as shown in **FIG 6:20**.

2 Using a screwdriver, lever out the selector shaft seal rings from the gearbox case. Use pliers to pull out both lockball plugs and remove balls and springs. With the transmission in first gear, drive the lockpins out of the selector forks and dogs as shown in **FIG 6:21**. From the rear of the gearbox, drive out both selector shafts with a brass drift, turning the speedometer drive housing to expose the ends of the shafts. In the same manner, drive out the reverse selector shaft. The reverse selector fork will remain in the gearbox case.

Reverse idler gear:

Turn the speedometer drive housing until the reverse idler gear shaft is exposed. Refer to **FIG 6:22** and use

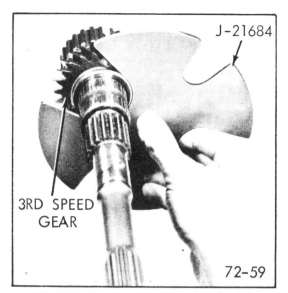

FIG 6:25 Pressing off small synchronizer hub

service tool J.22923 to push out the shaft towards the rear, collecting the lockball. Remove the shaft, reverse idler gear and selector fork from the gearbox case.

Third motion shaft assembly:

Before dismantling pull the gearbox case extension together with the third motion shaft assembly out of the gearbox case.

1 Remove the retaining ring from the groove in the speedometer drive housing and remove the third motion shaft assembly from the housing. **FIG 6:23** shows the components of the third motion shaft assembly. Remove the needle bearing, spacer ring, baulk ring, synchronizer sleeve, keys and front key retaining ring, all of which are a loose fit on the shaft.

2 Remove the circlips 3 and 28 and slide off the spacer and the speedometer drive gear 26. Remove the drive gear lockball from the shaft. Using service tool J.21684 or similar support, press the rear bearing 25 from the shaft, then remove spacer plate 23, retaining ring 24, first-speed gear and needle bearing, baulk ring, synchronizer sleeve, keys and key spring, all of which are a loose fit on the shaft.

3 With the press plate located below second-speed gear, press out the large synchronizer hub and the needle bearing inner sleeve as shown in **FIG 6:24**. Locate the press plate below third-speed gear and press out the small synchronizer hub as shown in **FIG 6:25**.

Reassembly:

Thoroughly clean all parts before reassembly, including the gearbox case. Check all parts for abnormal wear, nicks or scoring and bearings for roughness or binding. Use SAE.90 gear oil to lubricate parts during reassembly. Fit new baulk rings, synchronizer key springs and keys.

Third motion shaft assembly:

1 From the front of the shaft install third-speed gear and check that it turns freely. Fit the third-speed baulk ring

to the cone face of the gear. Fit the rear synchronizer key spring into the hub 7 so that the hooked end of the spring rests in one of the slots. Press the hub 7 onto the shaft as shown in **FIG 6:26**, indexing the marks made when dismantling. Secure the hub with the retaining ring.

2 Slide the second-speed gear 13 onto the shaft from the rear and check that it turns freely. Fit the second-speed baulk ring to the cone face of the gear (see **FIG 6:27**). Install both synchronizer key springs into first and second-speed synchronizer hub so the hooks on both springs rest in the same hub slot and the spring ends are opposite each other, as shown in **FIG 6:28**. Press the hub onto the shaft, indexing the marks made when dismantling. Using service tool J.22913 press the needle bearing inner sleeve onto the shaft.

3 With tool J.22913 fit the first and second-speed keys 17 and install first and second-speed sliding gear onto the synchronizer hub with the forked groove to the rear. Slide the needle bearing, baulk ring, first-speed gear, spacer plate (chamfer to the rear) and gearbox case extension retaining ring onto the shaft. Use tool J.22913 to press on the rear bearing.

4 Fit the speedometer drive gear and dished washer on the shaft and secure with the circlip. Install the third motion shaft assembly into the speedometer drive housing up to its stop, then fit the retaining ring as shown in **FIG 6:29**. Place the front third and fourth-speed synchronizer key spring in position. Fit the keys 6, noting that the arrows on the keys point towards the selector fork groove. Fit the third and fourth-speed

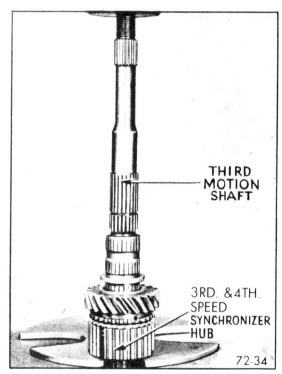

FIG 6:26 Pressing third and fourth-speed hub onto third motion shaft

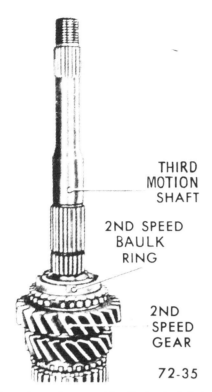

FIG 6:27   Second-speed gear and baulk ring installed

THIRD MOTION SHAFT

2ND SPEED BAULK RING

2ND SPEED GEAR

72-35

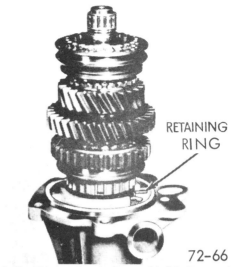

FIG 6:29   Third motion shaft assembly fitted to speedometer drive housing

RETAINING RING

72-66

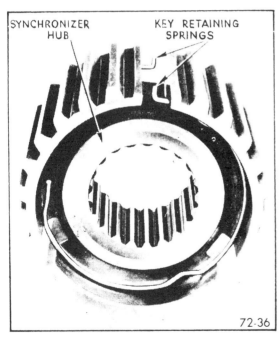

FIG 6:28   Both key springs installed

SYNCHRONIZER HUB

KEY RETAINING SPRINGS

72-36

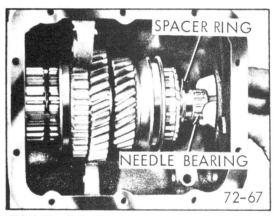

FIG 6:30   Fitting spacer ring and needle bearing to third motion shaft

SPACER RING

NEEDLE BEARING

72-67

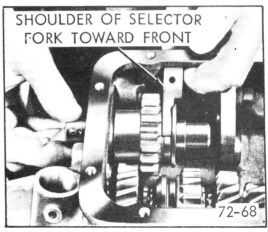

FIG 6:31   Fitting reverse selector fork

SHOULDER OF SELECTOR FORK TOWARD FRONT

72-68

FIG 6:32 Position of L-shaped selector dog

operating sleeve and the baulk ring over the synchronizer hub.

5 Fit a new gasket to the speedometer drive housing and slide the shaft assembly into the gearbox case. From the front, slide the spacer ring and needle bearing onto the shaft as shown in **FIG 6:30,** coating the needle bearing with grease before installation. Install clutch gear into the gearbox up to the circlip stop.

Reverse idler gear:

Turn the speedometer drive housing until the bore for the reverse idler gearshaft is exposed, place the lockball into the shaft and install the shaft from the rear of the case, fitting the reverse idler gear and selector fork as shown in **FIG 6:31.**

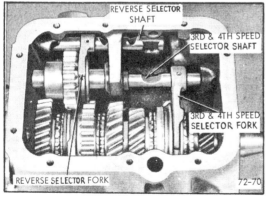

FIG 6:33 Third and fourth-speed selector shaft installed

Selector shafts and intermediate levers:

Inspect selector shafts for burrs and remove any found with emerycloth. Lightly oil the shafts before installation.

1 Insert the first and second-speed selector shaft with notches downward, pushing it from the front of the case through the L-shaped selector dog as shown in **FIG 6:32.** Push the selector shaft through the selector fork, positioning the shoulder toward the front of the case. Drive the lockpins into place, allowing them to produce $\frac{1}{16}$ to $\frac{5}{64}$ inch.

2 Insert the third and fourth-speed selector shaft, with the notches down, pushing the shaft through the third and fourth-speed selector fork. Drive the lockpin into position. **FIG 6:33** shows selector shaft installation and **FIGS 6:20** and **6:21** the positions of the lockpins.

3 Install the reverse selector shaft from the rear of the case, with the notches up, pushing it through the reverse selector fork. Drive in the lockpin. Refer to **FIG 6:20** and insert the selector shaft into the case, pushing it through the first and second-speed intermediate lever, then through the third and fourth-speed intermediate lever. Drive in the lockpins.

4 Engage the reverse speed intermediate lever, third and fourth-speed intermediate lever and install the pivot pin (see **FIG 6:19**). Reverse speed intermediate lever end play on the pin should be between .004 and .012 inch.

5 Insert both lockballs and springs into the bores in the gearbox case and drive in the plugs.

Laygear assembly:

1 Refer to **FIG 6:34** and coat the laygear thrust washers with grease and stick them to the gearbox case as

FIG 6:34 Laygear thrust washers installed

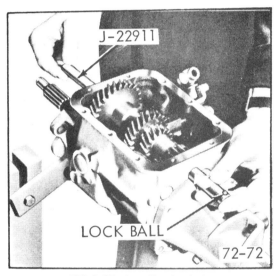

FIG 6:35 Installing layshaft

shown, noting that the lugs on the thrust washers must fit into the slots in the gearbox case. Turn the speedometer drive housing until the layshaft bore is exposed.

2 Place the lockball into the layshaft and insert the shaft from the rear of the gearbox so that the thrust washer is held in position. Hold the other thrust washer in position by inserting a short drift. Insert the laygear assembly with loading tool J.22911 installed into the gearbox case.

3 Refer to **FIG 6:35** and insert the layshaft into the laygear and drive the shaft into the case, pushing out the loading tool. Ensure that the locking ball is correctly installed.

4 Align the speedometer drive housing and bolt the housing to the gearbox case. Install the lockball and thrust spring into the top gearbox bore. Fit the gearbox case cover gasket, cover and fixing bolts.

Gearchange linkage:

The refitting of gearchange linkages is a reversal of the removal instructions given at the start of this Section. If the selector intermediate lever bush is worn, it can be renewed as follows: Refer to **FIG 6:36** and remove the

FIG 6:36 Removing selector intermediate lever bush

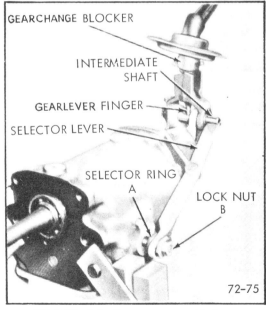

FIG 6:37 Adjusting reverse gear blocker

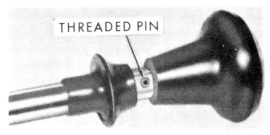

FIG 6:38 Threaded pin on gearlever knob

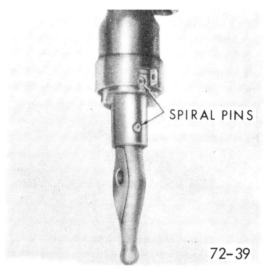

FIG 6:39 Spiral pins on gearlever

circlip securing the bush, then drive out the bush as shown. Drive in a new bush from the opposite side with the cut-out in the bush facing upwards. Refit the circlip.

6:9 Adjusting reverse gearchange blocker

Engage second gear. Refer to **FIG 6:37** and adjust selector ring 'A' so that the ball on the lower end of the gearlever finger has an equal clearance on both sides when seated into the intermediate lever hole. Loosen the selector ring an additional quarter turn and tighten the locknut 'B'.

6:10 Speedometer driven gear

Removing and refitting (gearbox removed):

Removal:

Remove the soft pin which retains the speedometer driven gear in the speedometer drive housing. Use service tool J.22929 to remove the driven gear as this tool screws onto the speedometer cable attachment and enables the sleeve to be removed without damage to the threads in the drive housing.

Refitting:

Install the driven gear in the reverse sequence to removal, noting the following: Use tool J.22929 when refitting the drive gear to prevent thread damage. Tap the soft retaining pin gently into position.

6:11 Dismantling and reassembling gearlever

Renewing control cable:

Remove the gearlever as described in **Section 6:7.**

1 Carefully pull off the gearlever knob and loosen the threaded pin shown in **FIG 6:38.** Refer to **FIG 6:39** and drive out the spiral pins shown. Take off the gearlever finger and pull the control cable out of the gearlever. The thrust spring may also be removed. Prior to installation, lubricate the sliding surface of the stop sleeve on the gearlever finger tube.

2 Install a new control cable through the gearlever and fasten it with the clamp sleeve so that the cut-out of the stop sleeve shows toward the left. Insert the long spiral pin noting that it must not protrude on either side.

3 With the threaded pin, clamp the control cable so that the pull ring is positioned on the gearchange lever tube and the clamping block on the pull ring. **Do not put any tension on the control cable.** The pull knob should have approximately $\frac{1}{16}$ inch free travel.

4 Attach the gearlever finger with the short spiral pin. Install the gearlever knob leaving a gap of $\frac{1}{4}$ inch between the knob and the plastic moulding.

Gearlever rubber dampening parts:

Removal and refitting:

Carefully pull off the gearlever knob and loosen the threaded pin shown in **FIG 6:38.** Remove the lower circlip from the gearlever tube and pull the tube off the gearlever finger. Remove the stop ring from the groove on the gearlever finger and remove the rubber dampener.

Refitting is a reversal of the removal instructions, noting the following: After the gearlever tube has been installed, clamp the control cable so that the pull ring is positioned on the gearlever tube and the clamping block on the pull ring, to avoid any axial play of the pull ring. Leave a gap of $\frac{1}{4}$ inch between the gearlever knob and the plastic moulding.

6:12 Fault diagnosis

(a) Jumping out of gear

1 Excessively worn groove in selector shaft
2 Gearbox misaligned or loose
3 Worn pilot bearing
4 Loose speedometer drive housing causing end play
5 Loose or worn bearings on third or first motion shaft
6 Worn synchronizer teeth or baulk rings

(b) Noisy transmission

1 Check 2 in (a)
2 Insufficient oil
3 Laygear or bearings worn or damaged
4 Worn or damaged third motion shaft bearings
5 First motion shaft worn or damaged
6 Worn gear or synchronizer teeth

(c) Difficulty in engaging gear

1 Incorrect clutch pedal adjustment
2 Worn selector shafts or forks
3 Worn synchromesh assemblies

(d) Oil leaks

1 Damaged joint washers
2 Worn or damaged oil seals
3 Damaged top cover face

CHAPTER 7

AUTOMATIC TRANSMISSION

7:1 Description

The Opel automatic transmission is supplied as an optional extra to take the place of the usual clutch and gearbox. A cutaway view of the transmission is shown in **FIG 7:1**. The automatic transmission utilizes a torque converter and a planetary gear set, with three multiple disc clutches and a single band to provide three forward speeds and reverse. Automatic gearchanges are controlled by road speed, engine vacuum and an accelerator pedal 'kick-down' connection to the transmission. The forward ratios are 2.4:1, 1.48:1 and 1.1 (direct), and 1.91:1 reverse.

The action of the torque converter shown in **FIG 7:2** is as follows. The pump, driven by the engine, transmits torque by means of the transmission fluid to the turbine which drives the automatic gearbox. The stator redirects the flow of fluid as it leaves the turbine so that it re-enters the pump at the most effective angle.

When the engine is idling, the converter pump is being driven slowly and the energy of the transmission fluid leaving it is therefore low, so little torque is imparted to the turbine. For this reason, with the engine idling and drive engaged the car will have little or no tendency to 'creep'. As the throttle is opened pump speed increases and the process of torque multiplication begins. As the turbine picks up speed and the slip between it and the pump becomes less, the torque multiplication reduces progressively until, when their speeds become substantially equal, the unit acts as a fluid coupling. In this condition the stator is no longer required to redirect the fluid flow and the roller clutch permits it to rotate with the pump and turbine.

Operation of the automatic transmission is controlled by the position of the selector lever in the quadrant. Six positions are provided. In **P** (Park) position the output shaft is mechanically locked to prevent the vehicle moving backward or forward and, for this reason, **P** should not be selected with the car moving. The engine may be started in the park position. **R** (Reverse) provides reverse drive. **N** (Neutral) position enables the engine to be started and operated without driving the vehicle. Selection of **D** (Drive) provides a start in first gear and automatic changes to second and top gears. Downchanges are similarly automatic but, should a rapid change-down be needed for a burst of acceleration a 'kick-down' change can be made by depressing the accelerator pedal to its fullest extent. **S** (Second) has the same starting ratio as the Drive position, but prevents the

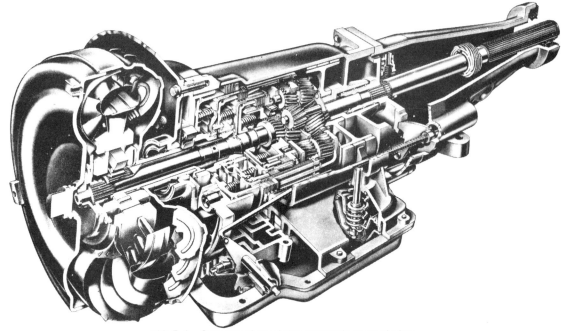

FIG 7:1　Cutaway view of the automatic transmission

transmission from changing above second gear, to retain second gear for acceleration or engine braking as desired, when travelling over undulating or winding roads. When **L** (Low) is selected no upward change will occur, this drive position being used for heavy pulling, steep climbs and maximum engine braking on descents. Both Low and Second positions can be selected at any

TURBINE
(DRIVEN MEMBER)

STATOR
(REACTION MEMBER)

CONVERTER
COVER

PUMP
(DRIVING MEMBER)

FIG 7:2　The torque converter

vehicle speed, but neither should be selected at a speed above that given for the gear in the Owners Manual, or engine rev/min may rise above the safe maximum.

If the car is to be towed, select **N** and do not exceed 35 mile/hr. If higher towing speeds are anticipated, towing for long distances, or if there has been transmission failure, the drive shaft must be disconnected or the car towed on its front wheels.

7:2 Maintenance

Transmission fluid:

Check the transmission fluid level every 6000 miles. The oil pan should be drained and the oil strainer renewed every 24,000 miles unless the vehicle is subject to hard driving or high temperature operating conditions, when the intervals should be 12,000 miles. The automatic transmission must be filled with Dexron Automatic Transmission Fluid. **Do not use any other type of fluid or oil in the transmission.**

Checking fluid level:

The automatic transmission is designed to operate with the fluid level at the 'FULL' mark at normal operating temperature, 180°F. This temperature will only be reached after approximately fifteen miles of driving. With the transmission at operating temperature proceed to check the fluid level as follows. Clean the area around the dipstick and start the engine with the control lever in the 'Park' position. **Do not race the engine.** Move the control lever through each position on the quadrant and return the lever to the 'Park' position. Immediately check the fluid level on the dipstick, with the engine idling and the vehicle on level ground. Add fluid if necessary, up to the 'FULL' mark.

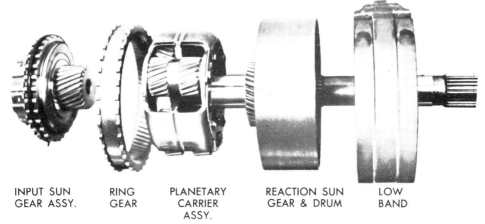

INPUT SUN GEAR ASSY.   RING GEAR   PLANETARY CARRIER ASSY.   REACTION SUN GEAR & DRUM   LOW BAND

FIG 7:3 The planetary gear assembly

If the vehicle cannot be driven sufficiently to bring the fluid up to normal operating temperature, the fluid level may be checked at room temperature (70°F) as just described but, when a reading is made, the fluid level should be $\frac{1}{4}$ inch below the 'ADD' mark on the dipstick. When the transmission reaches normal operating temperature the fluid level will then be at the level of the 'FULL' mark due to normal thermal expansion of the transmission fluid.

Do not overfill the transmission. Approximately one pint of fluid is sufficient to raise the level from 'ADD' to 'FULL'.

Renewing oil strainer:

Raise the car to provide access to the underside and support it in a safe manner. Have a container ready to catch the transmission fluid. Remove the oil pan and gasket then remove the oil strainer and gasket. Install a new oil strainer assembly and gasket. Thoroughly clean the oil pan with petrol or paraffin and dry off before replacing it, using a new gasket. Lower the car and refill the transmission as described previously.

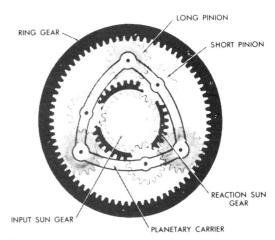

FIG 7:4 Meshing of the planetary, sun and ring gears

THIRD CLUTCH ASSEMBLY   THIRD CLUTCH HUB   SPRAG CLUTCH AND RETAINER ASSEMBLY

FIG 7:5 Third disc clutch and sprag clutch assemblies

O KAD

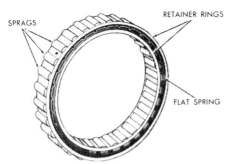

FIG 7:6 Sprag clutch details

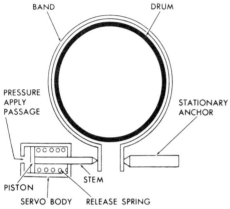

FIG 7:7 Band and operating mechanism

7:3 Power flow (mechanical)

The torque converter described in **Section 7:1** is connected to the engine by means of a plate bolted directly to the crankshaft and converter cover. The input shaft is splined into the hub of the turbine and delivers the output torque from the converter to the transmission

gear train. The planetary gear train carrier is welded to the output shaft which delivers torque from the transmission to the propeller shaft and thence to the rear wheels. **FIGS 7:3** and **7:4** show the layout of the planetary gear assembly through which power flow is accomplished by applying power to one member, holding another member thus making it a reaction member and obtaining the transmitted power from the third member. The short pinions are in constant mesh with both the input (front) sun gear and the long pinions. The long pinions are in constant mesh with the reaction (rear) sun gear, the short pinions and the ring gear. In order to provide the necessary input and reaction functions to produce the various speed ranges, the automatic transmission has three disc clutches, a band and a sprag (overrunning) clutch.

A disc clutch serves to connect or disconnect a rotating member with another rotating member or with a stationary member. A clutch of this type consists of driving and driven plates, a hub and either a drum or a housing, depending on whether the rotating member is to turn a drum or be stopped by contact with a housing. Operation is by means of an hydraulically operated piston which forces the driving and driven plates together, causing the hub to rotate with the drum or remain stationary with the housing. **FIG 7:5** shows the third clutch assembly on the left, with its clutch plates, piston and springs; the hub with input sun gear and, to the right, the sprag clutch assembly. The sprag clutch assembly consists of an inner and outer ring, sprags, retaining rings and a spring as shown in **FIG 7:6**. One diagonal dimension of each sprag is greater than the distance between the inner and outer rings, while the other diagonal is less. This causes the sprags to wedge and prevent rotation in one direction and to allow free rotation in the opposite direction. A band is used to hold one planetary member stationary with relation to the others. The band is connected to the transmission case (anchor) and is operated by a servo piston as shown in **FIG 7:7**. One band is used in the transmission to hold the reaction sun gear and drum stationary in first and second gear.

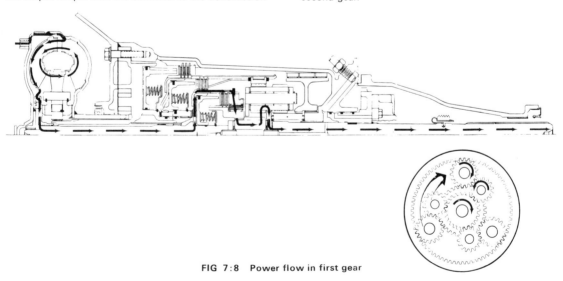

FIG 7:8 Power flow in first gear

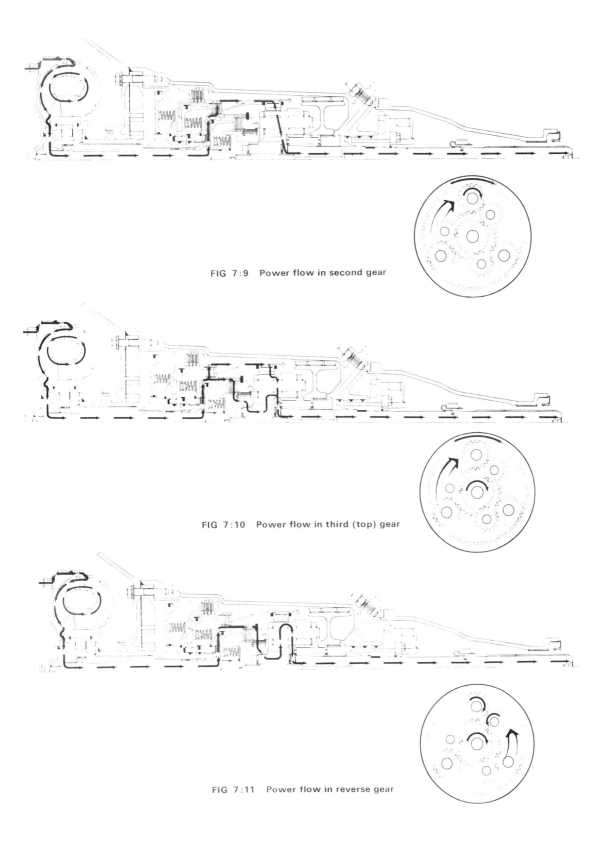

FIG 7:9   Power flow in second gear

FIG 7:10   Power flow in third (top) gear

FIG 7:11   Power flow in reverse gear

The following figures and descriptions show how the three forward ratios and reverse are obtained from the three disc clutches, the band and the sprag clutch. The line of arrows indicate the power flow from the crankshaft to the output shaft in each case, while the insets show the operation of the planetary gear assembly. In **N** (Neutral) and **P** (Park) positions, all clutches and the band are free and the sprag clutch is locked, but in **P** the parking gear pawl is engaged. Refer to **FIG 7:4** for details of the planetary gear assembly.

FIG 7:8, First gear. In **D** (Drive) range the band is applied and all clutches released. The reaction sun gear is held stationary. The input sun gear rotates clockwise turning the short pinions anticlockwise and the long pinions clockwise. The long pinions turn the ring gear clockwise and walk round the held reaction sun gear, driving the planetary carrier and the output shaft assembly clockwise. In **L** (Low) range the third clutch and the band are applied. The power flow is the same as **D**, but the third clutch prevents the sprag clutch from overrunning, to provide engine braking.

FIG 7:9, Second gear. In **D** (Drive) range the band and the second clutch are applied. The reaction sun gear is held stationary. The ring gear is the input and is driven clockwise turning the long pinions clockwise. The long pinions walk round the held reaction sun gear, driving the planetary carrier and the output shaft assembly clockwise. In **S** (Second) range the power flow is the same as in **D**.

FIG 7:10, Third gear. In **D** (Drive) range the band is released and the second and third clutches applied. The input is through the ring gear and the input sun gear, both being driven clockwise. In this condition the long and short pinions cannot rotate on their shafts, thus causing the planetary carrier, output shaft and gears to rotate clockwise as a solid unit to provide direct drive for top gear.

FIG 7:11, Reverse gear. In **R** (Reverse) range the reverse and third clutches are applied. The ring gear is held and the input sun gear is driven clockwise. This causes the short pinions to turn anticlockwise, turning the long pinions clockwise. The pinions then walk round the held ring gear, driving the planetary carrier and output shaft assembly anticlockwise.

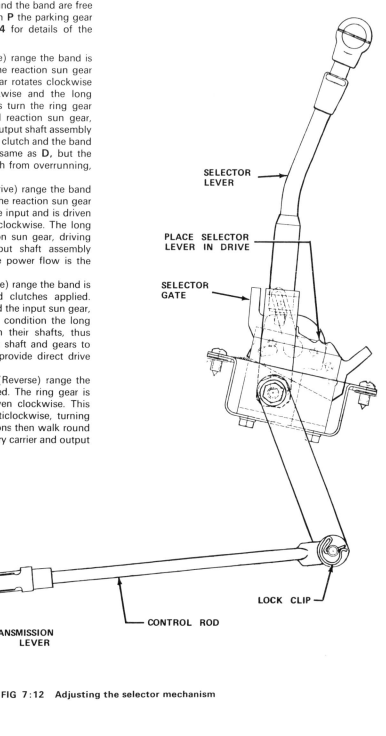

FIG 7:12 Adjusting the selector mechanism

7:4 Faulty performance

Those tests and adjustments which can be made by a reasonably competent owner are given in **Sections 7:5** and **7:7**. More serious performance faults which require pressure take-off points to be opened and pressure measurements taken to diagnose the fault, adjustment of the governor or clutches and band, partial or complete dismantling to replace worn or failed internal components dictate that the services of a fully equipped specialist should be enlisted. Quite apart from the specialized knowledge which is required, test equipment and a large number of special tools are essential. **It is advised that the automatic transmission should not be dismantled except by a Service Station.**

It should be noted that the torque converter is supplied as an assembly only, no internal parts being available separately.

7:5 Testing

Stationary tests:

Parking pawl:

With the car stationary on a gradient and the handbrake off, select **P**. The parking pawl should prevent the car from moving.

'Rocking':

With the car stationary apply slight throttle and select **D** and **R** alternately. As the gearchanges occur the car should 'rock' backwards and forwards.

Operational tests:

Governor speeds:

The following table gives the speeds at which gearchanges normally occur at the specified throttle settings. Select **D** and, by testing on a level road, check the actual speeds at which gearchanges occur.

Change	Throttle	Road speed (mile/hr)		
		Kadett	Rallye	GT
1 to 2	Light	10–14	11–13	12–14
2 to 3	Light	14–19	15–16	16–18
1 to 2	Full	38–50	40–45	42–47
2 to 3	Full	51–64	55–58	56–61
1 to 2	'Kick-down' held	37–48	39–44	40–46
2 to 3	'Kick-down' held	59–75	63–68	65–71
3 to 2	Light	12–16	13–15	14–16
2 to 1	Light	10–14	11–12	12–13

'Kick-down' is normally available up to approximately 58 mile/hr for the 3 to 2 change and approximately 34 mile/hr for the 2 to 1 change on all models.

Engine braking:

While driving at about 55 mile/hr in **D**, release the throttle and select **S**. This should result in rapid deceleration and increased engine speed. While driving at about 35 mile/hr in **D**, release the throttle and select **L**. Again, rapid deceleration and increased engine speed should result.

7:6 Fault diagnosis

This section contains a list of faults which may occur in the automatic transmission, followed by a list of possible causes. Although the owner will be in a position to deal with only a few of these himself, the list will assist him to consult knowledgeably with the specialist he selects to carry out the repairs. Before any attempt is made at diagnosis the fluid level must be checked as described in **Section 7:2**, and the selector and governor linkages correctly adjusted as described in **Section 7:7**.

Fault	Possible cause
No drive in any selector position	1, 2, 3, 4, 5, 6
No drive in **D** or **S**	7
No gearchange at any speed	16, 17, 18
Gearchange only at full throttle	11, 12, 15
Gearchange only at part throttle	13, 14
No light throttle 3 to 2 gearchange at low speeds	19
Upchange only from 1 to 2	20
Slipping 1 to 2 gearchange	21, 22, 23
Slipping 2 to 3 gearchange	24, 25, 26
Abrupt 1 to 2 gearchange	22, 27
Abrupt 2 to 3 gearchange	27
Abrupt 3 to 2 'kick-down' at high speed	28
Abrupt 3 to 2 no-throttle gearchange	29
'Flare' on high speed 'kick-down'	21, 24
'Flare' on low speed 'kick-down'	21, 24, 30
No 'kick-down'	14
No engine braking in **L**	31, 33
No engine braking in **S**	33
No parking lock in **P**	32, 33

Possible causes key:

1 Low fluid level
2 Clogged strainer
3 Inner manual valve disconnected
4 Input shaft broken
5 Pressure regulator malfunction
6 Failed pump
7 Sprag clutch faulty or installed backwards
8 Leak in pump suction circuit
9 Internal leak in pressure circuit
10 Priming valve stuck
11 Broken or disconnected vacuum line
12 Engine or accessory vacuum system leak
13 Detent pressure regulator valve stuck
14 Detent cable broken or improperly adjusted
15 Failed vacuum modulator
16 Governor valves stuck
17 1 to 2 change valve stuck in downchanged position
18 Bad leak in governor pressure passage
19 3 to 2 gearchange valve stuck
20 2 to 3 gearchange valve stuck
21 Low fluid pressure
22 1 to 2 accumulator valve stuck
23 Leaking second clutch piston seals or ball stuck open
24 Band adjustment loose
25 Leaking third clutch piston seals or ball stuck open
26 Worn input shaft bush
27 High fluid pressure
28 High speed downchange timing valve stuck open
29 Low speed downchange timing valve stuck open
30 High speed downchange timing valve stuck closed
31 Manual low control valve stuck
32 Faulty parking pawl, gear or lock actuator spring
33 Selector linkage improperly adjusted

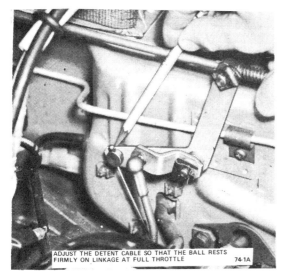

FIG 7:13 Adjusting the detent cable

FIG 7:14 Removing the heat shield

7:7 Adjustments

Selector linkage:

The selector lever and linkage components are shown in **FIG 7:12** and adjustment is carried out as follows: Remove the lock clip. Place both the selector lever and the transmission lever in **D** (Drive) positions as shown in the diagram. Adjust the control rod length until it fits freely over the pin in the lower selector lever. Refit the lock clip.

Detent cable:

The detent cable operates the 'kick-down' mechanism and is adjusted in the following manner. With the accelerator linkage in the full throttle position, adjust the nuts at the transmission end of the cable until the ball on the end of the cable rests firmly against the linkage as shown in **FIG 7:13**.

7:8 Removing and refitting

Kadett models:

Removal:

1 Disconnect the battery terminals. Disconnect the detent cable from the throttle linkage. Remove the two upper converter housing bolts. Remove the transmission filler tube and converter housing bolt. On 1.9 litre engines, remove the two upper starter bolts.

2 Raise the car and support both front and rear on floor stands. Remove the flywheel cover. Remove the drive shaft as described in **Chapter 8**. Remove the drain plug from the oil pan and drain the fluid into a suitable container.

3 Loosen the transmission support bracket and place a suitable jack under the transmission to hold it while the support bracket is removed. Lower the transmission

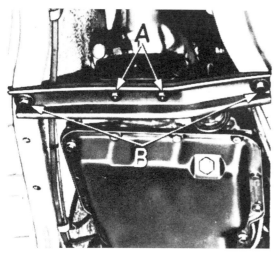

FIG 7:15 Transmission crossmember fixings

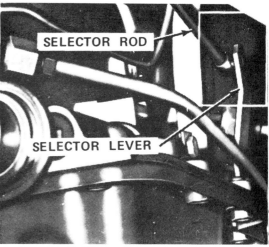

FIG 7:16 Detaching selector rod

enough for access, then remove the speedometer cable and modulator vacuum line. Remove the detent cable from the transmission, then remove the linkage from the selector lever.

4 Mark the flywheel and torque converter for reassembly in the same position and remove the converter to flywheel fixing bolts. Remove the converter housing to engine fixing bolts. Loosen the transmission from the engine. Disconnect the cooler lines at the transmission.

5 Move the transmission rearward and install torque converter holding tool J.21366. Lower the transmission and remove from under the car, keeping the rear of the transmission lower than the front to prevent the torque converter from falling.

Refitting:

Refitting is a reversal of the removal procedure, making sure that the torque converter and the flywheel are mated in their original positions, using the alignment marks made during removal. Torque wrench settings are 30 lb ft for the flywheel to converter bolts and 35 lb ft for the converter housing to engine bolts. Check the selector linkage and detent cable adjustments as described in **Section 7:7**. Check the transmission fluid level as described in **Section 7:2**.

GT models:

Removal:

1 Disconnect the battery terminals. Pull the throttle control rod off the ball pin. Raise the car and support both front and rear on floor stands. Refer to **FIG 7:14** and remove the heat shield from the righthand side to gain access for exhaust pipe removal. Detach the exhaust pipe from the manifold flange, unhook the rubber mountings from the tailpipe and silencer and allow the exhaust system to rest on the rear axle. Remove the drive shaft as described in **Chapter 8**.

2 Refer to **FIG 7:15** and detach the two nuts **A** attaching the rear engine support to the crossmember. Support the transmission with a suitable jack and remove the bolts **B** to detach the crossmember. Lower the transmission as far as possible, remove the drain plug and drain the fluid into a suitable container.

3 Refer to **FIG 7:16** and detach the selector rod from the ball pin on the outer transmission selector lever on the righthand side. Unscrew the front and rear oil cooler pipes from the transmission and plug them. Pull the modulator line off the diaphragm. Detach the detent cable connection at the accelerator pedal. Unscrew the detent cable connection retainer from the transmission and pull out the cable. Unhook the cable from the detent valve on the transmission.

4 Unscrew the speedometer cable and pull it from the housing. Detach the detent cable and the oil cooler pipes from the clips on the transmission oil pan. Unscrew the engine support brackets from the torque converter housing on both sides. Remove the converter housing cover plate.

5 Mark the torque converter and the flex plate for reassembly in the same position and unscrew the three converter to flex plate fixing bolts. Loosen the transmission from the engine. Move the transmission rearward and install torque converter holding tool J.21366. Lower the transmission and remove from under the car, keeping the rear of the transmission lower than the front to prevent the torque converter from falling.

Refitting:

Refitting is a reversal of the removal procedure, making sure that the torque converter and the flex plate are mated in their original positions, using the alignment marks made when dismantling. Check the selector linkage and detent cable adjustments as described in **Section 7:7**. Check the transmission fluid level as described in **Section 7:2**.

CHAPTER 8

PROPELLER SHAFT, REAR AXLE AND REAR SUSPENSION

PART 1—THE PROPELLER SHAFT

8:1 Description

The propeller shaft used with 1 and 1.1 litre models is of tubular steel with a splined sliding joint at the transmission end and a flanged universal joint at the differential end as shown in **FIG 8:1**. A thrust spring is used as shown for manual transmission applications. On earlier cars (Kadett 'A' range), the propeller shaft is enclosed by the engine rear support tube, which is attached to the gearbox and the central joint. The propeller shaft used with 1.5 and 1.9 litre engines is shown in **FIG 8:2** and has two universal joints, the front joint attaches to the transmission by a splined sliding joint and the rear to the drive pinion extension shaft flange by two U-bolts.

The torque tube which houses the drive pinion extension shaft is bolted to the differential housing. The central joint assembly contains a rubber mounted ballbearing.

8:2 Removing and refitting

All models except Kadett 'A' range:

Removing:

1 Raise the rear of the car and support it safely on floor stands placed under the rear jacking brackets. Disconnect the handbrake cable equalizer from the operating rod, as described in **Chapter 11**. On 1.1 litre cars, loosen the rear engine mount bolts and remove one of them, noting that one bolt must remain loosely installed to prevent damage to the heater housing as the transmission is tilted downwards.

2 Mark the mating parts of the universal joint and drive pinion extension shaft flanges to ensure correct reassembly, then remove the bolts or nuts.

3 Work the propeller shaft slightly forward, lower the rear end of the shaft and slide the assembly rearward. Remove the thrust spring which is fitted on the gearbox output shaft on manual transmission models.

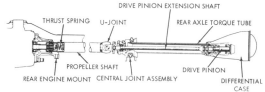

FIG 8:1 Propeller shaft, 1 and 1.1 litre models

FIG 8:2 Propeller shaft, 1.5 and 1.9 litre models

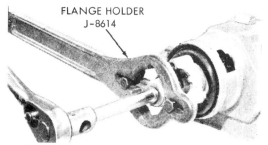

FIG 8:3 Removing drive pinion flange nut

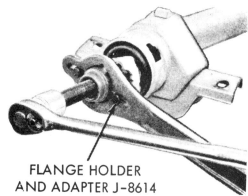

FIG 8:4 Removing the drive pinion flange

Fit a plug into the rear of the transmission to prevent loss of lubricant.

Refitting:

Refitting is the reverse of the removal instructions, noting the following points: On cars fitted with manual transmission fit the thrust spring to the gearbox output shaft before refitting the propeller shaft. For 1.1 litre models the spring must be fitted with the small end on the output shaft. When refitting the propeller shaft take care not to damage the rear gearbox oil seal. Index the alignment marks made on removal when refitting the

universal joint flange to the drive pinion flange. Tighten the flange fixing bolts to 18 lb ft for 1.1 litre cars or 11 lb ft for 1.5 and 1.9 litre cars.

Kadett 'A' models:
Removing:

1 Remove the carburetter control rod assembly. Raise the rear of the car and support it safely with floor stands placed under the side members behind the rear spring attachment points. Disconnect the handbrake cable equalizer from the operating rod as described in **Chapter 11** and detach the cable from all guide brackets on the underbody.
2 Disconnect both rear dampers from their support brackets. Detach the bracket retaining the brake pipe and hose assembly to the torque tube. The engine rear support tube can be detached by removing the four fixing bolts but, for the majority of drive shaft repairs this will not be necessary as the propeller shaft can be removed with the support tube in position.
3 Loosen the central joint pivot bolt a few turns. Support the central joint with a jack, placing a block of wood between the jack and the central joint to prevent damage, then remove the four support bracket fixing bolts. Remove the jack and allow the propeller shaft and support bracket assembly to hang free. Swing the support bracket downward and support the engine rear support tube with a floor stand.
4 Mark the mating parts of the pinion flange and the propeller shaft flange to ensure correct reassembly, then remove the bolts. Pull out the propeller shaft.

Refitting:

Refitting is the reverse of the removal instructions, noting the following points: Index the alignment marks made on removal when refitting the pinion flange to the propeller shaft flange and tighten the fixing bolts to a torque of 18 lb ft. Compress the road springs as described in **Section 8:3** when refitting the central joint assembly.

8:3 Dismantling and reassembly
Universal joints:

Mark the yoke and flange for correct alignment on reassembly and remove the four circlips that retain the trunnions and bearings. Using a drift, drive out the bearing assemblies and remove the spider. Replacement universal joint components are supplied in kit form including three sets of circlips of different thicknesses colour-coded white, yellow and green. Reassemble the universal joint in the reverse order of dismantling, pressing in the trunnions until the spider is centrally located and the circlip grooves are accessible. Install the thickest circlips possible to retain each trunnion to avoid play in the universal joint assembly, noting that each circlip fitted must be the same colour as that fitted opposite to ensure that the spider is centrally located.

The central joint:
Kadett 'A' models:
Dismantling:

1 Refer to **Section 8:2** and carry out instructions 1, 2, 3 and 4 for removing the propeller shaft on Kadett 'A' models.

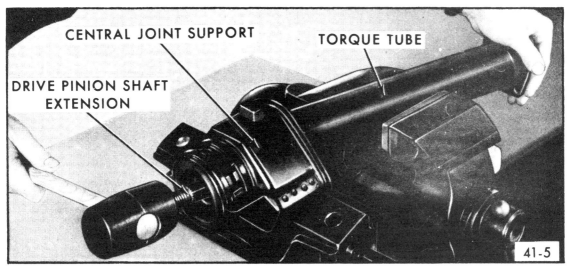

FIG 8:5   Removing drive pinion extension shaft

2 Remove the central joint support bracket to torque tube arm bolt, noting the sleeves positioned between the bracket and the central joint. Remove the bolts attaching the connecting link to the engine rear support tube and the torque tube arm. Lever out the rubber joint.

Reassembly:

Reassembly is the reverse of the dismantling procedure, noting the following points: When the central joint is reassembled place a jack under the torque tube and raise the assembly until the support bracket aligns with the threaded holes in the floor panel, and install the fixing bolts finger tight. Raise the car and support it on floor stands under the rear springs at the axle mounting points. Now load the luggage compartment sufficiently to straighten the springs and, with the load applied, tighten the support bracket to floor panel bolts to a torque of 30 lb ft and the central joint pivot bolt to 40 lb ft. Remove the weight from the luggage compartment.

All models except Kadett 'A' range:

Dismantling:

1 Raise the rear of the car and support it safely on floor stands placed under the axle tubes. Release the brake line bracket from the torque tube. Disconnect the handbrake equalizer from the operating rod as described in **Chapter 11.**
2 Mark the universal joint and flange to ensure correct reassembly and remove the fixing bolts to disconnect the propeller shaft. Support the torque tube with a jack, using minimum pressure. Remove the central joint to underbody attaching bolts and lower the torque tube. Remove the fixing bolts and detach the torque tube from the differential assembly, using care to avoid damaging the splines.
3 Refer to **FIGS 8:3** and **8:4** and remove the self-locking nut and the pinion flange using Service Tool J.8614. Remove the drive pinion extension shaft from the torque tube, using a soft-faced hammer as shown

in **FIG 8:5.** Remove the ballbearing from the rubber cushion. Remove the support bracket to support cushion bolts and pull the central joint support from the torque tube.

Reassembly:

Reassembly is a reversal of the dismantling procedure, noting the following points: Install the ballbearing with the flange facing towards the front and pack the area around the bearing with grease as shown in **FIG 8:6.** Install the support bracket onto the torque tube so that one cushion is in place, then lever the other cushion into place with a screwdriver. Use a new self-locking nut when refitting the flange to the drive pinion extension shaft, tightened to a torque of 73 lb ft on 1 and 1.1 litre cars or 87 lb ft on 1.5 and 1.9 litre cars.

Fit the torque tube assembly to the differential assembly using only three of the four bolts, the last bolt being used later to install the brake pipe bracket. Place a jack under the torque tube and raise it so that the central joint to under-body fixing bolts can be installed finger tight, then remove the jack. Press the rear of the car down several

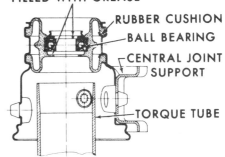

FIG 8:6   Torque tube bearing installed

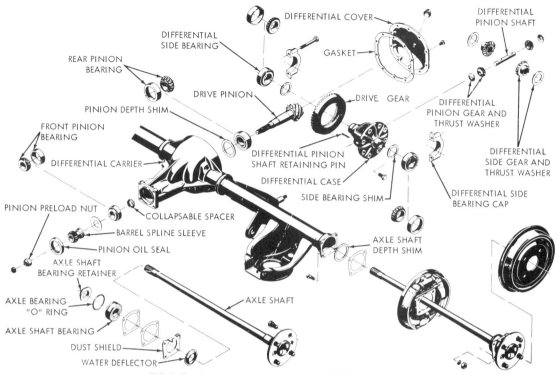

FIG 8:7   Rear axle components, 1 and 1.1 litre models

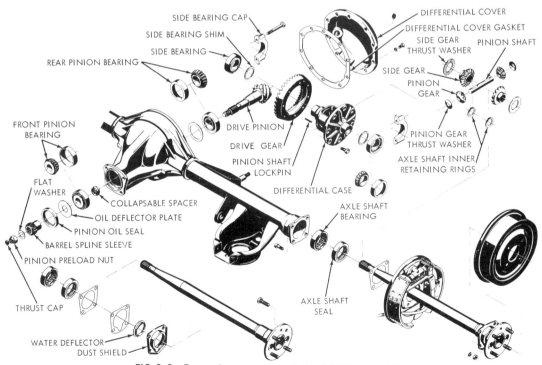

FIG 8:8   Rear axle components, 1.5 and 1.9 litre models

times to ensure that the springs are settled in their normal position and, with the car supported on the axle, tighten the bolts to a final torque of 36 lb ft.

PART 2—THE REAR AXLE

8:4 Description

The assembly is of the semi-floating type with shim adjustment for bearings and drive gear meshing. The components of the rear axle assembly are shown in **FIG 8:7** for 1 and 1.1 litre cars and **FIG 8:8** for 1.5 and 1.9 litre cars. The differential case houses two side gears meshed with two pinions. The pinion gears are held in place by a shaft anchored in the case by a lock pin. The inner ends of the axle shafts are splined into the side gears. On 1.5 and 1.9 litre cars the axle shafts are retained by a steel ring which bears against the face of the side gear. The outer end of the shafts have machined surfaces acting as inner races and seal surfaces for the roller bearing and oil seal which are pressed into the axle shaft housing.

On 1 and 1.1 litre cars the outer ends of the shafts are supported in the axle housing by thrust type ballbearings which are permanently lubricated and sealed on both sides. An O-ring seal is located between the bearing outer race and the housing and a retaining ring secures the bearing against the axle shaft shoulder.

The drive pinion is mounted in two roller bearings in the axle housing. The pinion setting is established by shims located between the differential carrier and the rear pinion bearing outer race.

The design of the rear axle assembly is such that the internal components can be removed and serviced with the rear axle assembly in position on the car. Check the oil level every 6000 miles.

8:5 Axle shafts

1 and 1.1 litre cars:

Removal:

Raise the rear of the car and support it safely on floor stands placed under the rear jacking brackets. Remove the road wheel and the brake drum. Refer to **FIG 8:9** and remove the four axle shaft retaining nuts through the access holes in the axle shaft flange. Install the axle shaft pulling tools J.2619 and J.8805 and withdraw the axle shaft.

Shaft bearing renewal:

With the axle shaft removed saw off part of the retaining ring and split the ring with a chisel as shown in **FIG 8:10,** being careful not to damage the axle shaft. Press off the bearing and water deflector.

Check the radial runout at the ballbearing seat and the axial runout of the axle shaft flange at its largest diameter. The permissible limit for radial runout is .002 inch and for axial runout .004 inch. If either of these tolerances is exceeded the axle shaft must be renewed.

Refit the dust shield with the flange towards the bearing and fit a new water deflector with the rolled edge towards the shaft flange. Press on the ballbearing with the oil seal facing the axle shaft splines. Finally, press on the new retaining ring with the larger diameter towards the bearing.

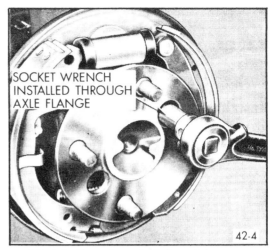

FIG 8:9   Removing axle shaft retaining nuts

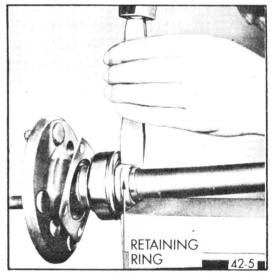

FIG 8:10   Removing bearing retaining ring

Refitting:

Refitting is a reversal of the removal instructions. Lubricate the splines and drive the axle shaft into the housing, using a soft-faced hammer.

1.5 and 1.9 litre cars:

Removal:

1 Raise the rear of the car and support it safely on floor stands placed under the rear jacking brackets. Remove the road wheel and the brake drum. Remove the differential cover and gasket and allow the oil to drain into a suitable container. Working through the access holes in the axle shaft flange, remove the four nuts and washers that attach the axle shaft retainer and backing plate to the axle housing, as shown in **FIG 8:9.**

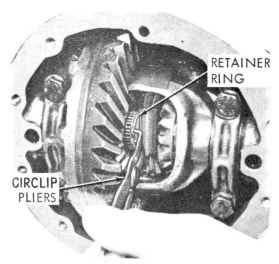

FIG 8:11　Removing axle shaft retaining ring

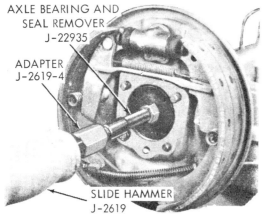

AXLE BEARING AND SEAL REMOVER J-22935

ADAPTER J-2619-4

SLIDE HAMMER J-2619

FIG 8:12　Removing axle shaft bearing and seal

2 Refer to **FIG 8:11** and remove the retaining ring from the inner end of the axle shaft. Install the axle shaft pulling tools J.2619 and J.8805 and withdraw the axle shaft.

Shaft bearing renewal:

Refer to **FIG 8:12** and remove the bearing and oil seal using the service tools shown. Make sure the bore in the axle housing is clean then drive in a new bearing. Coat the outer diameter of a new oil seal with jointing compound and press it into position.

Check the axle shaft radial runout at the bearing race and the axial runout of the axle shaft flange at its largest diameter. The permissible limit for radial runout is .001 inch and for axial runout .004 inch. If either of these tolerances is exceeded the axle shaft must be renewed.

Refitting:

Refitting is a reversal of the removal instructions. Fit a new gasket over the retaining bolts on the backing plate and install the axle shafts carefully to avoid damage to the oil seal. Fit a new gasket to the differential cover. Refill the rear axle with oil to the level of the filler plug.

8:6 Axle removal and refitting

Kadett 'A' and 'B' models:

Refer to **Sections 8:2** and **8:3** and disconnect the propeller shaft and remove the central joint assembly. Remove the road wheels. Disconnect the handbrake cable from all the connections under the car. Detach both dampers from the axle mountings and compress them upwards as far as possible. Remove the retainer from the brake pipe bracket and detach the brake hose from the brake pipe. Plug the hose and pipe to prevent loss of brake fluid. Remove the bolts attaching the axle to the rear spring brackets. Lift the axle and move to the left so that the right brake drum clears the spring, then lower the axle assembly and remove it from under the car.

Refitting is a reversal of the removal instructions, noting that it will be necessary to bleed the braking system as described in **Chapter 11** when refitting is completed.

All models except Kadett 'A' and 'B':

1 Raise the rear of the car and support it safely on floor stands placed under the rear jacking brackets. Leave the jack in position under the differential housing to support the weight of the axle assembly. Remove the road wheels and one brake drum. Disconnect the handbrake cable as described in **Chapter 11** and detach the cable from the actuating lever and backing plate on the brake assembly from which the drum has been removed. Disconnect the cable from the lower control arm brackets and pull the loose ends over the exhaust system.

2 Refer to **Part 3** of this Chapter and disconnect the dampers at their lower mountings, the panhard rod at the axle and the anti-roll bar if fitted. Mark the mating parts and disconnect the universal joint from the pinion flange and support the propeller shaft out of the way.

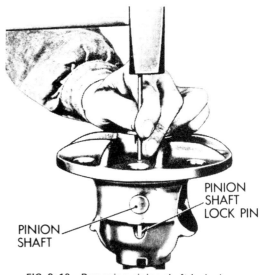

PINION SHAFT LOCK PIN

PINION SHAFT

FIG 8:13　Removing pinion shaft lock pin

3 Disconnect the brake hose from the brake pipe at the differential and remove the retaining clip. Lower the rear axle assembly sufficiently and remove the coil springs. Remove the bolts attaching the central joint support bracket to the underbody. Disconnect the lower control arms at the rear axle brackets then lower the axle assembly and remove it from under the car.

Refitting:

Refitting is a reversal of the removal instructions, noting the following points: Compress the rear springs as described in **Part 3** when refitting the control arms and the panhard rod. Bleed the brakes as described in **Chapter 11** when refitting the axle assembly has been completed.

8:7 The differential assembly

The removal and refitting of parts for service as described in this Section can be carried out with the rear axle assembly in the car. Refer to **FIG 8:7** or **8:8** to identify the components of the differential assembly.

Dismantling:

1 Raise the car and remove the axle shaft as described in **Section 8:5**. Remove the brake pipes and connector from the axle housing, plugging the pipes to prevent fluid loss. Disconnect the panhard rod from the axle housing. Remove the differential cover and gasket and allow the oil to drain into a suitable container.

2 Mark the side bearing caps to ensure correct reassembly and remove them. Using wooden levers, remove the differential assembly from the housing. Pull off the side bearings with J.22588 or similar puller and mark the bearings for correct reassembly if they are not to be renewed. Remove the bolts attaching the drive gear (crownwheel) to the differential case and use a brass drift to tap the drive gear from the case. Remove the pinion shaft lock pin as shown in **FIG 8:13** and remove the pinion shaft, pinion gears, side gears and thrust washers.

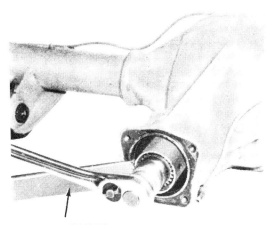

SPLINE HOLDER

FIG 8:14   Removing pinion preload nut

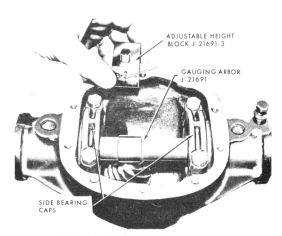

FIG 8:15   Pinion depth gauging tools

FIG 8:16   Pinion gear reference number

Drive pinion:

1 Refer to **Sections 8:2** and **8:3** and disconnect the propeller shaft and remove the central joint and torque tube. Using a suitable pointed tool, lever out the pinion oil seal. Place a screwdriver across the housing to lever against to avoid damage to the differential flange.

2 Using Service Tool J.22399 for 1 and 1.1 litre cars or J.22932 for 1.5 and 1.9 litre cars, hold the drive pinion as shown in **FIG 8:14** and remove the pinion preload nut and thrust cap. Drive out the pinion towards the inside of the housing. Use a drift to remove the pinion bearing outer races. Press the rear bearing from the pinion.

Reassembly:

Drive pinion:

1 Press the rear pinion bearing onto the pinion shaft and refit the pinion outer bearing races. Lubricate the inner pinion bearing and the outer races of both

FIG 8:17 Checking side gear clearance

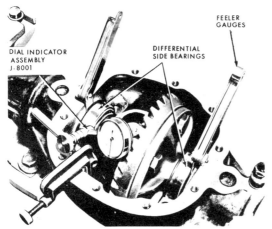

DIAL INDICATOR ASSEMBLY J-8001

DIFFERENTIAL SIDE BEARINGS

FEELER GAUGES

FIG 8:18 Checking side bearing clearance

bearings and insert the outer pinion bearing inner cone and the oil deflector. Install the drive pinion assembly without shims and, using the service tool to hold the pinion as shown in **FIG 8:14**, tighten the preload nut a little at a time, turning the pinion occasionally to seat the bearings. When the end play has been taken up, remove the tool and check the preload with a torque wrench. The torque required to turn the pinion should be 8 lb inch for new bearings or 4 lb inch for used bearings on 1 and 1.1 litre cars; 9 lb inch for new bearings or 6 lb inch for 1.5 and 1.9 litre cars. Gradually tighten the preload nut to obtain these figures.

2 The required thickness of shims to set the pinion depth is gauged as shown in **FIG 8:15**, using Service Tools shown. Install the gauging arbour in the side bearing outer bores and refit the bearing caps to a torque of 33 lb ft. Fit the adjustable height block between the pinion and the arbour then tighten the height block setscrew. Remove the height block and use a micrometer to measure its expanded height. Examine the face of the drive pinion to find the figure not underlined which is engraved on it, as shown in **FIG 8:16**.

This figure will have either a plus sign or a minus sign preceeding it. The figure is in hundredths of a millimetre and must be converted to inches using the conversion table in Technical Data in the Appendix. The figure thus obtained must be subtracted from the height block dimension if it was preceded by a plus sign on the pinion, or added to the height block dimension if it was preceded by a minus sign on the pinion. Having obtained this final figure, a constant must be subtracted from it which is 1.226 for 'A' models, 1.246 for 1.1 litre models and 1.468 for 1.5 and 1.9 litre models. The result of the calculations is the thickness of shims required to set the pinion depth.

3 Remove the drive pinion as previously described and fit shims to the thickness calculated. Fit a new collapsible spacer to the pinion shaft and install the pinion assembly and check the preload torque as previously described, being careful not to exceed the torque specified or the operation will have to be started again, using a new collapsible spacer. Immerse a new pinion oil seal in hypoid oil for three minutes then fit it in position. Refit the propeller shaft, central joint and torque tube as described in **Sections 8:2** and **8:3**.

Differential:

1 Using a feeler gauge, check the clearance between the side gears and the case. Select shims to obtain a maximum clearance of .006 inch measured as shown in **FIG 8:17**. Insert the differential gear shaft and secure it with the lock pin. Refit the drive gear to the differential case, tightening the bolts evenly and alternately to a final torque of 30 lb ft for 'A' and 'B' models, 47 lb ft for all other models. Drive gear runout should not exceed .003 inch.

2 Using two sets of feeler gauges and a dial gauge fitted at right angles to a drive gear tooth, check the thickness required for side bearing shims as shown in **FIG 8:18**. Adjust feeler gauge thickness from side to side until a drive gear backlash of .004 to .008 inch is obtained. Select shims to the thickness of the feelers and add .002 inch to each side for preload. Install the shims behind their respective bearings and fit the differential assembly into the housing. Fit the bearing caps and tighten to a torque of 33 lb ft.

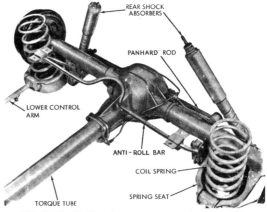

REAR SHOCK ABSORBERS

PANHARD ROD

LOWER CONTROL ARM

ANTI-ROLL BAR

COIL SPRING

SPRING SEAT

TORQUE TUBE

FIG 8:19 Coil spring rear suspension assembly

3 Refit the axle shafts as described in **Section 8:5**. Replace the differential cover, using a new gasket. Reassembly is a reversal of the dismantling procedure, noting that the brakes must be bled as described in **Chapter 11** on completion.

PART 3—THE REAR SUSPENSION

8:8 Description

Cars in the Kadett 'A' and 'B' ranges up to 1967 are fitted with semi-elliptical leaf springs and telescopic dampers. The springs are fitted with plastic pads between the leaves. Cars from 1968 onwards are fitted with a three link suspension arrangement consisting of coil springs, control arms, panhard rod and telescopic dampers as shown in **FIG 8:19**. Also shown is the anti-roll bar, fitted as standard to some models.

8:9 Spring removal and refitting

Kadett 'A' and 'B' range:

Removal:

Raise the car and support it safely on floor stands placed under the rear jacking brackets. Remove the road wheel. Loosen slightly the outer and inner nuts at the rear axle housing to spring attachment. Remove the U-bolt nuts, lockwashers and retaining plate, then remove U-bolts and the lower rubber pad. Remove the brake cable grommet from the bracket. Remove the front eye bolt, relieving tension from the spring with a jack. Remove the rear shackles, then remove the spring.

Refitting:

Refitting is a reversal of the removal procedure.

Later models:

Removal:

Raise the rear of the car with a jack under the differential housing. Support the car with floor stands under the rear jacking brackets, but leave the jack in position. Remove the road wheels and disconnect the dampers from the rear axle. Disconnect the shackles from the anti-roll bar, if fitted. It is not necessary to detach the panhard rod. Lower the axle assembly as far as possible without stressing the brake hose and remove the springs, tilting the axle assembly if necessary.

Refitting:

Refitting is a reversal of the removal procedure, noting the following points: Make sure that the damper rings are correctly positioned above and below the springs. Raise the rear axle assembly with the jack to compress the springs when refitting the dampers. Tighten anti-roll bar shackles with the car weight on the rear axle.

Control arms:

Disconnect the handbrake cable from the bracket on the control arm, then remove both fixing bolts and the control arm. Refit in the reverse order, but note that the rear springs must be compressed by placing a load of approximately 350 lbs in the luggage compartment before tightening the control arm fixing bolts to a torque of 18 lb ft.

8:10 The panhard rod

Remove the panhard rod with the car raised onto stands placed under the rear jacking points. Detach the panhard rod from its mounting points. When refitting the panhard rod, the rear springs must be compressed by placing a load of approximately 350 lbs in the luggage compartment before tightening the attaching bolts to a torque of 24 lb ft.

8:11 Rear dampers

The rear dampers are of the sealed type and require no servicing. If a damper becomes defective a replacement must be fitted.

Removal:

Remove the upper attaching nut, retainer and rubber grommet. Remove the lower attaching nut and rubber grommet retainer, compress the damper and remove it from the lower mounting pin.

Refitting:

Refitting is a reversal of the removal instructions, using new self-locking nuts.

PART 4—GENERAL

8:12 Fault diagnosis

(a) Noisy axle

1 Insufficient or incorrect lubricant
2 Worn bearings
3 Worn gears

(b) Excessive backlash

1 Worn gears or bearings
2 Worn axle shaft or side gear splines
3 Worn universal joints
4 Loose or broken wheel studs

(c) Oil leakage

1 Defective seals in axle tube
2 Defective drive pinion seal
3 Defective differential cover gasket

(d) Vibration

1 Propeller shaft out of balance
2 Worn universal joint bearings

(e) Rattles

1 Central joint mountings worn
2 Dampers loose
3 Loose spring clips
4 Worn bushes in spring eyes
5 Broken spring leaves (3, 4 and 5 pre-1968 models only)

(f) 'Settling'

1 Weak springs
2 Broken spring leaves
3 Badly worn shackle pins and bushes
4 Loose spring anchorages (2, 3 and 4 pre-1968 models only)

CHAPTER 9

THE FRONT SUSPENSION AND HUBS

9:1 Description

All models have independent front suspension with unequal length control arms and a transverse leaf spring. According to the model type, either a two-leaf or a three-leaf spring may be fitted. The entire front suspension is attached to the front crossmember as shown in **FIG 9:1** and can be removed as a complete unit. GT engines are not supported by mounting brackets but rest on a separate crossmember.

Ball joints are conventionally employed to provide pivoting joints between the control arms and steering swivels. Upward movement of the control arms is limited by rubber bumpers attached to the crossmember. The suspension is controlled by telescopic dampers which also serve to limit the downward travel of the control arms. All moving parts of the suspension including the ball joints need no periodic maintenance, either needing no lubrication at all or having been factory pre-lubricated for life.

9:2 Wheel hubs

Removal:

Jack-up the car and remove the road wheel. On cars with disc brakes, remove the two bolts holding the caliper to the steering swivel and wire the caliper to the suspension so the brake hose is not strained.

Remove the spindle grease cap. Remove the cotterpin and spindle nut and pull off the hub and drum or disc by hand. If new bearings are to be fitted, press out the bearings and outer races.

Refitting:

This is the reverse of the removal procedure. Re-grease the bearings and adjust the bearing end float.

Bearing end float:

Jack-up the car and remove the hub cap and the spindle grease cap. Remove the splitpin from the axle shaft nut and while rotating the wheel tighten the nut to a torque of 25 lb ft on Kadett 'A' and 'B' ranges or 18 lb ft for all later models. Loosen the nut until slight clearance can be felt then retighten the nut until the clearance just disappears. Fit a new splitpin and lock the nut.

9:3 Removing suspension assembly

1 Apply the handbrake and chock the rear wheels. Raise the front of the car and support it safely on floor stands placed under the front jacking brackets.

O KAD

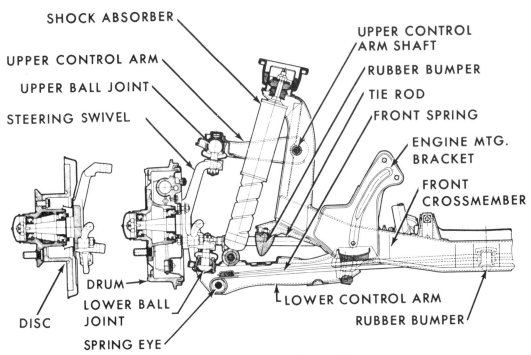

SHOCK ABSORBER

UPPER CONTROL ARM

UPPER BALL JOINT

STEERING SWIVEL

UPPER CONTROL ARM SHAFT

RUBBER BUMPER

TIE ROD

FRONT SPRING

ENGINE MTG. BRACKET

FRONT CROSSMEMBER

DRUM

LOWER BALL JOINT

DISC

SPRING EYE

LOWER CONTROL ARM

RUBBER BUMPER

FIG 9:1   Front suspension assembly

Support the engine and transmission assembly in its uppermost position with a floor stand at the rear of the engine. Alternatively, the engine and transmission assembly on 1.9 litre and GT models can be supported with engine holding tool J.23098 for the Kadett or J.23375 for the GT, as shown in **FIG 9:2**. Support the suspension crossmember with a jack.

2 On Kadett models, mark the relative positions of the steering mast to the flange and remove the clamp bolt as shown in **FIG 9:3**, then remove the mast guide stop bolt as shown in **FIG 9:4** and pull the steering column out of the mast flange until it is stopped by the indicator switch. Hold the column in this position by placing a block of wood between the steering wheel and the indicator housing. On GT models, loosen the steering mast at the lower universal joint and remove the clamp bolt as shown in **FIG 9:5**, then loosen the clamp at the upper universal joint and lift the steering mast upwards until it is free at the lower universal joint.

3 Disconnect the brake hoses as described in **Chapter 11**. Detach the dampers from their upper mounting points. On GT models remove the air cleaner and detach the radiator support on the crossmember. Remove the engine mounting bolts and rubber blocks. On earlier models release the clutch cable from the clip on the engine mount.

4 Make sure the jack is in position to support the crossmember, then remove the nuts securing the crossmember to the car frame and lower the front suspension assembly, making sure that the engine mounting bracket does not interfere with the starter cables.

Refitting:

Refitting the front suspension assembly is a reversal of the removal procedure. Tighten the crossmember to car frame attaching nuts to a torque of 36 lb ft. **Always use new self-locking nuts.** Push the steering column downwards until a clearance of $\frac{1}{8}$ inch is obtained between the steering wheel hub and the switch cover. With the steering wheel and the road wheels in the straight-ahead position, tighten the steering mast clamp bolt to a torque of 25 lb ft on pre-1968 cars or 15 lb ft on later cars. On GT models, tighten the clamp at the lower universal joint to a torque of 22 lb ft and the clamp at the upper universal joint to 14 lb ft. Use a new lockwasher when refitting the mast guide stop bolt.

Upon completion, bleed the brakes as described in **Chapter 11**.

9:4 Dismantling the assembly

All parts of the assembly can be removed and serviced with the assembly in the car but, in order to remove most parts of the front suspension it is necessary to stretch the front spring, using Service Tool J.21689.

Upper ball joint:

Removal:

Place a jack under the front spring eye and raise the car. Remove the road wheel. Remove the cotter pin and castellated nut from the upper ball joint stud. Press the ball stud from the steering swivel, using J.21687 or similar puller and remove two bolts attaching the ball

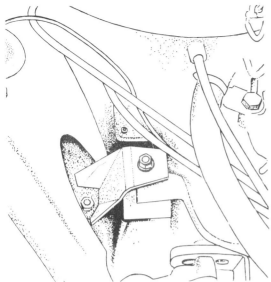

FIG 9:2 Engine holding fixture installed

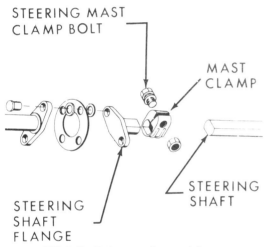

STEERING MAST CLAMP BOLT

MAST CLAMP

STEERING SHAFT

STEERING SHAFT FLANGE

FIG 9:3 Kadett steering mast flange

joint to the upper control arm, as shown in **FIG 9:6**. If there is excessive play in the ball joint or if the dust cap is torn or missing, the ball joint should be renewed.

Refitting:

Refitting is a reversal of the removal procedure. Install the ball joint with the off-centre holes in the flange towards the steering swivel spindle. Tighten the two ball joint attaching bolts to a torque of 18 lb ft. Tighten the castellated nut to a torque of 29 lb ft and lock with a new cotterpin. Check the castor and camber angles as described in **Section 9:5**.

Lower ball joint:

The maximum permissible axial play for a lower ball joint is .080 inch. If this figure is exceeded, or if the dust cap is torn or missing, the ball joint should be renewed.

Removal:

1 Raise the car and support it with floor stands at the rear of the front frame rails. Remove the road wheel.
2 Remove the cotter pin from the castellated nut on the ball joint stud and loosen the nut two turns. Using a hammer, hit the ball stud a sharp blow to loosen it. **Do not remove the nut.**
3 Install the front spring compressor J.21689 as shown in **FIG 9:7** and compress the spring until a distance of $3\frac{1}{8}$ inch is achieved between the compressor and the spring.
4 Disconnect the lower damper to control arm bolt and swing the damper out of the way. Remove the castellated nut from the ball joint stud. **Before removing the lower ball joint from the control arm, mark the position of the notch in the rim of the ball joint housing.** Lever off the dust cap retaining clip and carefully remove the dust cap. Press the ball stud out of the lower control arm.

Refitting:

1 Pressing only on the ball joint housing and not on the bottom plate, press the ball joint into place, making certain that the notch in the bottom plate aligns exactly with the mark made when dismantling. The notch must point towards the brake backing plate and must be aligned to within 2 deg. of the lower control arm centre-line. **If ball stud alignment is incorrect, binding or fracture of the ball stud will occur.**
2 Fit the dust cap to the lower ball joint and fill with chassis lubricant. Attach the retainer. Press the ball joint into the steering swivel, using tools J.9519.3 and J.21690. Install the castellated nut onto the ball joint stud and tighten to 45 lb ft, locking it with a new cotterpin. Remove the spring compressor. Check the castor and camber angles as described in **Section 9:5**.

Upper control arm:

Removal:

1 Raise the car and support it with floor stands at the rear of the front frame rails. Remove the road wheels. Install spring compressor and compress the spring

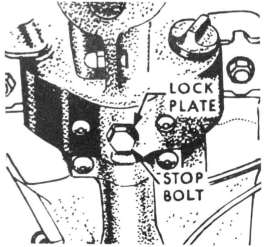

FIG 9:4 Steering mast guide stop bolt

LOCK PLATE

STOP BOLT

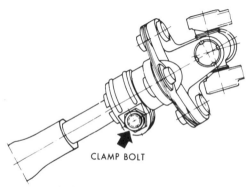

FIG 9:5 GT steering mast joint

FIG 9:6 Removing the upper ball joint

until there is a distance of $3\frac{1}{8}$ inch between the spring and compressor. Remove the upper ball joint as previously described. Support the brake assembly to avoid strain on the hose.

2 Remove the nut from the upper control arm shaft then remove the shaft and washers from the damper support. Avoid damaging the threads on the control arm shaft. Remove the upper control arm. Collect the inner toothed washers, noting their size and location for reassembly.

Refitting:

If the rubber bushings on the control arm are worn, the arm must be renewed. Refitting is a reversal of the removal procedure, noting the following:

Refer to **FIG 9:8** and replace components as shown, fitting the toothed washers to their original positions. Install the nut on the control arm shaft finger tight, then tighten the spring compressor to relieve tension on the control arm and tighten the shaft nut to 33 lb ft.

Lower control arm:
Removal:

1 Refer to the previous instructions for removing the lower ball joint and carry out instructions 1, 2 and 3. Disconnect and compress the damper.
2 Support the rail of the spring compressor with a jack and remove the lower control arm from the crossmember, noting that it may be necessary to remove the self-locking nuts with the aid of a punch.
3 Remove the lower ball stud nut. Slightly lower the jack to remove the spring and lower control arm assembly from the crossmember and steering swivel. Lower completely and remove the control arm to spring nuts. Release the compressor and remove the lower control arm.

Refitting:

Refitting is a reversal of the removal procedure, noting the following points: Torque the lower control arm to spring attaching bolts to 18 lb ft. On completion check the castor and camber angles as described in **Section 9:5**.

Steering swivel:
Removal:

1 Raise the car and support it with floor stands under the front frame rails. Refer to **Section 9:2** and remove the hub. Remove the brake backing plate (drum brake) from the swivel and wire it out of the way.
2 Compress the spring and remove the upper and lower ball joints as previously described. Disconnect the lower damper attaching bolt. Remove the steering swivel. Remove the disc brake dust shield from the swivel.

Refitting:

Refitting is a reversal of the removal instructions, noting the following: Fit a new gasket to the disc brake dust shield. Drum brake backing plate fixing bolts may be either M8 or M10 size. Torque M8 to 18 lb ft, M10 to 47 lb ft.

Front spring:
Removal and refitting:

Refer to the previous section for removing the lower control arms and carry out the instructions until both lower ball joints are detached from the steering swivels, then lower the compressor together with the spring and lower control arms. Remove the compressor and control arms. Refitting is a reversal of the removal procedure.

9:5 Adjustments

Before making castor and camber angle checks and adjustments the suspension ball joints and the front wheel bearings must be checked for excessive play and renewed or adjusted as necessary. The car must be standing on level ground and the front tyres should have approximately the same wear and be inflated to the recommended pressures. Castor and camber angles are given in Technical Data.

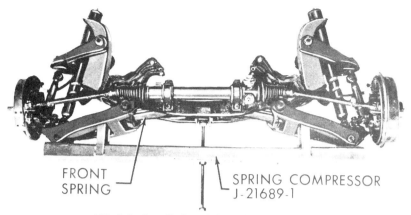

FRONT SPRING

SPRING COMPRESSOR J-21689-1

FIG 9:7   Installation of the spring compressor

Castor angle:

Use an approved gauge and check the castor angle. Adjustment is effected by changing the thickness of the toothed washers on both sides of the upper control arm shaft. Three washer sizes are available, .12, .24 and .36 inch. Raise the car, compress the front spring and remove the upper control arm shaft as previously described. Refer to **FIG 9:8** and install washers at the locations shown. To increase castor angle fit one of the thin washers at the front of the shaft and one of the thick washers at the rear. Decrease the angle by fitting a thick washer at the front and a thin washer at the rear. **Never use more than one washer at either location. The thickness of both washers must total .48 inch. Make sure that the crown of both washers faces inwards.**

Camber angle:

Camber is adjusted by turning the upper ball joint flange through 180 deg., which means that only two possible adjustments can be made. Camber is set at the factory to the smallest possible positive angle, so rotating the flange will increase the positive angle. Raise the car and support it on floor stands placed under both spring eyes. Remove the road wheel. Remove the upper ball joint from the control arm and steering swivel as previously described. Lift the upper control arm and turn the ball joint flange through 180 deg. Reassemble the suspension and recheck the camber.

9:6 Dampers

The telescopic dampers are of the sealed type and require no maintenance. Should a damper become unserviceable, a replacement must be fitted.

Removal:

Remove the air cleaner on GT models. Refer to **FIG 9:9** and remove the upper damper attaching nuts. Remove the lower attaching nut, bolt and lockwasher. Compress the damper and remove from the car.

Refitting:

Reverse the removal procedure, fitting new rubber grommets. Tighten the lower damper bolt to a torque of 30 lb ft, and tighten the upper attaching nut until the distance from the nut to the top of the stud is approximately $\frac{1}{2}$ inch as shown.

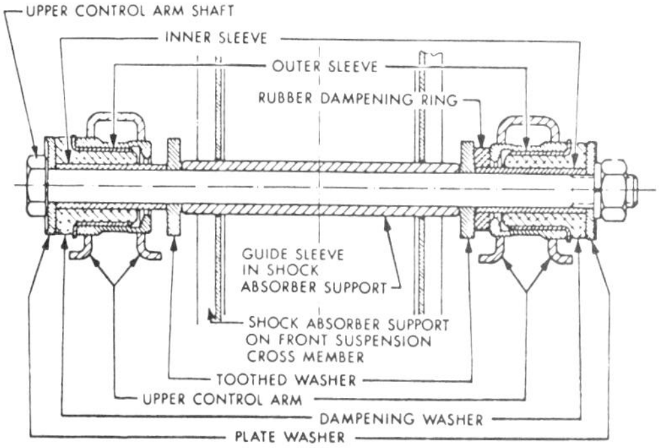

FIG 9:8 Upper control arm shaft, bushes and adjustment washers

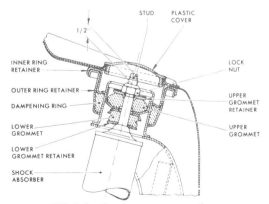

FIG 9:9   Damper upper mounting

9:7 Fault diagnosis

(a) Wheel wobble

1 Worn hub bearings
2 Broken or weak front spring
3 Uneven tyre wear
4 Worn suspension linkage
5 Loose wheel fixings
6 Incorrect tracking

(b) 'Bottoming' of suspension

1 Check 2 in (a)
2 Rebound rubbers worn or missing
3 Dampers not working

(c) Heavy steering

1 Defective wheel swivels
2 Wrong suspension geometry

(d) Excessive tyre wear

1 Check 4 and 6 in (a) and 2 in (c)

(e) Rattles

1 Check 2 in (a) and 1 in (c)
2 Worn bushes
3 Damper attachments loose

(f) Excessive rolling

1 Check 2 in (a) and 3 in (b)

CHAPTER 10

THE STEERING GEAR

10:1 Description

Rack and pinion steering is employed on all models. The pinion shaft is turned by the lower end of the steering mast and moves the rack to the left or right, transmitting the steering motion to the front wheels by means of the tie rods and steering arms. The rack and the pinion shaft are held in mesh by an adjustable thrust spring. The pinion is supported in the housing by a needle bearing in the upper part and a brass bush in the lower part. The rack moves in self-lubricating sintered metal bushes. The steering gear housing is held to the front crossmember by clamps fitted with rubber bushes. The layout of the steering gear assembly and tie rods is shown in **FIG 10:1**. A telescopic steering shaft was introduced with the 1967 models, the two sliding parts of the column being connected with plastic pins. Later models are equipped with the type of shock-absorbing column assembly shown in **FIG 10:2**. When a sufficiently high pressure acts upon either end of the column, the plastic pins **C** shear off and the outer jacket **B** compresses. A slide-off base is welded to the jacket and provided with three attachment slots. A metal piece **A**, attached to the base by plastic pins, is located in each of the slots. By this means the steering column assembly is prevented from being pushed into the car, but is free to move downwards when impact on the steering wheel shears the plastic pins. It is essential when servicing telescopic steering assemblies to avoid shocks or blows on either end of the column, as the plastic pins may be sheared off, necessitating renewal of the assembly.

10:2 Removing steering wheel

Removal:

Disconnect the battery, then lever out the horn button from the steering wheel and disconnect the horn wires. Release the tabwasher and remove the steering wheel nut, tabwasher and washer. Pull off the steering wheel, using tool J.21686 or similar puller as shown in **FIG 10:3**.

Refitting:

Make sure the wheels are in the straight-ahead position and centre the steering wheel when refitting. Tighten the steering wheel nut to a torque of 15 lb ft and lock with the tabwasher. Refit the horn button and connect the battery.

10:3 The steering column

The removal of the steering column assembly is necessary only for renewal of the complete assembly or the steering and ignition lock.

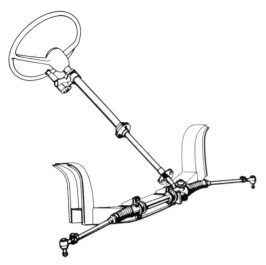

FIG 10:1 The steering gear assembly and tie rods

Removal (all models except GT):

1 Disconnect the battery and remove the air cleaner. Disconnect the choke cable from the carburetter and pull it into the passenger compartment. Disconnect the wires from the electrical switch on the steering and ignition lock.

2 On Kadett 'A' models, remove the steering and ignition lock cylinder by first turning the lock to the 'ON' position, then push the spring-loaded stop pin of the cylinder in and pull out the cylinder. Loosen the set-screw on the lock housing cover and take off the cover.
    On all other models the lock cylinder need not be removed, but make sure the cylinder is not in the 'LOCKED' position.

3 From under the car, remove the bolt from the clamp securing the flexible coupling to the steering mast shaft and mark both parts for correct refitting. Remove the stop bolt shown in **FIG 10:4** and pull the steering wheel approximately three inches rearwards and hold it in the withdrawn position with a block of wood.

4 **On Kadett 'A' models,** remove two nuts and lock-washers securing the column to the studs on the underside of the instrument panel, and loosen the bolts and nuts securing the braces to the cowling. Work the studs upward and free from the steering column bracket. Pull out the steering column assembly.
    On Kadett 'B' models, centre punch both shear-lock bolts shown in **FIG 10:5**, pilot drill them $\frac{1}{8}$ inch, then drill them off with a $\frac{5}{16}$ inch drill. Remove the steering column assembly, then screw out the bolt shafts from the underside of the instrument panel.
    On all later models, drill off the head of the rear slide-off base attaching bolt shown in **FIG 10:6**. Remove both attaching nuts shown in **FIG 10:7** and remove the steering column assembly, handling it carefully to avoid shocks or blows which could damage the energy absorbing parts.

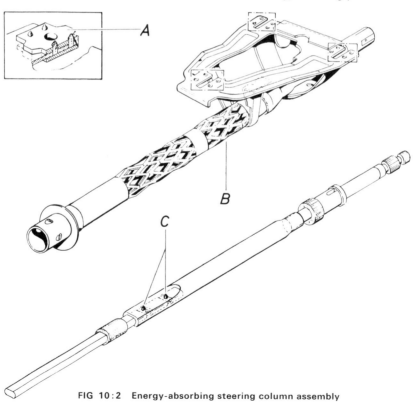

FIG 10:2 Energy-absorbing steering column assembly

FIG 10:3   Removing the steering wheel

FIG 10:5   Position of shear-lock bolts

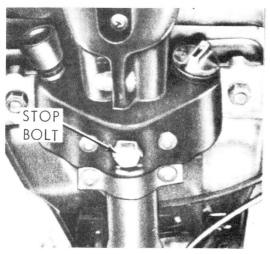

FIG 10:4   Steering column stop bolt

FIG 10:6   Slide-off base attaching bolt

Refitting:

Refitting is a reversal of the removal procedure, noting the following instructions.

On Kadett 'A' models, fit the steering column cover and loosely attach the bracket to the underside of the instrument panel. Install the steering and ignition lock cover and adjust it until the lock face protrudes between $\frac{1}{64}$ and $\frac{1}{32}$ inch. When reconnecting the steering mast shaft to the flexible coupling, index the alignment marks made on removal and allow a clearance of $\frac{1}{8}$ inch between the steering wheel and the switch housing cover, before tightening the clamp bolt to a torque of 23 lb ft. Lock the nut with the tabwasher. The correct fitting of the shaft to the flexible coupling, with the shaft cut-out parallel to the bolt hole, is shown in **FIG 10:8**.

On Kadett 'B' models, ensure that the indicator switch is in the neutral position and install the steering column assembly into the car. Refit the support using new shear-lock bolts as shown in **FIG 10:5**, installing the bolts finger tight. The toothed washer must be fitted between the support and the instrument panel as shown in **FIG 10:9**. Index the alignment marks previously made and insert the lower end of the steering mast shaft into the flexible coupling, but do not tighten the bolt. The correct fitting is shown in **FIG 10:8**. Push the mast into the flange and tighten the stop bolt. Check for free movement of the steering wheel. Adjust for a clearance of $\frac{1}{8}$ inch between the steering wheel and the switch housing cover, then tighten the flexible coupling clamp bolt to a torque of 25 lb ft and tab the nut. Tighten the shear-lock bolts until the hexagon head shears off.

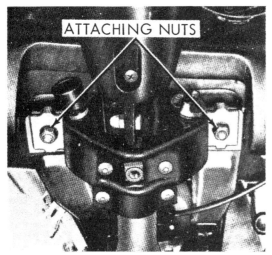

FIG 10:7 Column bracket attaching nuts

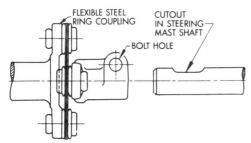

FIG 10:8 Flexible coupling assembly details

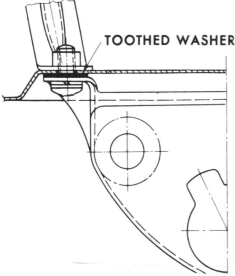

FIG 10:9 Positioning toothed washer between instrument panel and column support

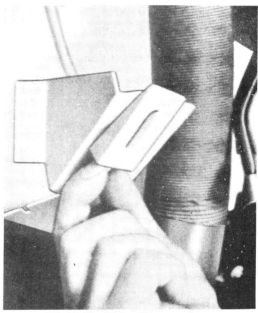

FIG 10:10 Slide-off base wedge

Tighten the shear-lock bolts until the hexagon head shears off.

On all later models, ensure that the indicator switch is in the neutral position and place the steering column assembly into the car, tightening the nuts shown in **FIG 10:7** to a torque of 7 lb ft. With the help of an assistant, insert the lower end of the steering mast shaft into the flexible coupling. Index the alignment marks previously made and adjust for a clearance of $\frac{1}{8}$ inch between the steering wheel and the switch housing cover, then tighten the clamp bolt to a torque of 15 lb ft. For compensation slide the aluminium wedge shown in **FIG 10:10** between the slide-off base and the bracket from the rear, then fit a new shear-lock bolt and tighten it until the hexagon head shears off, as shown in **FIG 10:6**. Secure the stop bolt with the tabwasher.

Removal (GT models):

1 Position the steering so that the wheels are straight-ahead. Disconnect the battery.
2 Refer to **FIG 10:11** and loosen the lower clamp bolt on the upper universal joint. Drill a $\frac{1}{8}$ inch pilot hole in the heads of both shear-lock bolts then drill off the heads with a $\frac{5}{16}$ inch drill. Disconnect the set plugs on the white ignition wire and the black direction signal wire.
3 Support the steering column assembly and remove both hexagon head bolts shown. Pull the steering column assembly off the centre steering shaft. Do not use force or the energy absorbing centre shaft may be damaged.

Refitting:

Refitting is a reversal of the removal procedure, noting the following: Make sure the earth wire is refitted, then tighten the hexagon headed bolts to a torque of 14 lb ft.

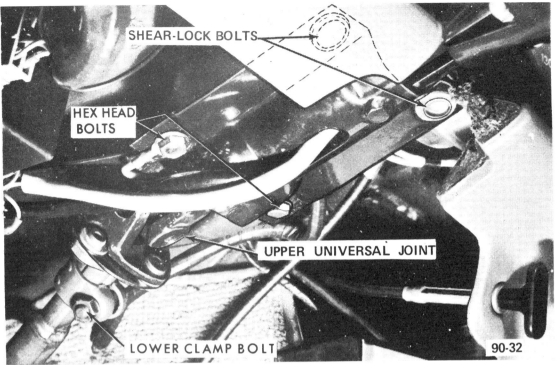

FIG 10:11　GT steering column attachment points

Fit new shear-lock bolts and tighten them until the heads shear off. Tighten the universal joint clamp bolt to a torque of 14 lb ft.

The centre steering shaft (GT):

Removal:

Position the steering so that the wheels are straight-ahead. Loosen the clamp bolt on the upper universal joint shown in **FIG 10:11**. Remove the upper clamp screw from the lower universal joint. Carefully push the centre steering shaft up into the upper joint until the lower end is free, then remove the shaft through the bottom of the car.

Refitting:

Refitting is a reversal of the removal instructions, tightening the lower universal joint bolt to a torque of 22 lb ft and the upper universal joint bolt to 14 lb ft.

10:4 Rack and pinion assembly

Removal:

1 Loosen the clamp bolt securing the flexible coupling to the steering shaft, removing the bolt on Kadett 'A' and 'B' models. Remove the stop bolt shown in **FIG 10:4** and pull the steering wheel approximately

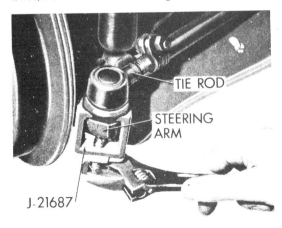

FIG 10:12　Removing steering arm ball joints

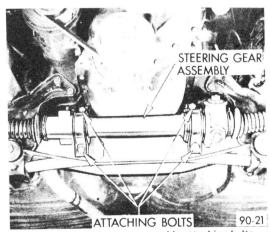

FIG 10:13　Steering gear assembly attaching bolts

O KAD

105

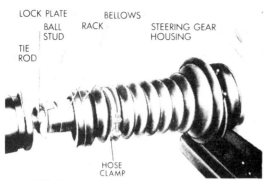

FIG 10:14 Tie rod attachment details

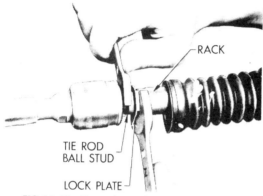

FIG 10:15 Removing and refitting the tie rod

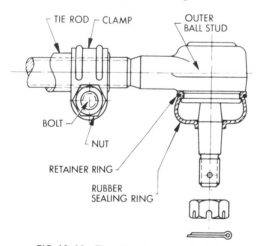

FIG 10:16 Tie rod and outer ball stud

three inches rearwards and hold it in the withdrawn position with a block of wood.

2 Remove the cotterpin and castellated nut from the tie rod end on each side of the car, then press the ball studs out of the steering arms as shown in **FIG 10:12**, using tool J.21687 or similar.

3 Remove the four steering gear assembly attaching bolts shown in **FIG 10:13** and lift off the assembly and tie rods.

Refitting:

Refitting is a reversal of the removal instructions, tightening the steering gear mounting bolts to a torque of 25 lb ft on Kadett 'A' and 'B' models, 18 lb ft on all later models. Connect the steering shaft to the flexible coupling as described in **Section 10:3**. Refit the ball stud to the steering arm, tighten the nut to a torque of 29 lb ft and lock with a new cotter pin.

Removing tie rods:

Tie rod removal may be carried out with the rack and pinion assembly either removed or installed. If the assembly is to remain on the car it is necessary to carry out the previous instruction 2 for removing the ball studs from the steering arms before proceeding as follows:

1 Clean the tie rods and the area around the steering gear assembly to prevent dirt from entering the assembly via the rack.

2 Refer to **FIG 10:14** and remove the clamp securing the rubber bellows to the tie rod and slip the bellows off the tie rod to expose the lock plate. Bend up the edges of the lock plate and unscrew the ball studs from the rack, holding the rack with a second spanner as shown in **FIG 10:15** to prevent damage to the rack teeth.

Refitting:

1 Install new lock plates onto the tie rod ball studs and screw the studs into the rack, holding the bent tab on the lock plate against the flat on the rack. Tighten the ball studs to a torque of 43 lb ft. Hold the rack as shown in **FIG 10:15** to prevent damage to the teeth. Bend the round edges of the lock plate over the flat on the ball stud.

2 Position the rubber bellows and clamps over the tie rods so that the wire ends of the clamp point in the same direction as the adjusting screw, making sure that the bellows are not twisted and will compress and expand properly. Refit the ball stud to the steering arm, tighten the nut to a torque of 29 lb ft and lock with a new cotterpin.

Dismantling tie rods:

Refer to **FIG 10:16** and loosen the tie rod clamp bolt and unscrew the ball stud. Remove the retainer ring from the ball stud and take off the rubber sealing ring. Reassembly is a reversal of the removal procedure.

Dismantling the rack and pinion assembly:

Refer to **FIG 10:17**.

1 Loosen the adjuster screw locknut and remove the adjuster screw from the housing. Take out the thrust spring and sintered bronze shell.

2 Hold the pinion shaft part of the assembly in a vice and remove the pinion nut, flat washer and special washer. Remove the pinion shaft from the gear assembly, then withdraw the rack.

3 Remove the O-rings from the retainer and pinion bushings and take out the thrust washer.

Reassembly:

Coat all moving parts with steering gear lubricant during reassembly and fill the long end of the housing with approximately $1\frac{3}{4}$ oz. of lubricant.

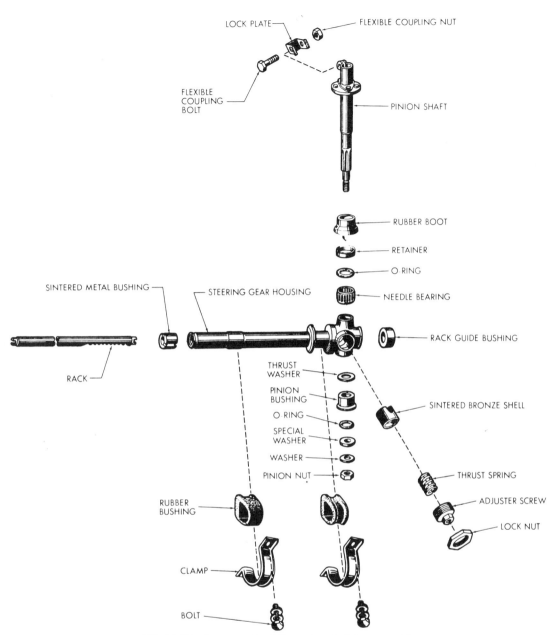

FIG 10:17 Components of the rack and pinion assembly

1 Hold the housing in a vice and fit new O-rings onto the retainer and pinion shaft bushings. Fit the thrust washer onto the pinion bushing.

2 Insert the toothless end of the rack into the short end of the housing until it protrudes equally from both ends of the housing. **Check to ensure that the three air channels in the sintered metal bushing are not obstructed by lubricant. If the air channels are blocked a vacuum may form which will draw the rubber bellows into the rack during operation.**

3 Fit the pinion shaft into the housing so that the spline on the shaft meshes with the twelfth tooth on the rack. The pinion shaft is best fitted with tool J.21712 to avoid possible damage to the O-ring in the bushing. Make sure the pinion is positioned with the bolt hole in the flexible coupling on top so that the bolt will be parallel with the rack.

4 Reassemble the special washer, flat washer and new pinion nut onto the pinion shaft and tighten the nut to a torque of 11 lb ft. **Do not overtighten the nut or the steering gear may get jammed.**

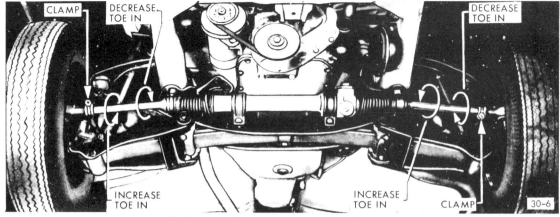

FIG 10:18   Adjusting the front wheel alignment

5 Fit the sintered bronze shell into place and fill the adjuster screw hole with lubricant. Reassemble the thrust spring, adjuster screw and locknut onto the housing. Refit the steering gear to the car before making final adjustments to the adjuster screw as described in the next section.

10:5 Lubrication and adjustment

Adjustment of the steering gear assembly is carried out by turning the adjuster screw in or out, which varies the backlash between the pinion and rack. Adjustment is as follows:

1 Set the steering to the high point by positioning the front wheels straight-ahead with the steering wheel spokes centred. The steering shaft flexible coupling bolt should then be parallel to the rack.
2 Loosen the locknut and turn in the adjuster screw until a resistance is felt. This causes the sintered bronze shell to preload the rack. Unscrew the adjuster screw $\frac{1}{8}$ to $\frac{1}{4}$ turn, then tighten the locknut.
3 Fill the area under the pinion shaft rubber boot with steering gear lubricant and slide the boot into position.

10:6 Tracking

When correctly adjusted the front wheels must toe-in $\frac{1}{16}$ to $\frac{1}{8}$ inch, and this can be checked and adjusted as follows: The car must be unladen and standing on level ground, with the tyres inflated to the recommended pressures. Set the steering to the straight-ahead position. With the steering wheel hub button removed the marking on the shaft end should be horizontal. Check the wheel alignment using an approved track setting gauge. Push the car forward until the wheels have turned through 180 deg. and recheck. If adjustment is required, refer to **FIG 10:18** and loosen the clamp bolts at each end of the tie rods and rotate the rods equally as shown until the alignment is correct. Tighten the clamp bolts and recheck the alignment.

10:7 Fault diagnosis

(a) Wheel wobble

1 Unbalanced wheels and tyres
2 Slack steering connections
3 Incorrect steering geometry
4 Excessive play in steering gear
5 Faulty suspension
6 Worn hub bearings

(b) Wander

1 Check 2, 3 and 4 in (a)
2 Uneven tyre pressures
3 Uneven tyre wear
4 Ineffective dampers

(c) Heavy steering

1 Check 3 in (a)
2 Very low tyre pressures
3 Neglected lubrication
4 Wheels out of track
5 Rack adjustment too tight
6 Inner steering column bent
7 Steering column bushes tight

(d) Lost motion

1 Loose steering wheel, worn splines
2 Worn rack and pinion teeth
3 Worn ball joints
4 Worn swivel hub joints
5 Worn flexible coupling
6 Worn universal joints (GT)
7 Slack pinion bearings

CHAPTER 11

THE BRAKING SYSTEM

11:1 Description

Kadett 'A' models are equipped with drum brakes on all four wheels. Disc brakes for the front wheels were introduced with the Kadett 'B' range in 1966 and may be fitted to these and all later models. The brakes on all four wheels are hydraulically operated by the brake pedal, the handbrake operating the rear brakes only through a mechanical linkage. Early models use a single master cylinder, cars from 1967 onwards being fitted with a dual master cylinder, with vacuum servo units available as an optional extra. The brake pedal is directly connected to the master cylinder where pressure on the fluid is generated and passed to the brakes by a system of metal and flexible pipes.

Drum brakes are of the same type for both front and rear wheels, having one leading and one trailing shoe to each brake. On all-drum braking systems the rear brakes are fitted with a smaller diameter wheel cylinder than the front brakes. This controls the tendency for the rear wheels to lock under heavy braking due to weight transfer to the front wheels. Drum brake systems require a minimum static pressure of $4\frac{1}{4}$ lbs on the brake fluid at all times to hold the wheel cylinder seals against the cylinder walls, preventing the entry of air or the loss of fluid.

This is achieved by the use of a check valve in the master cylinder.

Disc brakes have a fixed caliper with two self-adjusting friction pads between which the disc rotates. The friction pads are applied by two pistons operated by hydraulic pressure from the master cylinder, both pistons operating simultaneously to exert equal pressure on the pads. Disc brakes require that all pressure is released to disengage the pistons. When disc front brakes are used with rear drum brakes, two pressure lines are provided on single master cylinder systems to allow the complete release of pressure to the disc brakes, while maintaining the static pressure on the drum brakes by means of the check valve. On dual master cylinder installations two separate braking systems are employed for the front and rear brakes, using a check valve in the rear brake circuit on disc and drum arrangements, or two check valves on all-drum arrangements.

11:2 Maintenance

Regularly check the level of the fluid in the master cylinder supply tank and replenish if necessary up to the 'MAX' mark on the side of the tank. Make sure that the level is consistent in both parts of the tank on dual master

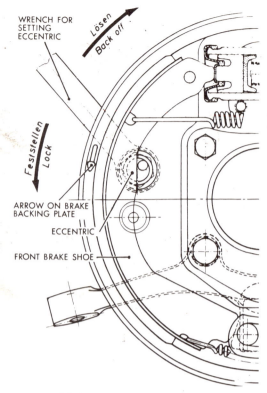

FIG 11:1 Drum brake adjustment

this time revolving the wheel in the backward direction. Lower the car and repeat the adjustment procedure on the other wheel(s).

Handbrake cable adjustment will be necessary whenever the cables have been disconnected for servicing, or if the cables have been stretched during a long period of use. Check the adjustment at the brake drum first, then adjust the handbrake cable as described in **Section 11:9** if the handbrake lever can be engaged more than eight clicks on the rachet under heavy pressure. The cable should be lubricated periodically to ensure that it moves freely in the equalizer.

11:3 Drum brakes

Removing the brake shoes:

When working on the front wheels, apply the handbrake and chock the rear wheels; when working on the rear wheels, chock the front wheels and release the handbrake.

1 Jack-up the car and remove the road wheel and the wheel hub. Remove the upper and lower brake shoe return springs. **FIG 11:2** shows the brake drum assembly. Kadett 'A' models do not have brake cylinder pushrods as shown, the shoes being operated directly from the cylinder pistons.

2 **On Kadett 'A' models,** remove the shoes by sliding them out of the clips. On the rear shoes disconnect the brake cable from the cable lever.

  On all other models, remove the shoes by removing the retaining pins and springs.

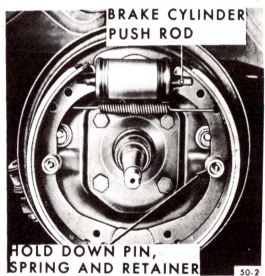

FIG 11:2 Removing and refitting brake shoes

cylinder installations. Wipe dirt from around the filler cap before removing it and check that the vent hole in the cap is unobstructed. If frequent topping up is required the system should be examined for leaks, but it should be noted that disc brake systems will need topping up more frequently than all-drum systems, due to the wheel cylinder movement compensating for friction pad wear. The recommended fluid is that complying to General Motors specification GM.4653M Type 375. **Never use anything but the recommended fluid.**

When brake pedal travel becomes excessive, adjust all the brakes on drum systems or the rear drums when disc front brakes are fitted. Adjustment is carried out as follows: Raise the car so that the wheel is clear of the ground. Refer to **FIG 11:1**. Revolve the wheel in a forward direction and turn the front brake shoe eccentric until the shoe contacts the brake drum, then turn the eccentric in the opposite direction until the drum is just free to turn. Turn the other eccentric to adjust the rear brake shoe,

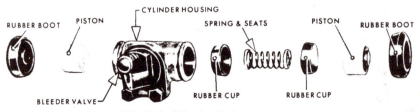

FIG 11:3 Wheel cylinder components

Refitting:

Clean the brake drum and backing plate thoroughly, using care to avoid dirt entering the wheel bearings. Make sure the return springs are correctly fitted to the webs and that the shoes register correctly in the wheel cylinder and pivot. Slacken off the brake adjuster completely before refitting the drum. Readjust the shoes when assembly is complete. Adjust the wheel bearing as described in **Section 9:2**.

Relining brake shoes:

If the linings are worn down to the rivets, renewal is necessary. It is not recommended that owners attempt to reline brake shoes themselves. It is important that the linings should be properly bedded to the shoes and ground for concentricity. For this reason it is best to obtain sets of replacement shoes, or have the relining carried out by a service station. **Do not allow grease, oil or brake fluid to contact brake linings.** If the linings are contaminated in any way they must be renewed as they cannot be successfully cleaned.

Servicing a wheel cylinder:

Remove the road wheel, drum and brake shoes. Disconnect the brake pipe or hose and use a plug to prevent loss of fluid. Remove the wheel cylinder from the brake backing plate. Refer to **FIG 11:3** and remove the boots, pistons, cups and spring from the cylinder, and the bleeder screw from the housing.

Discard the rubber boots and cups and thoroughly clean the remaining parts in the correct grade of brake fluid. Inspect the pistons and cylinder bore for scoring or corrosion. Light corrosion may be removed with fine steel wool, but if the corrosion is deep or if there is heavy scoring the part should be renewed.

Dip the internal parts in brake fluid and reassemble the cylinder. Use the fingers to insert the new rubber cups to avoid damaging the edges. Fit new rubber boots. Install the wheel cylinder onto the brake backing plate

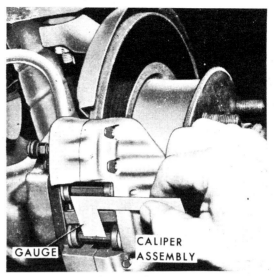

FIG 11:4   Checking friction pad wear

and connect the brake pipe or hose. Refit the shoes, drum and road wheel, then bleed the brakes as described in **Section 11:5**.

11:4 Disc brakes

Disc brake friction pad wear can be measured as follows: There is no need to remove the wheel. Make up a gauge $\frac{23}{32}$ inch across as shown in **FIG 11:4**. While an assistant presses the brake pedal, insert the gauge as shown between the upper and lower friction pad tabs at each caliper. If the gauge is a tight fit or will not fit between the tabs at all on any one of the tests, all four friction pads should be renewed. Do not renew the pads on one side only as uneven braking will result.

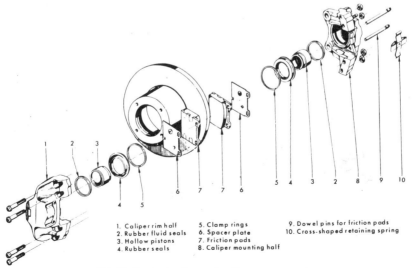

1. Caliper rim half
2. Rubber fluid seals
3. Hollow pistons
4. Rubber seals
5. Clamp rings
6. Spacer plate
7. Friction pads
8. Caliper mounting half
9. Dowel pins for friction pads
10. Cross-shaped retaining spring

FIG 11:5   Brake disc and caliper components

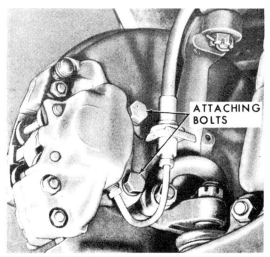

FIG 11:6   Caliper attaching bolts

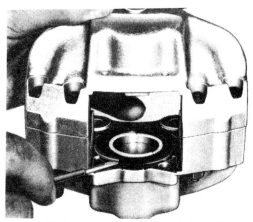

FIG 11:7   Removing the rubber seal clamp ring

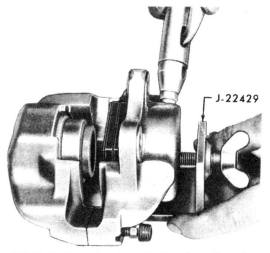

FIG 11:8   Removing rim half piston from the caliper

Renewing friction pads:

Raise the car and support it in a safe manner, then remove the front wheels. Refer to **FIG 11:5** and drive out the dowel pins towards the centre of the car. Refer to **FIG 11:5** and remove the cross-shaped spring 10 and the pads.

Before fitting new friction pads, clean the face of each piston 3 and ensure that the recesses for the pads in the caliper are free from dirt and rust. Open the bleeder screw on the caliper and push both pistons down into their bores. When the pistons bottom in the bores, close the bleeder screw. Using the bleeder screw in this way will prevent the fluid level from rising in the master cylinder supply tank. Fit new friction pads with spacer plates 6. Drive one dowel pin 9 through the friction pads and the caliper up to its stop, working from the inboard side. Fit a new spring 10 under the dowel pin then install the second dowel pin. **Any dowel pin which is not a tight fit in the caliper must be renewed.** Operate the brake pedal several times to adjust the brake. Check the level of fluid in the supply tank, topping up as necessary.

When new friction pads have been fitted avoid heavy braking except in emergencies during the first 125 miles in order that the pads may have time to bed down.

Removing and dismantling a caliper:

1 Jack-up the car and remove the road wheel. Remove the friction pads as previously described. Refer to **FIG 11:6** and remove the brake pipe from the caliper and both caliper attaching bolts. If both calipers are to be removed, keep their components separate for reassembly to the same caliper from which they were removed. **The calipers must not be separated into two halves during servicing.** All work is carried out with the two halves bolted together.
2 Remove the clamp rings from the rubber seals, using a screwdriver as shown in **FIG 11:7** then remove the rubber seals.
3 To remove the rim half piston from the caliper, use a clamp such as J.22429 as shown in **FIG 11:8** to hold the mounting half piston in position. Reconnect the brake pipe to the caliper and press the brake pedal gently until the piston emerges from the bore enough to be removed by hand. Alternatively, compressed air may be used to blow out the piston as shown, carefully regulating the air pressure. Remove the mounting half piston in the same manner, using the clamp and rubber plate to seal the bore in the rim half of the caliper.
4 Remove the rubber seals from the grooves in the caliper bores as shown in **FIG 11:9**. Check all parts including the bores in the caliper halves for rust or score marks. Slight rust spots can be removed from the pistons and bores with fine steel wool. Parts that are badly scored or corroded must be renewed.

Reassembling the caliper:

1 Thoroughly clean all internal parts with brake fluid. Refer to **FIG 11:5.** Fit new fluid seals 2, rubber seals 4 and clamp rings 5. Coat all parts with brake fluid during reassembly. Use the fingers to install the fluid seals in the grooves in the caliper bores.
2 With the fluid seals in position, clamp the caliper mounting half in a vice and push the piston into the

bore, with its hollow end outwards. Turn the piston so that the relieved edge faces downwards at an angle of 20 deg. To check the angle, use the friction pad spacer plate 6 as a gauge when fitting the piston. When the angle is correct, push the piston to the bottom of the bore.

3 Clamp the caliper rim half in the vice and install the second piston in the same manner. Fit the new rubber seals and clamp rings to both halves, making sure they are properly seated in the caliper collars.

4 Refit the caliper assembly to the car, tightening the fixing bolts to a torque of 72 lb ft. Attach the brake pipe to the caliper and bleed the brakes as described in **Section 11:5.**

Removing and refitting a brake disc:

Remove the road wheel. Remove the attaching bolts shown in **FIG 11:6** and detach the caliper from the steering swivel. Wire the caliper to the suspension to avoid straining the brake hose. Remove the hub and disc assembly together with the wheel bearings. Mount the assembly in a vice as shown in **FIG 11:10,** using gentle pressure to avoid bending the bolts. Mark the position of the disc on the drum for correct reassembly, then pull

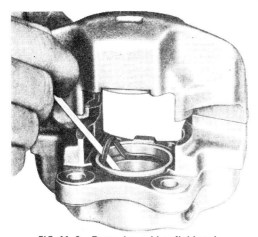

FIG 11:9 Removing rubber fluid seal

FIG 11:10 Removing brake disc from the hub

FIG 11:11 The brake disc shield

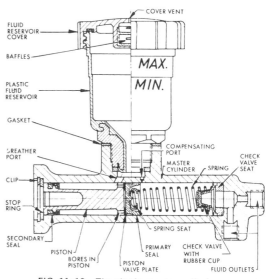

FIG 11:12 The single master cylinder

off the disc. **Do not drive off the disc due to possible distortion.** Disc runout should not exceed .004 inch.

When refitting the disc, check the mating surfaces of the disc and hub and remove any burrs or high spots by careful filing. Tighten the disc to hub bolts to a torque of 36 lb ft. Check the wheel bearings and repack with grease if necessary. Adjust the wheel bearings as described in **Section 9:2.** Using care to avoid damaging the friction pads, refit the caliper to the steering swivel, tightening the bolts to a torque of 72 lb ft.

Removing and refitting a brake disc shield:

Remove the brake disc as just described. Refer to **FIG 11:11** and remove the screw from the front and the bolt from the rear of the shield. Pull off the shield and the paper gaskets. When refitting, use new gaskets smeared with grease. Tighten the rear fixing bolt to a torque of 47 lb ft.

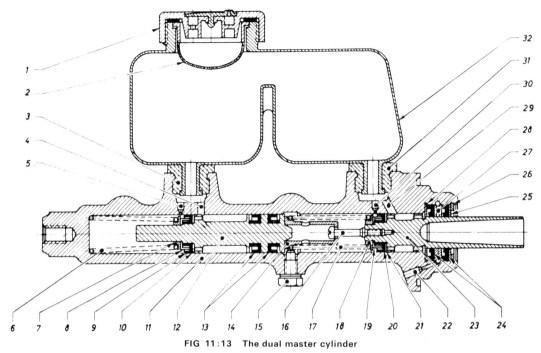

FIG 11:13 The dual master cylinder

Key to Fig 11:13 1 Filler cap 2 Filter 3 Sealing plug 4 Feed port 5 Compensating port 6 Thrust spring
7 Spring seat 8 Support ring 9 Seal 10 Plate 11 Housing 12 Intermediate piston 13 Seals
14 Stop sleeve 15 Stop screw 16 Stop screw 17 Thrust spring 18 Spring seat 19 Support ring 20 Seal
21 Plate 22 Drain port 23 Rear piston 24 Seals 25 Stop plate 26 Circlip 27 Intermediate ring
28 Stop plate 29 Feed port 30 Compensating port 31 Sealing plug 32 Brake fluid supply tank

11:5 Bleeding the system

This is not routine maintenance and is only necessary if air has entered the system due to parts being dismantled, or because the fluid level in the master cylinder supply tank has dropped too low. The need for bleeding is indicated by a spongy feeling of the brake pedal accompanied by poor braking performance. **Do not bleed the brakes with any drum or caliper removed.** Always bleed the brake nearest the master cylinder first.

1 Check the fluid level in the supply tank and refill if necessary, bringing the level to the 'MAX' mark on the tank. Clean all dirt from around the appropriate bleeder valve and remove the dust cap.

2 Attach a length of rubber or plastic tubing to the bleeder screw and lead the free end of the tubing into a clean glass jar. Get an assistant to apply pressure on the brake pedal, then open the bleeder screw to allow fluid to flow out of the system. When the brake pedal reaches the floor, tighten the bleeder screw and allow the pedal to return. Repeat the operation until the fluid flowing into the jar is free from air bubbles. Check and top up the brake fluid in the supply tank during the operation to ensure that the level does not drop too low.

3 On completion, top up the fluid to the correct level. **Discard all dirty fluid. If it is perfectly clean, let it stand for 24 hours before using it again to ensure that it is free of air bubbles.**

11:6 Single master cylinder

This is shown in section in **FIG 11:12**. The pushrod from the brake pedal operates directly on the master cylinder piston to push it down the cylinder bore. This pressurizes the fluid, which passes through the outlets into the brake lines connected to the wheel cylinders or calipers. When the piston returns fully the compensating port is opened allowing fluid from the supply tank to replace any lost in the pipes and cylinders. The check valve maintains a pressure in the brake pipes which is necessary to the operation of drum brake wheel cylinders, as described in **Section 11:1**.

Removal:

Remove the three brake lines from the master cylinder and tape the ends to prevent the entry of dirt. Remove the two bolts securing the master cylinder to the dash panel and lift out the master cylinder.

Dismantling:

Drain the fluid from the tank. Remove the circlip and stop ring then withdraw and separate the internal parts. Unscrew the supply tank, noting the lefthand thread.

Reassembling:

Thoroughly clean all internal parts with brake fluid. Renew all the rubber cups and seals. Check that the ports in the cylinder are unobstructed and carefully scrape off any burrs. Coat all parts liberally with brake fluid during reassembly.

Refitting:

Refit the master cylinder in the reverse order of removal, tightening the fixing bolts to a torque of 15 lb ft. Bleed the system as described in **Section 11:5**.

11:7 Dual master cylinder

This is shown in section in **FIG 11:13**. Operation is by pushrod from the brake pedal as described in **Section 11:1**.

Removal:

Disconnect the two brake lines from the master cylinder. On cars fitted with vacuum servo assistance, remove the front support attaching bolts, the cylinder to servo retaining nuts and lift out the master cylinder. On cars without vacuum servos, remove the attaching bolts and lift out the master cylinder.

Dismantling:

Drain and remove the supply tank and remove the sealing plugs from the housing. Screw the static pressure valve(s) from the housing. Push the piston into the cylinder until a thin rod can be inserted through the feed port to retain it. Remove the stopscrew 15 and circlip 26 and take out both pistons and springs. Remove stopscrew 16 from the rear brake piston and remove the component parts. Remove the component parts from the intermediate piston 12.

Reassembling:

1 Clean all internal parts with brake fluid and check them for wear or damage, renewing any unserviceable components. If the cylinder bore is scored or rusted

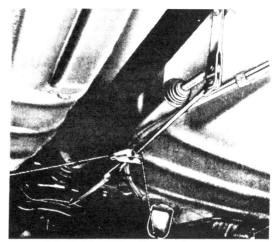

FIG 11:14   GT handbrake adjustment

the master cylinder assembly should be renewed. Always fit new rubber seals and static pressure valve(s).
2 Assemble the front and rear brake circuit pistons. Insert the intermediate piston together with the thrust spring and spring seat, noting that the smaller diameter of the thrust spring must face the piston. Push the piston into the housing against the spring and insert a thin rod into the feed port to retain it. Fit the stop screw into the housing and tighten it.
3 Insert the rear piston into the housing and fit the circlip. Check the piston for free movement, fitting washers under the head of the stop screw if required to ensure this. Gently push the piston into the housing and remove the thin rod from the feed port in the front brake circuit. Check that the compensating ports are free. Screw in new static pressure valve(s).

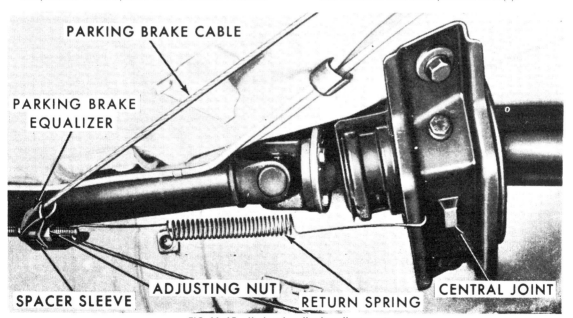

FIG 11:15   Kadett handbrake adjustment

4 Coat new sealing plugs with brake fluid and fit them into the housing. Push the supply tank into the plugs. Clean and refit the filter and filler cap.

Refitting:

Refit the master cylinder in the reverse order of removal, tightening the fixing bolts to a torque of 15 lb ft. Bleed the system as described in **Section 11:5.**

11:8 Vacuum servo unit

The vacuum servo unit is bolted to the dual master cylinder and operates to assist the pressure applied at the brake pedal. The vacuum cylinder in the servo is connected to the engine intake manifold by a hose which houses a vacuum control valve. If the vacuum servo unit or the control valve is defective they must be renewed as units as it is not possible for them to be repaired. To test the vacuum servo unit, switch off the engine and depress the brake pedal several times to clear all the vacuum from the unit. Hold a steady light pressure on the brake pedal and start the engine. If the servo is working correctly, the brake pedal should move further downward without further foot pressure, due to the build up of vacuum in the unit. Failure of the servo unit does not impair the efficiency of the braking system, but greater pedal pressure will be needed to stop the car.

Removing and refitting the vacuum servo:

Remove the dual master cylinder as described in **Section 11:7** and disconnect the servo unit from the master cylinder. Refit in the reverse order.

11:9 The handbrake

Normally, adjustment of the rear brake shoes will automatically take up excessive handbrake free movement. If not, check the rear brake shoes and reline them if they are badly worn. If the handbrake cable is still slack due to stretching, or if the cable has been refitted after a servicing operation, adjust it as follows. Make sure the rear brake shoes are correctly adjusted as instructed in **Section 11:2.** Pull up the handbrake lever three notches on the rachet. Refer to **FIG 11:14** for GT models or **FIG 11:15** for all other models. Lubricate the cable at the point where it passes through the equalizer to ensure even pressure to both rear brakes. Loosen the locknut then turn the adjusting nut until the rear wheels can just be turned by heavy hand pressure. Tighten the locknut and recheck handbrake operation.

Removing the handbrake cable:

Chock the front wheels and release the handbrake. Disconnect the cable from the rear brake connections. Unscrew the locknut and adjusting nut from the operating rod and remove the cable. Refitting is a reversal of the removal procedure.

11:10 Fault diagnosis

(a) 'Spongy' pedal

1 Leak in the system
2 Worn master cylinder
3 Leaking wheel cylinders
4 Air in the fluid system
5 Gaps between shoes and undersides of linings

(b) Excessive pedal movement

1 Check 1 and 4 in (a)
2 Excessive lining or pad wear
3 Very low fluid level in supply tank
4 Too much free movement of pedal

(c) Brakes grab or pull to one side

1 Distorted discs or drums
2 Wet or oily pads or linings
3 Loose backplate or caliper
4 Disc loose on hub
5 Worn suspension or steering connections
6 Mixed linings of different grades
7 Uneven tyre pressures
8 Broken shoe return springs
9 Seized handbrake cable
10 Seized wheel cylinder piston

CHAPTER 12

THE ELECTRICAL SYSTEM

12:1 Description

All models manufactured since 1966 are equipped with 12-volt electrical systems, earlier models in the Kadett 'A' range having 6-volt systems. The charging circuit is provided with regulating devices which may be adjusted if necessary, though it must be stressed that accurate meters are required when checking or altering their settings. The negative terminal of the battery is earthed.

There are wiring diagrams in Technical Data at the end of this manual which will enable those with electrical experience to trace and correct faults.

Instructions for servicing the electrical equipment are given in this Chapter, but it must be pointed out that it is not sensible to try to repair units which are seriously defective, electrically or mechanically. Such equipment should be replaced by new units which can be obtained on an exchange basis.

12:2 The battery

To maintain the performance of the battery it is essential to carry out the following operations, particularly in winter when heavy current demands must be met.

Keep the top and surrounding parts of the battery dry and clean as dampness can cause current leakage. Clean off corrosion from the metal parts of the battery mounting with diluted ammonia and coat them with anti-sulphuric paint. Clean the terminal posts and smear them with petroleum jelly before remaking the connections and tightening the terminal clamps securely. High electrical resistance due to corrosion at the terminals can be responsible for lack of sufficient current to operate the starter motor.

Test the condition of the cells with an hydrometer after topping up the electrolyte level with distilled water to just above the separators. **Never add neat acid. If it is necessary to prepare new electrolyte due to loss or spillage, add sulphuric acid to distilled water. It is highly dangerous to add water to acid.**

The indications from the readings of the specific gravity are as follows:

For climates below 27°C or 80°F:

Cell fully charged   —   Specific gravity 1.270 to 1.290
Cell half discharged —   Specific gravity 1.190 to 1.210
Cell discharged   —   Specific gravity 1.110 to 1.130

For climates above 27°C or 80°F:

Cell fully charged   —   Specific gravity 1.210 to 1.230
Cell half discharged —   Specific gravity 1.130 to 1.150
Cell discharged   —   Specific gravity 1.050 to 1.070

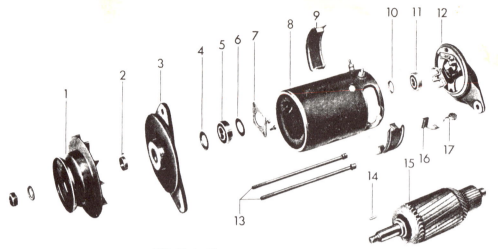

FIG 12:1   The generator components

Key to Fig 12:1   1 Pulley   2 Spacer   3 Drive end bracket   4 Oil deflector   5 Bearing   6 Coverplate
7 Retaining plate   8 Generator housing   9 Cover band   10 Sealing washer   11 Bearing   12 Commutator end bracket
13 Through-bolts   14 Key   15 Armature   16 Brush   17 Brush spring

These figures assume an electrolyte temperature of 60°F or 16°C. If the temperature of the electrolyte exceeds this, add .002 to the readings for each 5°F or 3°C rise. Subtract .002 for any corresponding drop below 60°F or 16°C.

All of the cells should read approximately the same. If one differs radically from the others it may be due to an internal fault or to spillage or leakage of the electrolyte.

If the battery is in a low state of charge, take the car for a long daylight run or put the battery on a charger at 5 amps with the vent plugs removed until it gasses freely. Do not use a naked light near the battery as the gas is inflammable. If the battery is to stand unused for long periods, give a refreshing charge every month. It will be ruined if it is left uncharged.

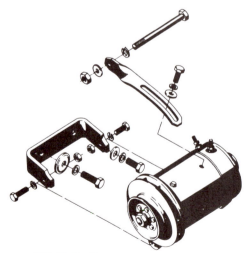

FIG 12:2   Generator mounting details

12:3 The generator

FIG 12:1 shows the components of the generator.

Testing when generator is not charging:

1 Refer to **Chapter 4, Section 4:4** and check that a loose drive belt is not the cause of the trouble.
2 Switch off all the lights and accessories. Start the engine and connect an ammeter in series with the battery and control box by disconnecting the red lead from the B+ control box terminal, then connecting the ammeter between the terminal and the red wire. Raise the engine speed and check the ammeter reading. The output for 12-volt systems should be 20 amps minimum at 2500 rev/min, for 6-volt systems 50 amps minimum at 2000 rev/min.
3 If the generator is in order, check the continuity of the cables to the control box. Remove the ammeter, reconnect the cable and test the control box as described in **Section 12:6.**

Removing the generator:

FIG 12:2 shows the installation of the generator. Remove the fan belt as described in **Chapter 4, Section 4:4,** then disconnect the battery earth strap. Disconnect the wires from the generator. Remove the adjuster bolt and washers and the two pivot bolts, nuts and washers then lift out the generator.

Dismantling the generator:

Refer to **FIG 12:1.** Remove the brush cover bands 9. Loosen the screw securing the connecting lead to the commutator end bracket and remove the through-bolts and end bracket from the housing. Remove the armature together with the drive end bracket from the housing. Remove the pulley securing nut and withdraw the pulley, using a suitable puller. Remove the key 14 from the shaft and pull off the drive end bracket. Remove the bearing retainer plate and press the bearing from the drive end bracket.

Servicing the brushgear:

Remove the brush cover bands. Lift the brushes up in their holders and secure them by positioning each spring at the side of its brush. Fit the commutator end bracket over the commutator and release the brushes. Hold back each spring in turn and move the brushes by pulling gently on their flexible connectors. If a brush moves sluggishly or sticks in its holder, remove it and ease the sides against a smooth file. Refit in its original position. Renew and bed to the commutator any brush which is less than the permissible minimum of .47 inch. Renew any brush spring which gives a spring balance reading of less than 16 oz.

Servicing the commutator:

A commutator in good condition will be smooth and free from pitting and burned segments. Clean with a cloth and petrol, and, if necessary, polish with fine glasspaper. **Do not use emerycloth.** Skim a badly worn commutator in a lathe, using a high speed and taking a light cut with a sharp tool. Remove the minimum amount to clean up, then polish with fine glasspaper. Undercut the insulation between the segments to a depth of .002 inch using a hacksaw blade ground to the thickness of the insulation.

The armature:

In the absence of armature testing facilities, the only check for faults which an owner can make is to substitute one which is known to be serviceable.

Field coils:

When testing with an ohmmeter, the reading should be between 3.5 and 3.85 ohms. If the reading is less than 3.5 ohms the field coils must be renewed by a service station.

Renewing bearings:

It is most unlikely that noticeable bearing wear will occur during the life of the generator. However, if bearing wear is encountered, the bearings in the commutator end bracket and the drive end bracket should be renewed.

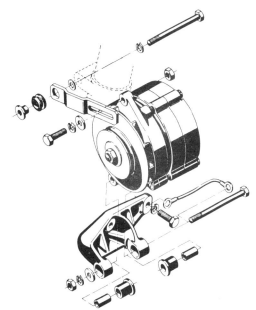

FIG 12:3 Alternator mounting details

Reassembling and refitting the generator:

This is the reverse of the dismantling procedure. If new brushes have been fitted, place a strip of fine glasspaper round the commutator and grind them in until they make good contact on their bearing faces. Reconnect the lead to the commutator end bracket and refit the brush cover bands. Adjust the fan belt tension as described in **Chapter 4, Section 4:4.**

12:4 The alternator

Alternators are fitted to Rallye models as standard and to all models fitted with electrically heated backlights. The installation is shown in **FIG 12:3.**

Testing when the alternator is not charging:

Refer to the previous section for testing the generator and carry out instructions 1, 2 and 3. The ammeter reading when testing an alternator should be 30 amps minimum at 2500 rev/min.

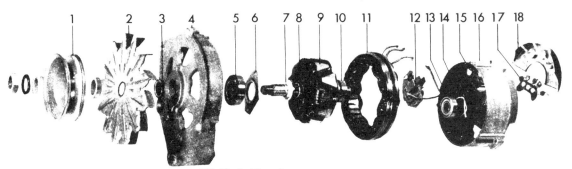

FIG 12:4 The alternator components

Key to Fig 12:4   1 Pulley   2 Cooling fan   3 Spacer   4 Drive end bracket   5 Bearing   6 Retaining plate
7 Spacer   8 Securing ring   9 Rotor   10 Slip rings   11 Stator   12 Brush holder   13 Bearing   14 Shim
15 Negative diodes   16 Rear end bracket   17 Field diodes   18 Positive diodes

FIG 12:5　Removing the alternator brush holder

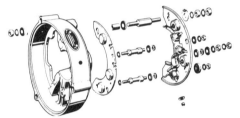

FIG 12:6　The diode support assemblies

Removing the alternator:

Remove the fan belt as described in **Chapter 4, Section 4:4,** then disconnect the battery earth strap. Disconnect the wires from the alternator. Remove the securing bolts and lift out the alternator.

Dismantling the alternator:

1 Refer to **FIG 12:4.** Unscrew the retaining nut and remove the pulley and fan from the rotor shaft. Remove the diode cover and brush holder as shown in **FIG 12:5.** Mark the drive end bracket, stator and rear end bracket to ensure correct reassembly, then remove the drive end bracket and rotor assembly. Use a puller to remove the drive end bracket from the rotor shaft.

2 From the rear of the alternator dismantle the diode holders into the order shown in **FIG 12:6.** Unscrew the bearing retainer and remove the ballbearing from the drive end bracket. Use a suitable puller to remove the rear bearing from the rotor shaft.

Servicing the alternator:

Brush gear:

Check the brushes and renew if worn to a length of $\frac{3}{8}$ inch or less. Unsolder the connecting wire and remove the old brush. When soldering the connecting wire for a

new brush, hold the wire with a pair of flat-nosed pliers to prevent the solder from flowing down the wire strands, otherwise the connecting wire will become rigid with the solder and the brush unserviceable.

Check that the brushes move freely in their holders. If a brush binds, remove it and ease the sides against a smooth file.

Slip rings:

The faces of the slip rings must be in a clean and polished condition. Clean them with fine emerycloth and polish them. To avoid causing flat surfaces on the slip rings this operation is best carried out while spinning the rotor in a lathe.

Rotor:

Test the rotor windings and slip rings using a test lamp or ohmmeter as shown in **FIG 12:7.** A test lamp must not light up; an ohmmeter should indicate near infinite resistance. Test the rotor windings for a shortcircuit by connecting the ohmmeter between the two slip rings. The reading obtained should be between 4.0 and 4.4 ohms. If any test is failed, the rotor and slip rings assembly must be renewed.

Stator:

Test the stator windings by connecting a test lamp or ohmmeter between each wire in turn, and the casing. A test lamp must not light up; an ohmmeter should indicate near infinite resistance. Check the stator windings for a shortcircuit, using a low reading ohmmeter. Check two phases at a time, connecting the ohmmeter between the wire ends alternately. The readings obtained should be between .26 and .29 ohms. If any test is failed, the stator assembly must be renewed.

Diodes:

If the alternator current output is low, one or more of the diodes may be defective. **FIG 12:8** shows the diode configuration in the charging circuit. Disconnect each diode before testing, otherwise it will not be possible to determine which diode is at fault. Use a 12-volt supply and test lamp bulb. Connect the test lamp between the diode connection and housing, then reverse the connections. The test lamp should light up brightly in one direction, but should not light at all in the reverse direction. Diodes in each set of three should pass and block current in the same directions as the others in the set. Any diode that fails the tests given must be renewed by a service station, using special press equipment.

Reassembling and refitting the alternator:

This is the reversal of the dismantling procedure. Reconnect any diodes that were disconnected, using a very hot soldering iron and working quickly to avoid damaging the diodes, which are very sensitive to heat. Lubricate both bearings with high melting point grease. Adjust the fan belt tension as described in **Chapter 4, Section 4:4.**

12:5 The starter

The starter is a brush type series wound motor equipped with an overrunning clutch and operated by a solenoid. The armature shaft is supported in sintered bronze bushes which are factory packed with lubricant and require no servicing between overhauls. **FIG 12:9** shows the components of the starter. When the starter is operated from the ignition switch, the engagement lever moves the pinion into mesh with the flywheel ring gear. When the pinion meshes with the flywheel ring gear teeth, the solenoid contact disc closes the circuit and the starter motor operates to turn the engine over. When the engine starts, the speed of the flywheel causes the pinion to overrun the clutch and armature. The pinion continues to be engaged until the engagement lever is released, when it returns under spring action.

Tests for a starter which does not operate:

Check that the battery is in good condition and fully charged and that its connections are clean and tight. Switch on the headlights and operate the starter switch. Current is reaching the starter if the lights go dim, in which case it will be necessary to remove the starter for servicing. If the lights do not go dim, check the switch and the starter cables. Check the brushes by the method described later, it not being necessary to remove the starter to do this. If the switch, cables and brushes are in order, the starter must be removed and serviced.

Removing the starter:

Kadett 'A' models:

1 Disconnect the battery. Disconnect the exhaust pipe from the manifold flange and move the exhaust pipe downward out of the way.
2 Remove the nut and washer from the battery terminal on the starter solenoid and remove the cable and wire. Remove the control wire from the '50' terminal on the solenoid.
3 Remove two bolts from the starter drive housing flange and remove the starter by moving it forward and upward, rotating the solenoid outwards while doing so.

1.1 litre models:

1 Disconnect the battery and remove the air cleaner. Disconnect the choke cable.
2 Raise the front of the car and support it in a safe manner. Detach the right engine mount from its attachment on the car body. Disconnect the exhaust tailpipe at the rear of the car. Loosen one bolt and remove the other bolt from the left engine mount.
3 Raise the engine on the starter side and remove the engine mount bracket to crankcase bolts. Remove the bracket for access to the starter.
4 Disconnect the starter wiring and remove the starter mounting bolts. Remove the starter from the car.

1.5 and 1.9 litre models:

1 Disconnect the battery. Disconnect the starter wiring and remove the starter support bracket. Remove two starter bolts, one nut and lockwashers as shown in **FIG 12:10.**
2 To provide clearance, drive out the starter stud as shown in **FIG 12:11,** then remove the starter.

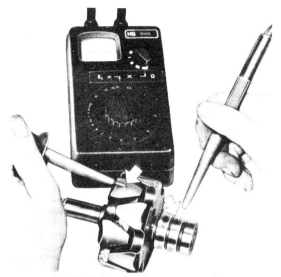

FIG 12:7   Testing the rotor assembly

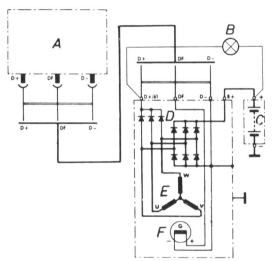

FIG 12:8   Alternator charging circuit

Servicing the brush gear:

Removal:

Kadett 'A' models:

Remove the cover band from the starter and disconnect and remove the two insulated brushes from the field coils.

1.1 litre models:

Remove the cover band from the starter. Remove the screws attaching the four brushes to their holders and remove them.

1.5 and 1.9 litre models:

If the starter has not been removed from the car it will be necessary to remove the front starter bracket. Detach the wire connection from the solenoid switch and unscrew

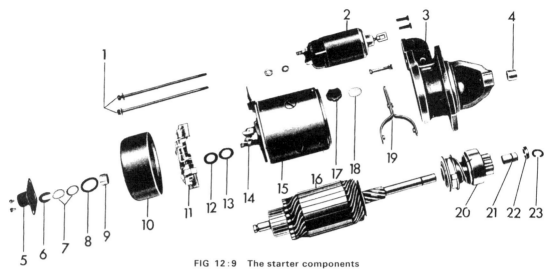

FIG 12:9   The starter components

Key to Fig 12:9   1 Through-bolts   2 Solenoid   3 Drive end bracket   4 Bush   5 End cap   6 Retainer
7 Shims   8 Rubber seal ring   9 Bush   10 Commutator end bracket   11 Negative brush plate   12 Fibre washer
13 Washer   14 Positive brushes on field coils   15 Starter motor housing   16 Armature   17 Rubber washer
18 Washer   19 Engagement lever   20 Pinion and clutch   21 Bush   22 Thrust washer   23 Retainer

the commutator end housing cover. Take the retainer and compensating washers off the armature shaft, noting the rubber seal ring, as shown in **FIG 12:12**. Unscrew both through-bolts and remove the commutator end housing. Remove the brushes from their holders and remove the brush holder plate from the armature, noting the compensating washers.

Servicing:

Mark the brushes to ensure refitting in their original positions, if they are not to be renewed. If a brush is worn to a length of $\frac{1}{2}$ inch or less it must be renewed. If a brush moves sluggishly in its housing, remove it and ease the sides against a smooth file. Check the tension of the brush springs, which should be between 28 and 32 oz on Kadett 'A' and 1.1 litre models; between 40 and 46 oz on 1.5 and 1.9 litre models. Solder new brushes into position as described in **Section 12:4** for the alternator.

Refitting the brush gear is a reversal of the removal procedure in all cases.

Dismantling the starter:

1 Refer to the appropriate previous section and remove the brush gear. Remove the screws attaching the small cover at the end of the shaft and remove the cover. Remove the lockwasher and shim from the shaft and remove the two through-bolts. Remove the commutator end bracket then remove the brush holder plate, collecting the shims between the plate and commutator.

2 Detach the solenoid by removing the screws shown in **FIG 12:12**. Remove the rubber and metal plate from the drive end bracket. Remove the engagement lever pivot pin. Remove the engagement lever and the armature from the drive end bracket.

3 Drive back the retaining ring on the armature shaft and remove the circlip. Pull off the retaining ring, overrunning clutch and pinion.

Servicing the starter:

The commutator:

Follow the procedure described in **Section 12:3** for the generator commutator. If the starter commutator is skimmed in a lathe, care must be taken not to reduce the diameter of the commutator below 1.25 inches. If cleaning up would remove enough metal to reduce the diameter below this figure the armature must be renewed.

The armature:

A damaged armature should always be renewed. No attempt should be made to straighten a bent shaft or to machine the core.

Testing the field coils:

Test the continuity with a 12-volt supply and test lamp between the terminal post and each field brush in turn. Test for insulation breakdown by connecting a test lamp between the terminal post and the starter body. If the lamp lights, defective insulation is indicated. The renewal of field coils should be entrusted to a service station.

Starter bearings:

Press out the old bearing bushes. Allow the new bushes to stand fully immersed in engine oil for at least 30 minutes before pressing them into the brackets. Press them in with a shouldered mandrel having a polished pilot of the same diameter as the armature shaft and slightly longer than the bushes.

Pinion and clutch assembly:

Do not clean the overruning clutch with solvents as this would wash the grease from inside the clutch. Coat the armature shaft splines and the contact areas for the engagement lever with high melting point grease.

Reassembling and refitting the starter:

These operations are the reverse of the dismantling and removal procedures.

12:6 The control box

The control box on cars equipped with alternators contains only a voltage regulator, the use of diodes in the alternator making a cut-out relay unnecessary. The alternator charging circuit is shown in **FIG 12:8**.

On cars equipped with generators, the control box contains a voltage regulator and a cut-out relay. The generator charging circuit is shown in **FIG 12:13**.

Checking the charging circuit:

Do not disturb the control box settings until the generator or alternator has been checked as described in **Sections 12:3** or **12:4**.

It must be stressed that the use of first grade electrical meters is essential to check and make any necessary adjustments to the control box. All checks and adjustments must be made as quickly as possible to avoid errors due to heating up of the operating coils. If the control box fails to respond correctly to any adjustment it should be examined at a service station.

Adjusting the voltage regulator:

1 Remove the red battery lead from the control box B+ terminal. Connect the voltmeter positive lead to the B+ terminal and the negative lead to earth on the base of the control box.
2 Start the engine and slowly increase its speed while observing the voltmeter. The reading should be between 7 and 7.5 volts for 6-volt systems; between 13.5 and 14.5 volts for 12-volt systems. If the reading is not within the specified range, remove the control box cover and adjust the voltage regulator armature spring to obtain a reading between the figures quoted. If the reading fluctuates, the contacts are dirty and must be cleaned as described later.
3 Replace the control box cover and recheck the setting.

Adjusting the cut-out relay (generator systems only):

1 Connect the voltmeter positive lead to the control box terminal 61 and the negative lead to earth. Connect an ammeter in series with the B+ terminal and disconnect the red wire.
2 Start the engine and increase the speed while observing the voltmeter. The voltage will increase until the cut-out relay points close, then drop slightly as the circuit is completed to the battery. The highest voltage reading just before it drops off is the closing voltage. This voltage should be between 5.9 and 6.5 volts for 6-volt systems; between 12.3 and 13.4 volts for 12-volt systems. If the voltage as tested is not between these limits, remove the control box cover and adjust the closing voltage by bending the cut-out relay spring support. Increase the tension on the spring to increase the closing voltage, decrease tension to decrease the voltage.
3 Replace the control box cover and recheck the setting.

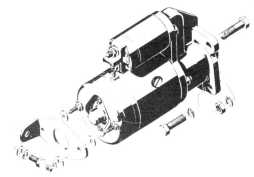

FIG 12:10   Starter installation, 1.5 and 1.9 litre cars

FIG 12:11   Removing starter stud

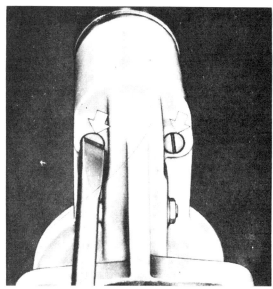

FIG 12:12   Removing the starter solenoid switch

O KAD

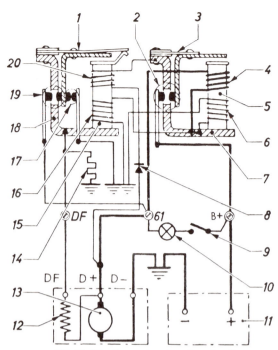

FIG 12:13 Generator charging circuit

Key to Fig 12:13 1 Voltage regulator spring   2 Cut-out
relay points   3 Cut-out relay spring   4 Cut-out relay
current coil   5 Iron core of cut-out relay   6 Cut-out relay
voltage coil   7 Cut-out relay armature support   8 Variode
9 Ignition switch   10 Charging indicator lamp   11 Battery
12 Field coils   13 Generator armature   14 Resistor
15 Iron core of regulator   16 Regulator voltage coil
17 Regulator lower points   18 Regulator armature support
19 Regulator upper points   20 Regulator control coil

Cleaning contact points:

Clean the contact points in the voltage regulator and
cut-out relay with fine glasspaper. Clean off all dust with
methylated spirits.

12:7 Fuses

On Kadett 'A' models the fuses are located in a box
attached to the left front wheelhousing. On all later
models the fuses are installed behind the kick-pad in the
passenger compartment and are accessible through the
opening provided. Extra fuses are located in the appropriate relay switches in the engine compartment for
foglamps (8 amps) and electrically heated backlight (16
amps) if these accessories are fitted.

Models from 1967 onwards are also equipped with
fusible links in certain sections of the wiring as shown in
FIG 12:14. These prevent long sections of wiring from
being burned out in the event of a shortcircuit. The only
section of wiring which can burn out under these
conditions is the short length between the fusible link
and the component it serves. When an electrical failure
occurs, check the links after ensuring that the main fuses
are intact, and renew any found burnt out. Also renew the
short length of wire between the link and the component
if it has been damaged by the shortcircuit. Cut the old
link from the wiring and solder a new link into place, with
a new length of wire if necessary.

12:8 The horn

The horn contacts can be examined by levering the
horn button from the centre of the steering wheel. Make
sure the contacts are clean and that they operate
correctly when the horn button is pressed. To remove the
horn, remove the front grill and the horn bracket fixing
bolt. Disconnect the wires and remove the horn. Refit in
reverse sequence to removal.

12:9 Windscreen wipers

The wiper assembly consists of a permanent magnet
type motor with a reduction gearbox driving the wiper
arms through a crank and connecting rod mechanism.

Kadett 'A' and early Kadett 'B' models are fitted with
single-speed wiper motors, later Kadett 'B' models and
all models from 1967 onwards are fitted with two-speed
motors. **FIG 12:15** shows the components of the two-
speed motor. The single-speed motor differs by having
only one positive brush 19 and spring 21, and fixing screws
instead of rubber mounts 22.

Apart from renewal of wiper blades the wiper assembly
needs no routine maintenance.

Checking the wiper operation:

If the motor is completely inoperative, check the fuse
and the connections at the fuse block and wiper switch.
Disconnect the wire from the motor terminal 53, turn on
the ignition and wiper switches and use a voltmeter to
check the voltage available to the motor, which should be
the full voltage of the battery if it is properly charged.
A further check can be made by connecting a temporary
lead between the battery and terminal 53. If the motor
then runs the fault is in the wiring circuit or switch. If not,
the motor must be removed for service.

If the wiper operation is sluggish, detach the linkage
crank arm from the motor and operate the wipers by hand
to check for binds in the linkage.

Removing wiper arms:

The arms are splined to their shafts. On GT models,
undo the attaching nuts and remove the arms. On all
other models, tilt the arm away from the windscreen, then
lift the retaining spring with the aid of a screwdriver and
remove the arm.

Removing the wiper linkage:

All models except GT:

Remove the wiper arms. For access to the linkage on the
left side, remove the instrument housing which is held by
screws on Kadett 'A' models, clips on all others. For access
to linkage on the right side, remove the glove box. Remove
the fixing screws and the linkage. Inspect all rubber
gaskets, plastic rings, washers and clips renewing any
that are worn.

GT models:

Remove the wiper arms. Remove the three bolts from
the panels around each wiper arm shaft and drop the
linkage from the panel. Remove the screws from the left
and centre linkage covering panels and remove the centre
panel. Remove the left panel together with the linkage
and wiper motor complete. Remove the linkage from the
motor shaft. Inspect all parts, renewing any that are worn.

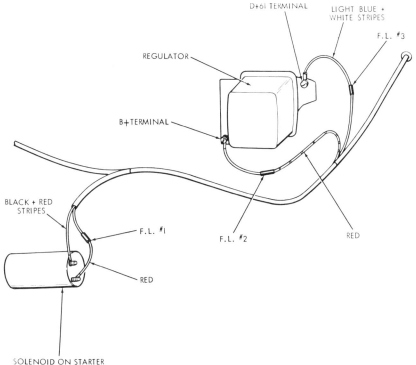

D+6l TERMINAL

LIGHT BLUE +
WHITE STRIPES

F.L. #3

REGULATOR

B+TERMINAL

BLACK + RED
STRIPES

F.L. #1

F.L. #2

RED

RED

SOLENOID ON STARTER

FIG 12:14   Locations of the fusible links

Removing the motor:

All models except GT:

Detach the crank arm from the motor drive shaft. Remove the electrical connections and the three nuts attaching the motor to the panel. Refit in the reverse order, making sure that the earth wire is attached to the terminal plate screw.

GT models:

Remove the wiper linkage as previously described. Disconnect the electrical connections and remove the three bolts attaching the motor to the panel.

Servicing the motor:

Refer to **FIG 12:15** and remove the two screws 24 and detach the transmission housing together with the armature from the motor housing. Check that the brushes are free and that the springs function adequately. Renew the brushes if they are .24 inch or less in length. To remove a negative brush, remove the retaining screw from the commutator end frame. To remove a positive brush the lead must be cut off at the brush holder. New positive brushes must be soldered into position, making sure that the solder does not run down the flexible lead, as this would stiffen the lead and make the brush unserviceable. Clean the commutator with a cloth moistened in petrol. Lightly oil the armature shaft. The transmission should be lubricated with grease which meets GM specification 02383.

12:10 Headlamps

On all models except GT, remove the headlamp rim then remove the retaining screws and the headlamp. On GT models, rotate the headlamp to the open position and remove the headlamp housing, then remove the retaining screws and the headlamp. Refit headlamp lens units with the '2' mark uppermost.

Headlamps should be set so that, when the car is normally loaded, the beams are parallel to each other and to the road. Two screws are provided for trimming which move the mounting ring in the body against spring pressure. Accurate setting is best carried out by a service station having special beam-setting equipment.

12:11 Panel and warning lights

The removal of the instrument panel will give access for the replacement of instrument and warning lights.

Removal, Kadett 'A' models:

Drain the cooling system and remove the temperature unit from the cylinder head. Loosen the clamps and detach the capillary tube. Pull the tube and temperature unit into the car. Disconnect the speedometer cable and the wires from the panel units, then pull the bulbs from their retainers. Remove the fixing nut and remove the instrument panel towards the front of the car. Refit in reverse sequence.

Removal, all models except 'A' and GT:

Disconnect the speedometer cable at the instrument panel. From behind the panel, apply equal pressure to

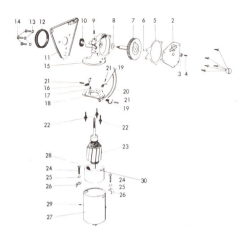

FIG 12:15   The wiper motor components

Key to Fig 12:15 1 Attaching screws 2 Transmission cover
3 Nut   4 Adjuster screw   5 Gasket   6 Ball
7 Driven gear   8 Washer   9 Adjuster screw   10 Sleeve
11 Mounting plate   12 Gasket   13 Toothed washers
14 Attaching screws   15 Transmission housing
16 Negative brush   17 Attaching screw   18 Retaining plate
19 Positive brush   20 Wire   21 Thrust spring
22 Rubber mounts   23 Armature   24 Attaching screws
25 Lockwasher   26 Angle brackets   27 Motor housing
28 Magnet ring   29 Magnet threaded pin locators
30 North pole paint marking on this side

compress the four retaining clips and tilt the panel out towards the rear of the car. Disconnect the wires from the terminals, noting their location for correct refitting. Refit in reverse sequence.

Removal, GT models:

Remove the two access covers from each side of the central console, and remove the two screws. Detach the steering assembly from the instrument panel as described in **Chapter 10,** and swing it together with the steering wheel towards the floor of the car. Disconnect the speedometer cable and remove the flasher unit. Remove the radio knobs and nuts from their shafts. Remove the instrument panel assembly, which is retained by push buttons at the top and a thumb nut at the lower left corner. Remove the instrument and parking light switch, then disconnect the wires from the terminals, noting their location for correct refitting. Refit in reverse sequence.

12:12 Flasher and traffic hazard warning lights
Flasher unit:

The flasher unit, in which a switch is operated by alternate heating and cooling of an actuating wire, is housed in a small cylindrical container behind the dashboard. A small relay to flash the pilot light is incorporated.

In case of trouble check the bulbs and the main fuses. If one bulb is defective the other bulb and the pilot light will flash at twice the normal speed, which will indicate this fault. If the flasher unit is defective it must be renewed. Mark the connection before removing the old unit to ensure the new unit is correctly wired.

Traffic hazard warning system:

This system, when fitted, operates in conjunction with flashing direction indicator lights. When the hazard

warning light switch on the instrument panel is turned on, all four flasher lights operate simultaneously through the flasher unit. The system will operate with the ignition switched off so that, if necessary, the car can be locked up and the lights left flashing in the event of a breakdown. As the system is meant as a warning to other traffic of a stationary vehicle, the hazard warning should not be switched on when the car is moving.

12:13 Fuel, pressure and temperature gauges

These gauges are accessible after removing the instrument panel as described in **Section 12:11.** To avoid accidental shortcircuits, it is advisable to disconnect the battery before inspecting or removing an instrument or gauge.

12:14 Electrically heated backlight

The electrically heated backlight is operated by a switch on the dashboard, operation being possible only with the engine running. These backlight assemblies, due to their large current draw, can only be fitted as an extra to cars equipped with alternator charging systems. The electrical circuit for these fittings is incorporated in the wiring diagrams in the Appendix.

12:15 Lighting circuits
Lamps give insufficient light:

Refer to **Section 12:2** and check the condition of the battery. Recharge if necessary. Check the setting of the headlamps as described in **Section 12:10.** Renew any bulbs that have darkened with age.

Bulbs burn out frequently:

Refer to **Section 12:6** and check the control box settings.

Lamps light when switched on but gradually fade:

Refer to **Section 12:2** and check the battery as it is not capable of supplying current for any length of time.

Lamp brilliance varies with the speed of the car:

Check the condition of the battery and its connections. Make sure they are tight and renew any faulty cables.

12:16 Fault diagnosis
(a) Battery discharged

1 Terminal connections loose or dirty
2 Shorts in lighting circuit
3 Generator or alternator not charging
4 Control box faulty
5 Battery internally defective

(b) Insufficient charging rate

1 Check 1 and 4 in (a)
2 Drive belt slipping

(c) Battery will not hold charge

1 Low electrolyte level
2 Battery plates sulphated
3 Electrolyte leakage from cracked case
4 Battery plate separators defective

(d) **Battery overcharged**

1 Control box needs adjusting

(e) **Generator or alternator output low or nil**

1 Belt broken or slipping
2 Control box out of adjustment
3 Worn bearings, loose polepieces
4 Commutator worn, burned or shorted
5 Armature shaft bent or worn
6 Insulation proud between commutator segments
7 Brushes sticking, springs weak or broken
8 Field coil windings broken, shorted or burned
9 Alternator diode(s) defective

(f) **Starter motor lacks power or will not turn**

1 Battery discharged, loose cable connections
2 Starter pinion jammed in flywheel ring gear
3 Starter switch or solenoid faulty
4 Brushes worn or sticking, leads detached or shorting
5 Commutator dirty or worn
6 Starter shaft bent
7 Engine abnormally stiff, perhaps due to rebore

(g) **Starter runs but does not turn engine**

1 Pinion engagement mechanism faulty
2 Broken teeth on pinion or flywheel gears

(h) **Noisy starter pinion when engine is running**

1 Pinion return mechanism faulty

(j) **Starter motor inoperative**

1 Check 1 and 4 in (f)
2 Armature or field coils faulty

(k) **Starter motor rough or noisy**

1 Mounting bolts loose
2 Damaged pinion or flywheel teeth
3 Pinion engagement mechanism faulty

(l) **Lamps inoperative or erratic**

1 Battery low, bulbs burned out
2 Faulty earthing of lamps or battery
3 Lighting switch faulty, loose or broken connections

(m) **Wiper motor sluggish, taking high current**

1 Faulty armature
2 Commutator dirty or shorting
3 Brushes worn or sticking, springs weak or broken
4 Lack of lubrication
5 Linkage worn or binding
6 Wiper motor fixing bolts loose
7 Motor transmission binding, no armature shaft end float

(n) **Wiper motor runs but does not drive arms**

1 Wiper linkage faulty
2 Transmission components worn

(o) **Fuel, temperature or pressure gauges do not work**

1 Check wiring for continuity
2 Check instruments and transmitters for continuity

CHAPTER 13

THE BODYWORK

13:1 Bodywork finish

Large scale repairs to body panels are best left to expert panel beaters. Even small dents can be tricky, as too much hammering will stretch the metal and make things worse instead of better. Filling minor dents and scratches is probably the best method of restoring the surface. The touching up of paintwork is well within the powers of most owners, particularly as self-spraying cans of paint in the correct colours are now readily available. A paint may change colour with age and it is better to spray a whole wing rather than touch up a small area.

Before spraying, remove all traces of wax polish with white spirit. More drastic treatment is required if silicone polishes have been applied. Use a primer surfacer or paste stopper according to the amount of filling required, and when it is dry, rub it down with 400 grade 'Wet or Dry' paper until the surface is smooth and flush with the surrounding area. Spend time on getting the best finish possible as this will control the final effect. Apply the retouching paint, keeping it wet in the centre and light and dry round the edges. After a few hours of drying, use a cutting compound to remove the dry spray and finish with liquid polish.

13:2 Removing door trim

Remove the window regulator handle by depressing the door trim pad and inserting a small screwdriver or service tool J.7797 between the plastic spacer and the regulator handle to lever off the spring retainer. Remove the door release handle by inserting a screwdriver behind the escutcheon and levering it loose. Remove the fixing screws and lift off the armrest. Remove two screws and take off the upper moulding. Remove the door trim pad. Refitting is the reversal of removal.

13:3 Window winding mechanism
Removal:

1 Remove the door trim as described in **Section 13:2** and peel off the paper backing from the door.
2 Loosen the sheave adjustable bracket screw shown in **FIG 13:1** and push the bracket as far as possible towards the top. Remove the two screws and clamping plate securing the cable to the channel bracket. Slide the door glass up and prop it in position.
3 Refer to **FIG 13:2** and loosen the adjusting screws securing the cable lower pulley bracket in position. Slide the pulley bracket upwards and slip the cable off

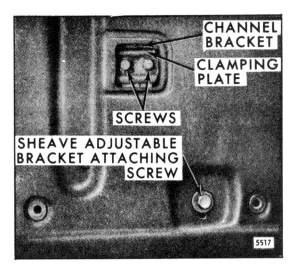

FIG 13:1 Winder mechanism adjustable bracket and clamping plate screws

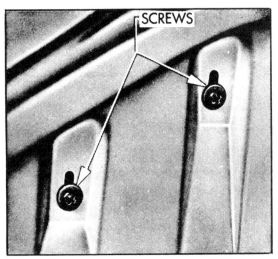

FIG 13:2 Lower pulley bracket adjusting screws

both upper and lower pulleys. **FIG 13:3** shows the installation of cable and regulator mechanism.

4 Remove the three screws shown in **FIG 13:4** and lift out the mechanism.

Refitting:

Wind one half of the cable around the regulator pulley and secure by wedging the wound end of the cable in the lug in the regulator mechanism. On a left side door, wind one half of the cable in an anticlockwise direction until the outboard grooves in the pulley are filled. On a right side door, wind the cable onto the pulley in a similar manner but in a clockwise direction. **FIG 13:5** shows the cable winding on a left side door, **FIG 13:6** the winding for a right side door.

Install the regulator mechanism onto the door panel and lubricate the cable with graphite grease. Complete the installation in the reverse order of removal.

13:4 Door hinges and lock mechanisms

Hinges:

The removal and refitting of door hinges must be entrusted to an Opel Main Dealer, as the operation requires the door to be carefully aligned and the hinge welded into position. However, the door can be removed if required by driving out the hinge pins as follows. File the underside of the door to locate the link rivet, then drive out the rivet with a punch. Use service tool J.21688 to drive out both door hinge pins and lift off the door. Refit in the reverse order, securing the door check link with an appropriate rivet or a bolt, lockwasher and nut. Make sure that the plastic plugs are replaced after installing the hinge pins.

Door locks:

Removal:

Remove the trim panel as described in **Section 13:2**. Remove the outer door handle by levering out the retainer as shown in **FIG 13:7**. Pull the door weatherstrip off the window frame as required. Loosen the two clamp screws

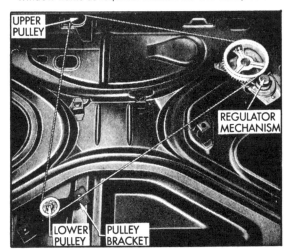

FIG 13:3 Installation of the cable and regulator mechanism

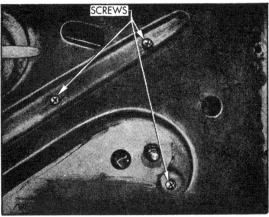

FIG 13:4 Location of the regulator attaching screws

shown in **FIG 13:1**. Disconnect the remote control connecting rod, then remove the three attaching screws and lift out the door lock. Refit in the reverse order, checking the operation of the lock mechanism before shutting the door.

13:5 Removing door glasses

1 Remove the window regulator handle, inner door handle, armrest and door trim as described in **Section 13:2**. Do not loosen the ventilator window attachment.

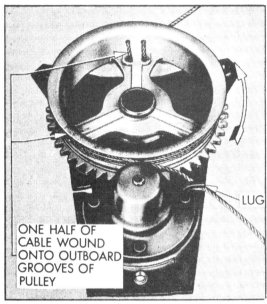

FIG 13:5   Direction of cable winding, left side door

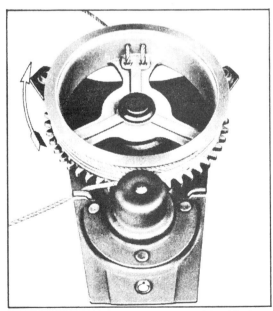

FIG 13:6   Direction of cable winding, right side door

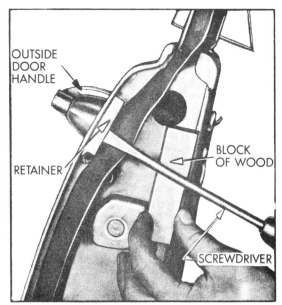

FIG 13:7   Removing the outer door handle

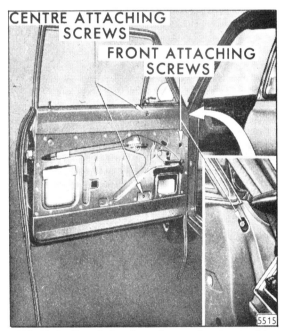

FIG 13:8   The window frame front and centre attaching screws

2 Pull the door weatherstrip off the window frame as required. On any operation where the window frame has to be removed to gain access to other parts, it is permissible to cut the weatherstrip at areas where the frame fits the door panel, in order to facilitate removal. Remove the window frame front and centre attaching screws as shown in **FIG 13:8** and the rear attaching screws as shown in **FIG 13:9**.

O KAD

FIG 13:9   The window frame rear attaching screws

3 Lower the glass to its bottom stop and slowly pull out the frame. If removal of upper or side glass insulation channel is required, lever it out and remove any tabs which may remain in the channel. To remove the door glass, remove the two screws and the clamping plate shown in **FIG 13:10** which secures the cable to the channel bracket and lift out the glass. The rubber strip on the outer door panel may be removed by pulling it up out of its slot.

Refitting:

Refit the glass in the reverse order of removal, noting the following. When installing the window frame, position it so that it is evenly aligned in the door opening. Secure the weatherstrip in position with rubber solution.

Removing ventilators:

Remove the trim panel as described in **Section 13:2**. Unscrew both nuts and take off washers and spring from the ventilator pivot shaft as shown in **FIG 13:11**. File off the lower part of the rivet securing the ventilator to the window frame and drive out the rivet. Remove the ventilator and pull out the weatherstrip. Refit in the reverse order, tightening the nut on the ventilator pivot shaft until sufficient resistance is felt at the ventilator.

13:6 Fitting windscreen glass

To remove the original glass, lift the wiper arms clear and remove the interior mirror. Push the upper and lower

reveal moulding escutcheon aside and lever off the moulding. Loosen the rubber channel from the body with the aid of a flat bladed tool. Starting at the upper lefthand corner, gradually push the windscreen outwards until it is free.

Before fitting a new windscreen glass, clean the windscreen aperture flange of all old sealer and make sure that there are no particles of broken glass in the sealing rubber channels. Fit the rubber to the glass with the lip for the reveal moulding on the outside as shown in **FIG 13:12**. Thread a length of strong blind cord around the rubber channel groove into which the flange of the

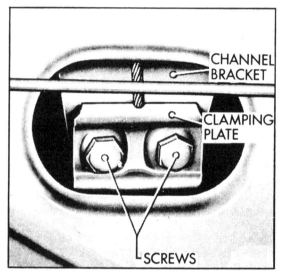

FIG 13:10   Channel bracket to cable clamp screws

FIG 13:11   Removing the ventilator

aperture fits. Cross the ends of the cord at the lower centre of the windscreen. Lubricate the rubber channel flange with a soap-and-water solution to facilitate fitting.

Place the windscreen and rubber channel onto the flange at the bottom of the aperture and centre it. Apply steady hand pressure to the glass while an assistant pulls the cord to lip the rubber channel over the flange in the aperture. **Work equally on each side of the windscreen. Do not fit one end and then try to fit the other.** Use a pressure gun to inject sealing compound between the glass and the rubber and between the rubber and the flange. Remove excess compound with a rag and

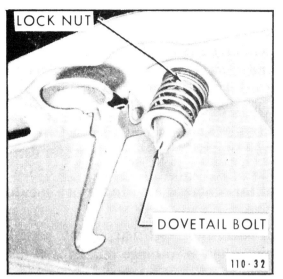

FIG 13:14   Dovetail bolt and bonnet safety catch

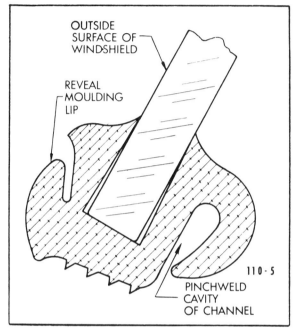

FIG 13:12   Fitting the windscreen rubber to the glass

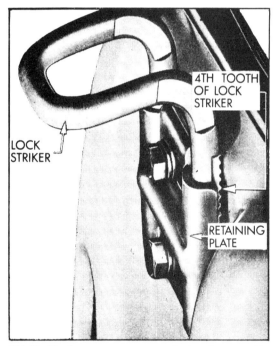

FIG 13:15   Luggage compartment lock striker assembly

white spirit. Do not use thinners as this will damage the paintwork. Refit the reveal moulding, using a hook to lip it under the rubber.

13:7 Fitting a backlight glass

The removal and refitting of a backlight glass is similar to that for a windscreen glass, so reference should be made to the previous section for details of the necessary procedures.

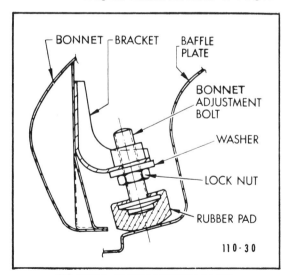

FIG 13:13   Bonnet adjustment bolts

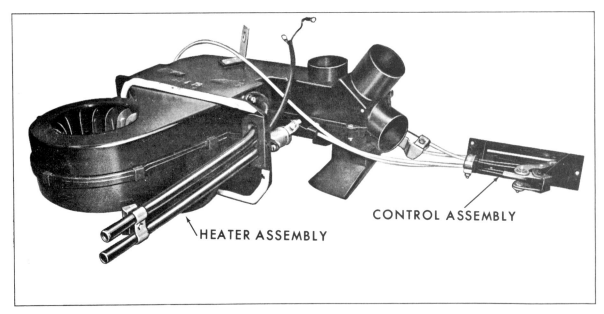

FIG 13:16   The heater control system, GT models

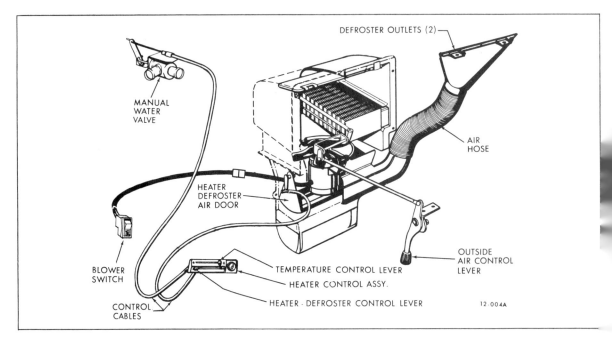

FIG 13:17   The heater control system, all models except GT

13:8 Bonnet and luggage compartment locks

Adjusting the bonnet lock:

Close the bonnet and check that its front edges are level with the corresponding edges of the front wings. If not, slacken the locknut shown in **FIG 13:13** and adjust the bolts until the bonnet is correctly aligned. Retighten the locknuts. Check the closed bonnet for looseness and if necessary slacken the locknut and adjust the dovetail bolt shown in **FIG 13:14** to correct the condition. Retighten the locknut.

Adjusting the luggage compartment lock:

Refer to **FIG 13:15**. Loosen the lock striker retaining plate and position it so that it is central, with the fourth tooth from the top of the striker at the edge of the plate. Partially close the luggage compartment lid and check that the latch engages the lock striker properly, repositioning the striker plate if necessary to the left or right. Fully close the lid and check that the rubber stops just touch down without being compressed, repositioning the striker up or down if necessary.

13:9 Removing the facia

The instrument panel:

Full details for the removal and refitting of the instrument panel on all models is given in **Chapter 12, Section 12:11**.

Removing the glove box:

Remove the glove box to dash panel attaching screws and lower the glove box from the facia.

To remove the glove box lock, remove the glove box as just described then remove both nuts from the glove box lock studs and lift the lock assembly from the facia panel. Refit in the reverse order.

13:10 The heater

Adjusting the heater controls:

The layout of the heater control system is shown in **FIG 13:16** for GT models, **FIG 13:17** for all other models. In all cases adjustment of the control cables is by slackening the cable clamps and moving the outer cables in or out as required, to provide full travel of the operating levers. When the correct adjustment is obtained, tighten the cable clamps and recheck the adjustment.

APPENDIX

TECHNICAL DATA

Engine   Fuel system   Ignition system   Clutch
Transmission   Suspension   Steering   Brakes
Electrical equipment   Capacities

WIRING DIAGRAMS

HINTS ON MAINTENANCE AND OVERHAUL

GLOSSARY OF TERMS

INDEX

TECHNICAL DATA

Dimensions are in inches unless otherwise stated

ENGINE

Bore and stroke:

1 litre 1962—65	72.14 x 60.96 mm (2.84 x 2.40 inch)
1.1 litre 1966—70	74.93 x 60.96 mm (2.95 x 2.40 inch)
1.5 litre	82.55 x 69.85 mm (3.25 x 2.75 inch)
1.9 litre	92.96 x 69.85 mm (3.66 x 2.75 inch)

Compression ratio:

1 litre Kadett 1962—65	7.8:1
1 litre Sport 1962—65	8.8:1
1.1 litre Kadett 1966—67	7.8:1
1.1 litre Super Kadett 1966—67	8.8:1
1.1 litre Rallye 1966—67	9.2:1
1.1 litre 1968—69 and 1970 R	8.2:1
1.1 litre SR 1970	9.2:1
1.5 litre and 1.9 litre	9.0:1

Crankshaft:

Main journal diameter:

1 and 1.1 litre	2.126
1.5 and 1.9 litre	2.283

Main bearings:

1 and 1.1 litre	Three thinwall, steel-backed
1.5 and 1.9 litre	Five thinwall, steel-backed
Material	Tri-metal

Diametrical clearance:

1 and 1.1 litre	.0004 to .0022
1.5 and 1.9 litre	.0009 to .0025
Undersizes	Various, selected by journal measurement

End float, all models	.004 to .008

Crankpin journal diameter:

1 and 1.1 litre	1.77
1.5 and 1.9 litre	2.046

Connecting rods:

Big-end bearings	Thinwall, steel-backed
Material	Tri-metal

Big-end bearing diametrical clearance:

1 and 1.1 litre	.0006 to .0025
1.5 and 1.9 litre	.0009 to .0025

Big-end end float:

1 and 1.1 litre	.004 to .010
1.5 and 1.9 litre	.0043 to .0095

Pistons:

Type:

1 and 1.1 litre	Light alloy with steel expansion strip
1.5 and 1.9 litre	Light alloy, slotted

Clearance:

1 and 1.1 litre	.0004 to .0008
1.5 and 1.9 litre	.0012
Oversizes available	Various, selected by bore measurement

Pistons rings, 1 and 1.1 litre:

Top ring	Squared, chrome-plated
Second ring	Tapered
Oil control ring	Slotted scraper

Piston rings, 1.5 and 1.9 litre:
Top ring	Rectangular, chrome-plated
Second ring	Tapered
Oil control rings	Three; one slotted, two scraper

Fitted gap, 1 and 1.1 litre:
Top and second rings	.01 to .016
Oil control ring	.008 to .014

Fitted gap 1.5 litre:
Top and second rings	.0118 to .0177
Oil control rings	.0098 to .0157

Fitted gap 1.9 litre:
Top and second rings	.0018 to .0216
Oil control rings	.0098 to .0157
Ring to groove clearance, all models:	
Top ring	.0024 to .0034
Second ring	.0013 to .0025
Oil control ring	.0013 to .0025
Gudgeon pin fit in connecting rod	Press-fit

Camshafts:
Bearing type	Three steel-backed, whitemetal lined
End float:	
1 and 1.1 litre	.007 to .013
1.5 and 1.9 litre	.004 to .04
Bearing diametrical clearance	.001 to .003
Drive	Chain

Valves:
Seat angle, inlet and exhaust	45 deg.
Head diameter, inlet:	
1 and 1.1 litre	1.259
1.5 litre	1.496
1.9 litre	1.574
Head diameter, exhaust:	
1 and 1.1 litre	1.063
1.5 litre	1.259
1.9 litre	1.338
Clearance in guide:	
Inlet, 1 and 1.1 litre	.0006 to .0018
Exhaust, 1 and 1.1 litre	.0014 to .0026
Inlet, 1.5 and 1.9 litre	.001 to .0025
Exhaust, 1.5 and 1.9 litre	.002 to .0035

Valve guides:
1 and 1.1 litre:
Standard production	.2766 to .2774
Oversize 1, production and service	.2795 to .2803
Oversize 2, production and service	.2825 to .2833
Oversize A, service only	.2864 to .2872

1.5 and 1.9 litre:
Standard production	.3553 to .3563
Oversize 1, production and service	.3583 to .3593
Oversize 2, production and service	.3612 to .3622
Oversize A, service only	.3671 to .3681
Valve timing and clearance:	
Timing marks, 1 and 1.1 litre	Marks on timing wheels
Timing marks, 1.5 and 1.9 litre	Marks on timing wheels and chaincase
Rocker clearance, 1 and 1.1 litre:	
Inlet	.006 hot
Exhaust	.010 hot

Rocker clearance, 1.5 and 1.9 litre:
Inlet	...	...	...	...	...	.012 hot
Exhaust	...	...	...	...	...	.012 hot

Rocker clearance *for pre-setting only:*
Inlet, 1 and 1.1 litre	...	...	...	...	.008
Exhaust, 1 and 1.1 litre	...	...	...	...	.012
Inlet, 1.5 and 1.9 litre	...	...	...	...	.012
Exhaust, 1.5 and 1.9 litre	...	...	...	...	.012
Oil pump type ...	...	...	...	...	Internal gear
Oil filter...	...	...	...	...	Fullflow with renewable element

FUEL SYSTEM

Carburetter(s):
1 litre 1962–65 ...	...	...	...	Opel single
1.1 litre Kadett and Super 1966–67	...	...		Solex single
1.1 litre Rallye 1966–67 ...	...	...	...	Solex twin
1.1 litre 1968–69	...	...	...	Solex single
1.1 litre R and SR 1970 ...	...	...	...	Solex twin
1.5 litre ...	...	...	...	Solex two barrel, manual choke
1.9 litre ...	...	...	...	Solex two barrel, automatic choke

Jet sizes, 1962–65 models
					Standard	*High performance*
Main jet	...	...	...	...	36	75
Main jet for operation above 3500 ft		...	...	...	44	44
Metering rod	...	...	...	...	712	797
Metering rod for operation above 3500 ft		...		...	173	173
Nozzle jet	...	...	...	...	75	200
Idle well jet	...	...	...	...	42	50
Full load jet	...	...	...	...	42	50
Pump jet ...	...	...	...	...	75	200

Jet sizes, 1966–67 models:
					Kadett	*Super Kadett*	*Rallye*
Main jet	...	...	...	...	X117.5	X130	117.5
Idle jet ...	...	...	...	...	g50	g50	55
High-speed bleeder jet		...	...	...	100	110	110

Jet sizes, 1.1 litre models:
					1968	*1969*	*1970*	*1970 SR*
Main jet	...	...	...	...	X132.5	X132.5	X107.5	X115
High-speed air jet	...	...	...	...	700	70	130	110
Idle jet ...	...	...	...	...	47.5	45	45	50

Jet sizes, 1.5 and 1.9 litre:
					1.5	*1.9*
Primary main jet	...	...	...	...	X110	X117.5
Secondary main jet	...	...	...	...	X975	X155
Primary high-speed air jet	...	...	...	...	120	120
Secondary high-speed air jet	...	...	...	...	100	80
Primary idle jet	...	...	...	...	g52.5	g50
Secondary idle jet	...	...	...	...	g75	g75
Fuel pump type	...	...	...	...	Mechanical drive	

IGNITION SYSTEM

Sparking plugs:
1 litre 1962–65 ...	...	...	...	...	AC.45.F
1.1 litre 1966–67	...	...	...	...	AC.43.FO
1.1 litre 1968–70	...	...	...	...	AC.43.FS
1.5 litre ...	...	...	...	...	AC.42.XLS
1.9 litre ...	...	...	...	...	AC.43.FS
Gap (all models) ...	...	...	...	...	.030

O KAD

Distributor:

Type	Bosch
1 litre 1962–65	VJU.4.BR.43
1.1 litre 1966–67	1.FU.4.(R)
1.1 litre 1968–70	VJU.4.(R)
1.5 and 1.9 litre	JFU.4
Contact points gap	.018
Firing order	1–3–4–2, No. 1 is the front cylinder

CLUTCH

Clutch:

Type	Single dry plate with diaphragm spring
Diameter of plate	$6\frac{3}{4}$
Operation	Cable
Pedal free travel	$\frac{3}{4}$ to 1

TRANSMISSION

Gearbox:

Number of forward speeds	Four
Synchromesh	All four forward speeds

Overall gearbox ratios:

1 litre models:

Top	1:1
Third	1.406:1
Second	2.156:1
First	3.764:1
Reverse	3.797:1

1.1 litre models:

Top	1:1
Third	1.432:1
Second	2.215:1
First	3.867:1
Reverse	3.900:1

1.5 and 1.9 litre models:

Top	1:1
Third	1.366:1
Second	2.156:1
First	3.428:1
Reverse	3.317:1

Automatic transmission:

Top	1:1
Second	1.48:1
First	2.4:1
Reverse	1.91:1

Differential ratios:

1962–67 models:

Kadett	3.89:1
Station Wagon and Rallye	4.125:1

1968 models:

1.1 litre	3.89:1
1.5 litre	3.67:1
1.9 litre	3.18:1

1969–70 models:

1.1 litre standard	3.89:1
1.1 litre R and SR	4.11:1
1.9 litre manual transmission	3.18:1 or 3.44:1 (optional ratios)
1.9 litre automatic transmission	3.18:1, 3.44:1 or 3.67:1 (optional ratios)

SUSPENSION

Front suspension:

Type ... ... Independent, transverse leaf spring

Rear suspension:

Type:

    1962–67 ... ... Semi-elliptic cantilever

    1968–70 ... ... Coil springs, trailing arms and panhard rod

Dampers ... ... Hydraulic, telescopic

STEERING

Steering:

Type ... ... Rack and pinion

Steering angles, static unladen condition:

    Camber ... ... $\frac{3}{4}$ deg. $\pm \frac{1}{2}$ deg.

    Castor ... ... $1\frac{1}{2}$ deg. ± 1 deg.

    Toe-in ... ... $\frac{1}{32}$ to $\frac{1}{8}$

BRAKES

Type:

1962–65 models... ... ... Hydraulic, drum front and rear

1966–70 models... ... ... Hydraulic, drum front and rear or optional disc front and drum rear

Drum diameter:

    1 and 1.1 litre models 7.87

    1.5 and 1.9 litre models 9.06

Disc brake diameter, all models 9.37

Static fluid pressure on drum brake systems with

    pedal released ... ... $4\frac{1}{4}$ lb minimum

Brake fluid: ... ... GM.4653M type 375 (Opel B.040032)

ELECTRICAL EQUIPMENT

Battery:

1962–65 models ... ... 6-volt 66 amp/hr

1966–70 models... ... ... 12-volt 44 amp/hr

Earthing system, all models ... ... Negative

Starter motor:

Type:

    1962–65 models ... ... AL/EDD 0.4/6 R.9

    1966–70 models ... ... DD 12.VO .5 PS

    1.1 litre 1968–69 ... ... DD(R) 12.VO .5 PS

    1.1 litre 1970 ... ... 12 VO .5 PS

    1.5 and 1.9 litre 1968–69 ... ... EF(R) 12 VO .8 PS

    1.9 litre 1970 ... ... EF 12 VO .8 PS

Generator:

Type:

    1962–65 models ... ... LJ/GEG 200/6/2600 FR 33

    1966–67 models ... ... EG 14 V 25A27

    1968–70 1.1 litre ... ... EG (R) 14V 25A27

    1968–70 1.5 and 1.9 litre ... ... EG (R) 14 V 25A25

Alternator:

Type:

    1966–69 models K114V35A20

    1970 models K114V28A20

Control box, generator systems:
Type:
1962–65 models	...	...	...	...	RS/VA 200/6 A1
1966–70 models	...	...	...	...	VA14V25A

Control box, alternator systems:
Type:
1966–68 models	...	...	...	...	RS/ADN1/14V
1969 models ...	...	...	...	...	ADN1/14V
1970 models ...	...	...	...	...	ADN1/14V 28A

CAPACITIES

	US	IMP
Engine:		
1 and 1.1 litre	5 pints	4.2 pints
1.5 and 1.9 litre	6 pints	5 pints
Gearbox:		
1 litre	1.3 pints	1 pint
1.1 litre	$1\frac{1}{2}$ pints	$1\frac{1}{4}$ pints
1.5 and 1.9 litre	$2\frac{1}{2}$ pints	2 pints
Automatic transmission	13 pints	$10\frac{3}{4}$ pints
Rear axle:		
1 litre	1 pint	.84 pints
1.1 litre	$1\frac{1}{2}$ pints	$1\frac{1}{4}$ pints
1.5 and 1.9 litre	$2\frac{1}{2}$ pints	2 pints
Cooling system:		
1 and 1.1 litre, without heater	10 pints	$8\frac{1}{4}$ pints
1.5 and 1.9 litre, without heater	12 pints	10 pints
Heater, all models	1 pint	.84 pints
Fuel tank:		
1 litre	$8\frac{1}{2}$ gallons	7 gallons
1.1, 1.5 and 1.9 litre	$10\frac{1}{2}$ gallons	9 gallons
1970 GT models	$13\frac{1}{2}$ gallons	11 gallons

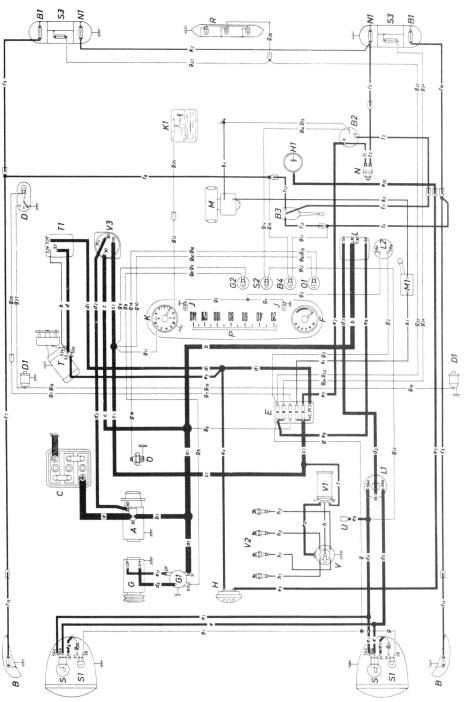

FIG 14:1   Wiring diagram for Kadett A models 1962—65

Key to Fig 14:1

A	Starter
B	Front direction signal lamp
B₁	Rear direction signal lamp
B₂	Direction signal flasher unit
B₃	Direction signal switch
B₄	Direction signal indicator lamp
C	Battery
D	Interior lamp
D₁	Interior lamp switch
E	Fuse box
F	Temperature indicator
G	Generator
G₁	Regulator
G₂	Charging indicator lamp
H	Horn
H₁	Horn button
J	Instruments lights
K	Fuel gauge dash unit
K₁	Fuel gauge tank unit
L	Light switch
L₁	Dipswitch
L₂	Instrument light switch
M	Heater motor
M₁	Heater motor switch
N	Stop lamp
N₁	Stop lamp switch
O	Oil pressure switch
O₁	Oil pressure indicator lamp
P	Speedometer with odometer
R	Licence plate lamp
S	Headlamps
S₁	Parking lights
S₂	High beam indicator lamp
S₃	Tail lamp
T	Windshield wiper motor
T₁	Windshield wiper motor switch
U	Connection for passing signal or fog lamp relay
V	Ignition distributor
V₁	Ignition coil
V₂	Spark plugs
V₃	Steering and ignition lock

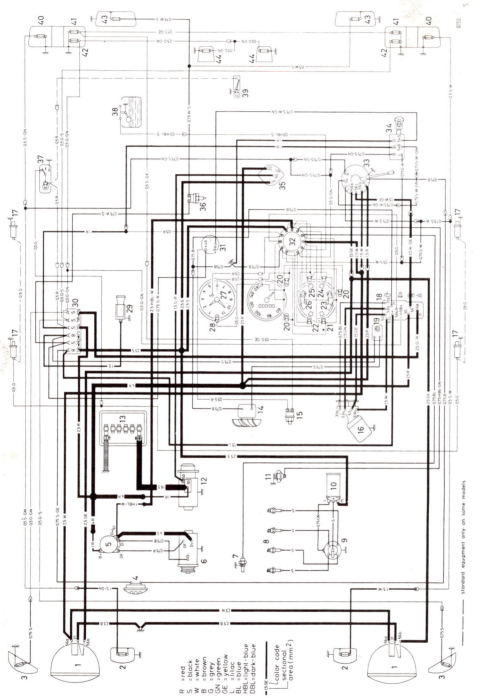

FIG 14 : 2   Wiring diagram for standard Kadett 1966–67

Key to Fig 14 : 2 1 Headlight 2 Front direction signal lamp 3 Parking lamp 4 Horn 5 Regulator 6 Generator 7 Temperature sending unit 8 Spark plugs 9 Distributor 10 Coil 11 Oil pressure switch 12 Starter 13 Battery 14 Heater blower motor 15 Stop light switch 16 Wiper motor 17 Interior lamp switch 18 Lights and windshield wiper switch 19 Heater blower motor switch 20 Instrument light 21 High beam lamp 22 Direction signal indicator light 23 Temperature gauge 24 Oil pressure light 25 Generator light 26 Fuel gauge 27 Clock 28 Clock light 29 Cigar lighter 30 Fuse box 31 Direction signal flasher 32 Printed circuit 33 Combined switch for turn signal, dipswitch, horn and passing signal 34 Hazard warning switch 35 Steering, ignition lock 36 Reversing lamp switch 37 Dome light 38 Fuel gauge, tank unit 39 Luggage compartment light 40 Rear turn signal light 41 Stop light 42 Tail light 43 Reversing light 44 Licence plate light

Color code
R = red
S = black
W = white
B = brown
G = grey
GN = green
GE = yellow
L = lilac
BL = blue
HBL = light-blue
DBL = dark-blue

sectional
area (mm²)

standard equipment only on some models

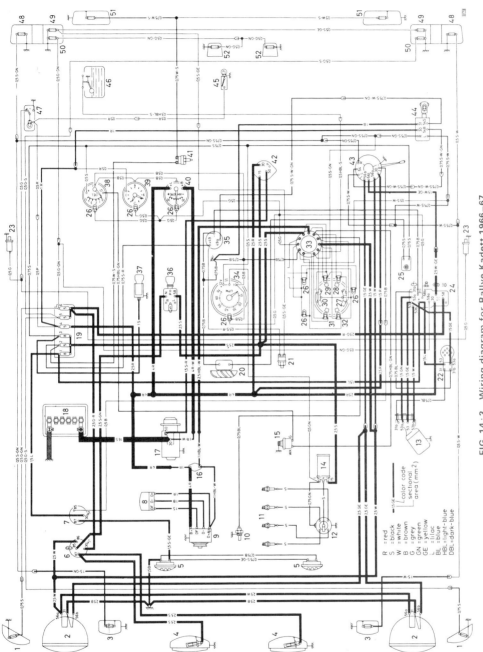

FIG 14:3   Wiring diagram for Rallye Kadett 1966-67

Key to Fig 14:3 1 Parking lamp 2 Headlight 3 Front direction signal lamp 4 Fog lamp 5 Horn 6 Fog lamp relay 7 Horn relay 8 Alternator/regulator
9 Alternator 10 Temperature sending unit 11 Spark plug 12 Distributor 13 Stop light switch 14 Coil 15 Oil pressure switch 16 Connector 17 Starter
18 Battery 19 Fuse box 20 Heater blower motor 21 Stop light switch 22 Electric windshield wiper switch (foot pump) 23 Interior lamp switch
24 Lights and windshield wiper switch 25 Heater blower motor switch 26 Instrument light 27 Temperature gauge 28 Oil pressure gauge 29 Generator light
30 Fuel gauge 31 Direction signal indicator light 32 High beam lamp 33 Printed circuit 34 Tachometer 35 Direction signal flasher 36 Fog light switch
37 Cigar lighter 38 Oil pressure gauge 39 Clock 40 Ammeter 41 Reversing lamp switch 42 Steering, ignition lock
43 Combination switch for direction signal, dipswitch, horn and passing signal 44 Hazard warning switch 45 Luggage compartment light (not USA imported)
46 Fuel gauge, tank unit 47 Dome light 48 Rear turn signal light 49 Stop light 50 Tail light 51 Reversing light 52 Licence plate light

color code
sectional
area (mm 2)

R   = red
W = white
B   = black
G   = grey
GN = green
GE = yellow
L   = lilac
BL = blue
HBL = light-blue
DBL = dark-blue

O KAD

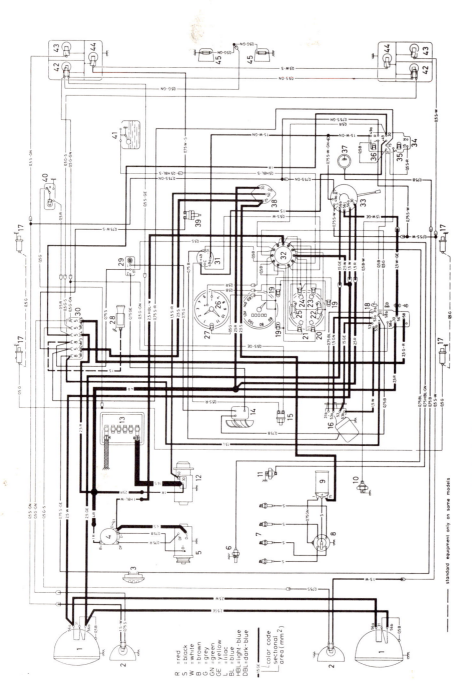

FIG 14:4 Wiring diagram for standard Kadett 1968

Key to Fig 14:4 1 Headlight 2 Front direction signal lamp and parking lamp 3 Horn 4 Regulator 5 Generator 6 Temperature sending unit
7 Spark plugs 8 Distributor 9 Ignition coil 10 Brake warning light control switch 11 Oil pressure switch 12 Starter 13 Battery 14 Heater blower motor
15 Stop light switch 16 Windshield wiper motor 17 Interior lamp switch 18 Combined lights and windshield wiper switch 19 Instrument lamps
20 High beam indicator lamp 21 Direction signal indicator lamp 22 Temperature gauge 23 Oil pressure indicator lamp 24 Generator light
25 Fuel gauge dash unit 26 Electric clock 27 Electric clock light 28 Cigar lighter 29 Heater blower switch 30 Fuse box 31 Direction signal flasher unit
32 Printed circuit 33 Combination switch for turn signal and dipswitch 34 Combined fog light, brake warning light and hazard warning light switch
35 Brake warning switch light 36 Hazard warning switch light 37 Horn button 38 Ignition and starter switch 39 Reversing lamp switch
41 Fuel gauge/tank unit 42 Tail and stop lamp 43 Direction signal lamp 44 Reversing lamp 45 Licence plate lamp 40 Dome light

R = red
S = black
W = white
B = brown
G = grey
GN = green
GE = yellow
L = lilac
BL = blue
HBL = light-blue
DBL = dark-blue

color code
sectional area (mm²)

standard equipment only on some models

148

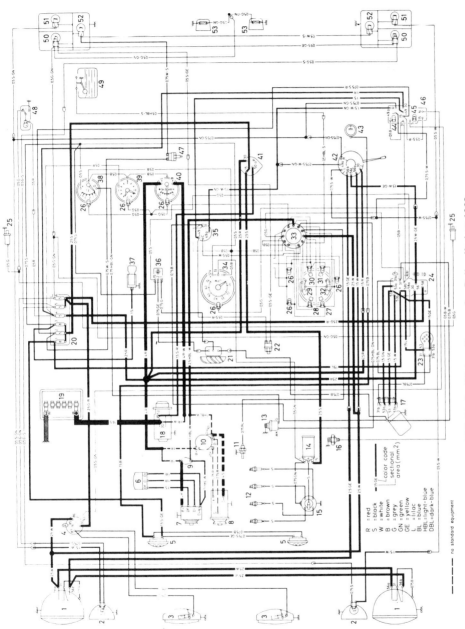

FIG 14:5 Wiring diagram for Rallye Kadett 1968

Key to Fig 14:5

1 Headlight	2 Front direction signal lamp and parking lamp
3 Fog light	4 Fog light relay
5 Horn	6 AC regulator
7 AC regulator	8 DC generator
9 Connector	10 DC regulator
11 Temperature sending unit	12 Spark plugs
13 Oil pressure switch	14 Ignition coil
15 Distributor	16 Brake warning light control switch
17 Windshield wiper motor	18 Starter
19 Battery	20 Stop light switch
21 Heater blower motor	22 Heater blower motor
23 Electric windshield wiper switch (foot pump)	24 Combined lights and windshield wiper switch
25 Interior and indicator lamp	26 Instrument light
27 High beam indicator lamp	28 Direction signal indicator lamp
29 Fuel gauge dash unit	30 Generator light
31 Oil pressure indicator lamp	32 Temperature gauge
33 Printed circuit	34 Tachometer
35 Direction signal flasher unit	36 Heater blower motor
37 Cigar lighter	38 Oil pressure gauge
39 Electric clock	40 Ammeter
41 Ignition and start switch	42 Combination switch for turn signal and dipswitch
43 Horn button	44 Hazard warning switch light
45 Brake warning switch light	46 Combined fog light, brake warning light and hazard warning light switch
47 Reversing lamp switch	48 Dome light
49 Fuel gauge/tank unit	50 Tail and stop lamp
51 Direction signal lamp	52 Reversing lamp
53 Licence plate lamp	

Color code
sectional
area (mm^2)

R = red
W = white
S = black
B = brown
G = grey
GE = yellow
GN = green
L = lilac
BL = blue
HBL = light-blue
DBL = dark-blue

------- no standard equipment

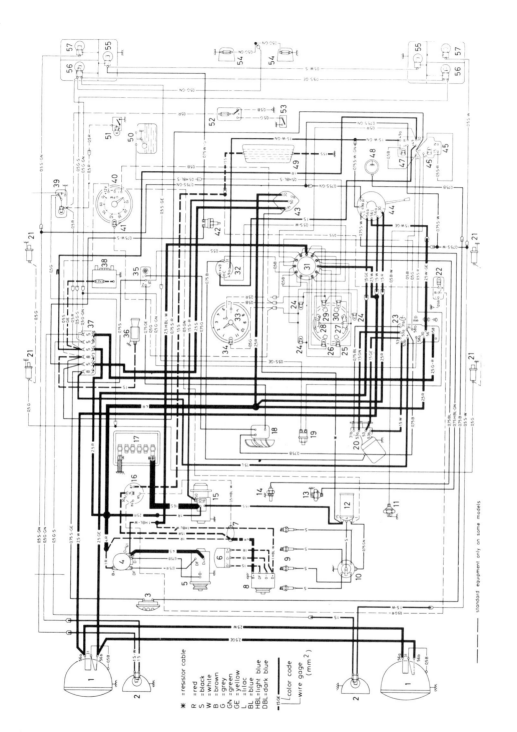

FIG 14:6 Wiring diagram for the standard Kadett 1969–70, including accessories

Key to Fig 14:6
1 Headlight   2 Front direction signal lamp and parking lamp   3 Horn   4 Regulator   5 Generator   6 Alternator   7 Connector
8 Alternator/regulator   9 Spark plugs   10 Distributor   11 Low brake indicator switch   12 Coil   13 Oil pressure switch   14 Temperature sending unit
15 Starter   16 Electrically heated back window relay   17 Battery   18 Heater blower motor   19 Stop light switch   20 Windshield wiper motor
21 Door jamb switch   22 Electrically heated back window switch   23 Combined lights and windshield wiper switch   24 Licence plate lamp
55 Reversing lamp   56 Tail and stop lamp   57 Direction signal lamp

color code
wire gage (mm²)

✱ = resistor cable

R = red
S = black
W = white
B = brown
G = grey
GN = green
GE = yellow
L = lilac
BL = blue
HBL = light blue
DBL = dark blue

standard equipment only on some models

150

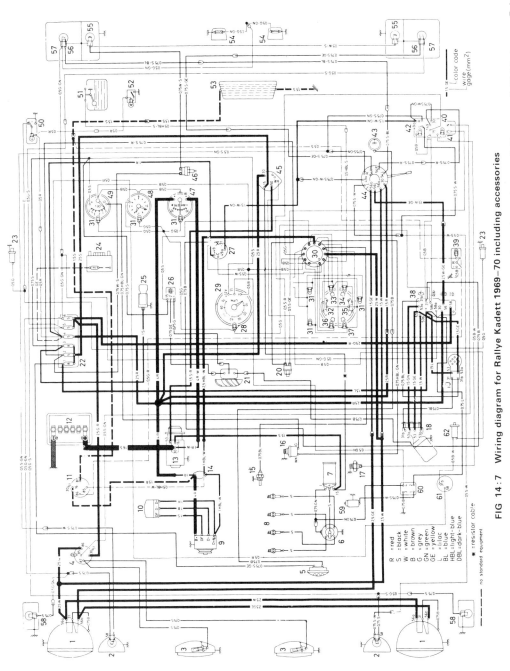

FIG 14:7 Wiring diagram for Rallye Kadett 1969–70 including accessories

Key to Fig 14:7   1 Headlamp   2 Direction signal lamp and parking lamp   3 Fog lamp   4 Battery   5 Horn   6 Distributor   7 Ignition coil
8 Spark plugs   9 AC generator   10 Regulator   11 Electrically heated back window relay   12 Starter   13 Starter   14 Terminal   15 Temperature sending unit
16 Oil pressure switch   17 Brake warning light switch   18 Winshield wiper motor   19 Wiper switch and pump assembly   20 Stop lamp switch
21 Blower motor   22 Fuse box   23 Interior lamp switch   24 Radio   25 Cigar lighter   26 Blower motor switch   27 Direction signal flasher unit
28 Tachometer lamp   29 Tachometer   30 Multiple plug   31 Instrument lamps   32 Fuel gauge dash unit   33 Charging indicator lamp
34 Oil pressure indicator lamp   35 Temperature indicator   36 Direction signal indicator lamp   37 Headlamp high beam indicator lamp
38 Windshield wiper instrument light and light switch   39 Electrically heated back window with warning lamp   40 Fog lamp switch   41 Brake warning light
42 Hazard warning light switch   43 Horn button   44 Signal switch   45 Ignition and starter switch   46 Reversing lamp switch   47 Ammeter   48 Electric clock
49 Oil pressure gauge   50 Interior lamp   51 Fuel gauge tank unit   52 Luggage compartment lamp   53 Electrically heated back window   54 Licence plate lamp
55 Reversing lamp   56 Direction signal lamp   57 Tail lamp   58 Side marker light   59 Solenoid valve   60 Solenoid valve relay   61 Warning buzzer
62 Warning buzzer switch

R = red
S = black
W = white
B = brown
G = grey
GN = green
GE = yellow
L = lilac
BL = blue
HBL = light-blue
DBL = dark-blue

★ = no standard equipment

--- = resistor cable

color code

wire
gage (mm²)

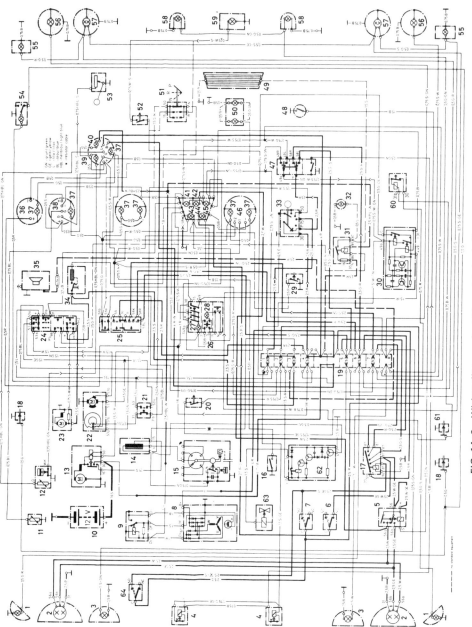

FIG 14:8   Wiring diagram for GT models including accessories

Key to Fig 14:8   1 Side marker and parking light   2 Headlamp high and low beams   3 Direction signal lamp   4 Horn   5 Dipswitch relay
6 Headlamp indicator lamp switch   7 Headlamp relay switch   8 AC generator   9 Regulator   10 Battery   11 Temperature   12 Oil pressure sender
13 Starter   14 Ignition coil   15 Distributor   16 Brake warning light control switch   17 Headlamp relay   18 Interior lamp switch   19 Fuse box
25 Parking light and instrument light switch   26 Hazard warning flasher, brake system warning light system   27 Hazard warning flasher indicator lamp
28 Brake system warning light   29 Clutch warning switch   30 Flasher unit   31 Heated back window relay   32 Heated back window indicator unit
33 Oil pressure gauge with oil pressure indicator lamp   34 Cigar lighter   35 Radio   36 Electric clock   37 Instrument lights   38 Temperature indicator and fuel gauge dash unit
39 Oil pressure gauge with oil pressure indicator lamp   40 Ammeter with charging indicator light   41 Right direction signal indicator lamp
42 Headlamp high beam indicator lamp   43 Parking brake and clutch indicator lamp   44 Headlamp high beam indicator lamp
45 Left direction signal indicator lamp   47 Signal switch   48 Horn switch   49 Heated back window   50 Selector lever indicator
51 Selector lever switch   52 Reversing lamp switch   53 Fuel gauge tank unit   54 Interior lamp   55 Side marking light   56 Direction signal lamp
57 Stop and tail lamp   58 Licence plate lamp   59 Reversing lamp   60 Warning buzzer   61 Warning buzzer relay   62 Tachometer relay
63 Solenoid valve   64 Headlamp relay switch

Inches	Decimals	Milli-metres	Inches to Millimetres Inches	mm	Millimetres to Inches mm	Inches
1/64	.015625	.3969	.001	.0254	.01	.00039
1/32	.03125	.7937	.002	.0508	.02	.00079
3/64	.046875	1.1906	.003	.0762	.03	.00118
1/16	.0625	1.5875	.004	.1016	.04	.00157
5/64	.078125	1.9844	.005	.1270	.05	.00197
3/32	.09375	2.3812	.006	.1524	.06	.00236
7/64	.109375	2.7781	.007	.1778	.07	.00276
1/8	.125	3.1750	.008	.2032	.08	.00315
9/64	.140625	3.5719	.009	.2286	.09	.00354
5/32	.15625	3.9687	.01	.254	.1	.00394
11/64	.171875	4.3656	.02	.508	.2	.00787
3/16	.1875	4.7625	.03	.762	.3	.01181
13/64	.203125	5·1594	.04	1.016	.4	.01575
7/32	.21875	5.5562	.05	1.270	.5	.01969
15/64	.234375	5.9531	.06	1.524	.6	.02362
1/4	.25	6.3500	.07	1.778	.7	.02756
17/64	.265625	6.7469	.08	2.032	.8	.03150
9/32	.28125	7.1437	.09	2.286	.9	.03543
19/64	.296875	7.5406	.1	2.54	1	.03937
5/16	.3125	7.9375	.2	5.08	2	.07874
21/64	.328125	8.3344	.3	7.62	3	.11811
11/32	.34375	8.7312	.4	10.16	4	.15748
23/64	.359375	9.1281	.5	12.70	5	.19685
3/8	.375	9.5250	.6	15.24	6	.23622
25/64	.390625	9.9219	.7	17.78	7	.27559
13/32	.40625	10.3187	.8	20.32	8	.31496
27/64	.421875	10.7156	.9	22.86	9	.35433
7/16	.4375	11.1125	1	25.4	10	.39370
29/64	.453125	11.5094	2	50.8	11	.43307
15/32	.46875	11.9062	3	76.2	12	.47244
31/64	.484375	12.3031	4	101.6	13	.51181
1/2	.5	12.7000	5	127.0	14	.55118
33/64	.515625	13.0969	6	152.4	15	.59055
17/32	.53125	13.4937	7	177.8	16	.62992
35/64	.546875	13.8906	8	203.2	17	.66929
9/16	.5625	14.2875	9	228.6	18	.70866
37/64	.578125	14.6844	10	254.0	19	.74803
19/32	.59375	15.0812	11	279.4	20	.78740
39/64	.609375	15.4781	12	304.8	21	.82677
5/8	.625	15.8750	13	330.2	22	.86614
41/64	.640625	16.2719	14	355.6	23	.90551
21/32	.65625	16.6687	15	381.0	24	.94488
43/64	.671875	17.0656	16	406.4	25	.98425
11/16	.6875	17.4625	17	431.8	26	1.02362
45/64	.703125	17.8594	18	457.2	27	1.06299
23/32	.71875	18.2562	19	482.6	28	1.10236
47/64	.734375	18.6531	20	508.0	29	1.14173
3/4	.75	19.0500	21	533.4	30	1.18110
49/64	.765625	19.4469	22	558.8	31	1.22047
25/32	.78125	19.8437	23	584.2	32	1.25984
51/64	.796875	20.2406	24	609.6	33	1.29921
13/16	.8125	20.6375	25	635.0	34	1.33858
53/64	.828125	21.0344	26	660.4	35	1.37795
27/32	.84375	21.4312	27	685.8	36	1.41732
55/64	.859375	21.8281	28	711.2	37	1.4567
7/8	.875	22.2250	29	736.6	38	1.4961
57/64	.890625	22.6219	30	762.0	39	1.5354
29/32	.90625	23.0187	31	787.4	40	1.5748
59/64	.921875	23.4156	32	812.8	41	1.6142
15/16	.9375	23.8125	33	838.2	42	1.6535
61/64	.953125	24.2094	34	863.6	43	1.6929
31/32	.96875	24.6062	35	889.0	44	1.7323
63/64	.984375	25.0031	36	914.4	45	1.7717

UNITS	Pints to Litres	Gallons to Litres	Litres to Pints	Litres to Gallons	Miles to Kilometres	Kilometres to Miles	Lbs. per sq. In. to Kg. per sq. Cm.	Kg. per sq. Cm. to Lbs. per sq. In.
1	.57	4.55	1.76	.22	1.61	.62	.07	14.22
2	1.14	9.09	3.52	.44	3.22	1.24	.14	28.50
3	1.70	13.64	5.28	.66	4.83	1.86	.21	42.67
4	2.27	18.18	7.04	.88	6.44	2.49	.28	56.89
5	2.84	22.73	8.80	1.10	8.05	3.11	.35	71.12
6	3.41	27.28	10.56	1.32	9.66	3.73	.42	85.34
7	3.98	31.82	12.32	1.54	11.27	4.35	.49	99.56
8	4.55	36.37	14.08	1.76	12.88	4.97	.56	113.79
9		40.91	15.84	1.98	14.48	5.59	.63	128.00
10		45.46	17.60	2.20	16.09	6.21	.70	142.23
20				4.40	32.19	12.43	1.41	284.47
30				6.60	48.28	18.64	2.11	426.70
40				8.80	64.37	24.85		
50					80.47	31.07		
60					96.56	37.28		
70					112.65	43.50		
80					128.75	49.71		
90					144.84	55.92		
100					160.93	62.14		

UNITS	Lb ft to kgm	Kgm to lb ft	UNITS	Lb ft to kgm	Kgm to lb ft
1	.138	7.233	7	.967	50.631
2	.276	14.466	8	1.106	57.864
3	.414	21.699	9	1.244	65.097
4	.553	28.932	10	1.382	72.330
5	.691	36.165	20	2.765	144.660
6	.829	43.398	30	4.147	216.990

HINTS ON MAINTENANCE AND OVERHAUL

There are few things more rewarding than the restoration of a vehicle's original peak of efficiency and smooth performance.

The following notes are intended to help the owner to reach that state of perfection. Providing that he possesses the basic manual skills he should have no difficulty in performing most of the operations detailed in this manual. It must be stressed, however, that where recommended in the manual, highly-skilled operations ought to be entrusted to experts, who have the necessary equipment, to carry out the work satisfactorily.

Quality of workmanship:

The hazardous driving conditions on the roads to-day demand that vehicles should be as nearly perfect, mechanically, as possible. It is therefore most important that amateur work be carried out with care, bearing in mind the often inadequate working conditions, and also the inferior tools which may have to be used. It is easy to counsel perfection in all things, and we recognize that it may be setting an impossibly high standard. We do, however, suggest that every care should be taken to ensure that a vehicle is as safe to take on the road as it is humanly possible to make it.

Safe working conditions:

Even though a vehicle may be stationary, it is still potentially dangerous if certain sensible precautions are not taken when working on it while it is supported on jacks or blocks. It is indeed preferable not to use jacks alone, but to supplement them with carefully placed blocks, so that there will be plenty of support if the car rolls off the jacks during a strenuous manoeuvre. Axle stands are an excellent way of providing a rigid base which is not readily disturbed. Piles of bricks are a dangerous substitute. Be careful not to get under heavy loads on lifting tackle, the load could fall. It is preferable not to work alone when lifting an engine, or when working underneath a vehicle which is supported well off the ground. To be trapped, particularly under the vehicle, may have unpleasant results if help is not quickly forthcoming. Make some provision, however humble, to deal with fires. Always disconnect a battery if there is a likelihood of electrical shorts. These may start a fire if there is leaking fuel about. This applies particularly to leads which can carry a heavy current, like those in the starter circuit. While on the subject of electricity, we must also stress the danger of using equipment which is run off the mains and which has no earth or has faulty wiring or connections. So many workshops have damp floors, and electrical shocks are of such a nature that it is sometimes impossible to let go of a live lead or piece of equipment due to the muscular spasms which take place.

Work demanding special care:

This involves the servicing of braking, steering and suspension systems. On the road, failure of the braking system may be disastrous. Make quite sure that there can be no possibility of failure through the bursting of rusty brake pipes or rotten hoses, nor to a sudden loss of pressure due to defective seals or valves.

Problems:

The chief problems which may face an operator are:
1 External dirt.
2 Difficulty in undoing tight fixings.
3 Dismantling unfamiliar mechanisms.
4 Deciding in what respect parts are defective.
5 Confusion about the correct order for reassembly.
6 Adjusting running clearance.
7 Road testing.
8 Final tuning.

Practical suggestions to solve the problems:

1 Preliminary cleaning of large parts—engines, transmissions, steering, suspensions, etc.,—should be carried out before removal from the car. Where road dirt and mud alone are present, wash clean with a high-pressure water jet, brushing to remove stubborn adhesions, and allow to drain and dry. Where oil or grease is also present, wash down with a proprietary compound (Gunk, Teepol etc.,) applying with a stiff brush—an old paint brush is suitable—into all crevices. Cover the distributor and ignition coils with a polythene bag and then apply a strong water jet to clear the loosened deposits. Allow to drain and dry. The assemblies will then be sufficiently clean to remove and transfer to the bench for the next stage.

On the bench, further cleaning can be carried out, first wiping the parts as free as possible from grease with old newspaper. Avoid using rag or cotton waste which can leave clogging fibres behind. Any remaining grease can be removed with a brush dipped in paraffin. If necessary, traces of paraffin can be removed by carbon tetrachloride. Avoid using paraffin or petrol in large quantities for cleaning in enclosed areas, such as garages, on account of the high fire risk.

When all exteriors have been cleaned, and not before, dismantling can be commenced. This ensures that dirt will not enter into interiors and orifices revealed by dismantling. In the next phases, where components have to be cleaned, use carbon tetrachloride in preference to petrol and keep the containers covered except when in use. After the components have been cleaned, plug small holes with tapered hard wood plugs cut to size and blank off larger orifices with grease-proof paper and masking tape. Do not use soft wood plugs or matchsticks as they may break.

2 It is not advisable to hammer on the end of a screw thread, but if it must be done, first screw on a nut to protect the thread, and use a lead hammer. This applies particularly to the removal of tapered cotters. Nuts and bolts seem to 'grow' together, especially in exhaust systems. If penetrating oil does not work, try the judicious application of heat, but be careful of starting a fire. Asbestos sheet or cloth is useful to isolate heat.

Tight bushes or pieces of tail-pipe rusted into a silencer can be removed by splitting them with an open-ended hacksaw. Tight screws can sometimes be started by a tap from a hammer on the end of a suitable screwdriver. Many tight fittings will yield to the judicious use of a hammer, but it must be a soft-faced hammer if damage is to be avoided, use a heavy block on the opposite side to absorb shock. Any parts of the steering system which have been damaged should be renewed, as attempts to repair them may lead to cracking and subsequent failure, and steering ball joints should be disconnected using a recommended tool to prevent damage.

3 It often happens that an owner is baffled when trying to dismantle an unfamiliar piece of equipment. So many modern devices are pressed together or assembled by spinning-over flanges, that they must be sawn apart. The intention is that the whole assembly must be renewed. However, parts which appear to be in one piece to the naked eye, may reveal close-fitting joint lines when inspected with a magnifying glass, and, this may provide the necessary clue to dismantling. Left-handed screw threads are used where rotational forces would tend to unscrew a right-handed screw thread.

Be very careful when dismantling mechanisms which may come apart suddenly. Work in an enclosed space where the parts will be contained, and drape a piece of cloth over the device if springs are likely to fly in all directions. Mark everything which might be reassembled in the wrong position, scratched symbols may be used on unstressed parts, or a sequence of tiny dots from a centre punch can be useful. Stressed parts should never be scratched or centre-popped as this may lead to cracking under working conditions. Store parts which look alike in the correct order for reassembly. Never rely upon memory to assist in the assembly of complicated mechanisms, especially when they will be dismantled for a long time, but make notes, and drawings to supplement the diagrams in the manual, and put labels on detached wires. Rust stains may indicate unlubricated wear. This can sometimes be seen round the outside edge of a bearing cup in a universal joint. Look for bright rubbing marks on parts which normally should not make heavy contact. These might prove that something is bent or running out of truth. For example, there might be bright marks on one side of a piston, at the top near the ring grooves, and others at the bottom of the skirt on the other side. This could well be the clue to a bent connecting rod. Suspected cracks can be proved by heating the component in a light oil to approximately 100°C, removing, drying off, and dusting with french chalk, if a crack is present the oil retained in the crack will stain the french chalk.

4 In determining wear, and the degree, against the permissible limits set in the manual, accurate measurement can only be achieved by the use of a micrometer. In many cases, the wear is given to the fourth place of decimals; that is in ten-thousandths of an inch. This can be read by the vernier scale on the barrel of a good micrometer. Bore diameters are more difficult to determine. If, however, the matching shaft is accurately measured, the degree of play in the bore can be felt as a guide to its suitability. In other cases, the shank of a twist drill of known diameter is a handy check.

Many methods have been devised for determining the clearance between bearing surfaces. To-day the best and simplest is by the use of Plastigage, obtainable from most garages. A thin plastic thread is laid between the two surfaces and the bearing is tightened, flattening the thread. On removal, the width of the thread is

compared with a scale supplied with the thread and the clearance is read off directly. Sometimes joint faces leak persistently, even after gasket renewal. The fault will then be traceable to distortion, dirt or burrs. Studs which are screwed into soft metal frequently raise burrs at the point of entry. A quick cure for this is to chamfer the edge of the hole in the part which fits over the stud.

5 **Always check a replacement part with the original one before it is fitted.**

If parts are not marked, and the order for reassembly is not known, a little detective work will help. Look for marks which are due to wear to see if they can be mated. Joint faces may not be identical due to manufacturing errors, and parts which overlap may be stained, giving a clue to the correct position. Most fixings leave identifying marks especially if they were painted over on assembly. It is then easier to decide whether a nut, for instance, has a plain, a spring, or a shakeproof washer under it. All running surfaces become 'bedded' together after long spells of work and tiny imperfections on one part will be found to have left corresponding marks on the other. This is particularly true of shafts and bearings and even a score on a cylinder wall will show on the piston.

6 Checking end float or rocker clearances by feeler gauge may not always give accurate results because of wear. For instance, the rocker tip which bears on a valve stem may be deeply pitted, in which case the feeler will simply be bridging a depression. Thrust washers may also wear depressions in opposing faces to make accurate measurement difficult. End float is then easier to check by using a dial gauge. It is common practice to adjust end play in bearing assemblies, like front hubs with taper rollers, by doing up the axle nut until the hub becomes stiff to turn and then backing it off a little. Do not use this method with ballbearing hubs as the assembly is often preloaded by tightening the axle nut to its fullest extent. If the splitpin hole will not line up, file the base of the nut a little.

Steering assemblies often wear in the straight-ahead position. If any part is adjusted, make sure that it remains free when moved from lock to lock. Do not be surprised if an assembly like a steering gearbox, which is known to be carefully adjusted outside the car, becomes stiff when it is bolted in place. This will be due to distortion of the case by the pull of the mounting bolts, particularly if the mounting points are not all touching together. This problem may be met in other equipment and is cured by careful attention to the alignment of mounting points.

When a spanner is stamped with a size and A/F it means that the dimension is the width between the jaws and has no connection with ANF, which is the designation for the American National Fine thread. Coarse threads like Whitworth are rarely used on cars to-day except for studs which screw into soft aluminium or cast iron. For this reason it might be found that the top end of a cylinder head stud has a fine thread and the lower end a coarse thread to screw into the cylinder block. If the car has mainly UNF threads then it is likely that any coarse threads will be UNC, which are not the same as Whitworth. Small sizes have the same number of threads in Whitworth and UNC, but in the $\frac{1}{2}$ inch size for example, there are twelve threads to the inch in the former and thirteen in the latter.

7 After a major overhaul, particularly if a great deal of work has been done on the braking, steering and suspension systems, it is advisable to approach the problem of testing with care. If the braking system has been overhauled, apply heavy pressure to the brake pedal and get a second operator to check every possible source of leakage. The brakes may work extremely well, but a leak could cause complete failure after a few miles.

Do not fit the hub caps until every wheel nut has been checked for tightness, and make sure the tyre pressures are correct. Check the levels of coolant, lubricants and hydraulic fluids. Being satisfied that all is well, take the car on the road and test the brakes at once. Check the steering and the action of the handbrake. Do all this at moderate speeds on quiet roads, and make sure there is no other vehicle behind you when you try a rapid stop.

Finally, remember that many parts settle down after a time, so check for tightness of all fixings after the car has been on the road for a hundred miles or so.

8 It is useless to tune an engine which has not reached its normal running temperature. In the same way, the tune of an engine which is stiff after a rebore will be different when the engine is again running free. Remember too, that rocker clearances on pushrod operated valve gear will change when the cylinder head nuts are tightened after an initial period of running with a new head gasket.

Trouble may not always be due to what seems the obvious cause. Ignition, carburation and mechanical condition are interdependent and spitting back through the carburetter, which might be attributed to a weak mixture, can be caused by a sticking inlet valve.

For one final hint on tuning, never adjust more than one thing at a time or it will be impossible to tell which adjustment produced the desired result.

GLOSSARY OF TERMS

Allen key Cranked hexagonal bar for turning socket head screws.

Alternator Rotary machine for generating alternating current electricity. Car alternators embody silicon diodes to rectify the AC output to DC for energizing the field and supplying the load.

Ambient temperature Surrounding atmospheric temperature.

Annulus A ring-shaped element. The outer gear of an epicyclic train.

Armature The rotating member, comprising shaft, windings and commutator, of a generator or motor. The moving element of a relay or solenoid.

Axial In line with, or pertaining to, an axis.

Backlash Play between meshing gears.

Balance lever Lever in which the force applied at the centre is divided equally between connections to the ends.

Bendix pinion Self-meshing and disengaging pinion on the shaft of an inertia type starter motor.

Bevel pinion Conical shaped gearwheel designed to mesh with a similar gear whose axis usually is at 90 deg. to its own.

bhp Brake horse power, as measured on a dynamometer.

bmep Brake mean effective pressure. The average pressure exerted on a piston during the working stroke.

Brake cylinder Cylinder with hydraulically operated piston(s) acting on brake shoes or pads.

Brake regulator Control valve fitted to some hydraulic braking systems to limit pressure applied to rear brakes to prevent the rear wheels locking when heavily braking.

Camber Angle at which a front wheel is tilted from the vertical.

Capacitor Modern term for condenser. Used across ignition make-and-break to produce a hot spark at the plug.

Castellated Top face of a nut, slotted across the flats to take a locking pin.

Castor Angle at which the kingpin or swivel pin is tilted from the vertical when viewed from one side.

cc Cubic centimetres. In engine capacity, the area of the bore in sq cm multiplied by the stroke in cm and the number of cylinders.

Clevis Forked connector with pin. Commonly used in handbrake and similar connections.

Collet Ring or collar, usually split, to encircle a groove in a stem or shaft where it is retained by an outer ring or seating. Used to secure the springs to the valves in the cylinder head of a car.

Commutator A segmented collar or faceplate on the armature of a generator or motor through which current is conveyed from or to the windings via the brushes. A current reversing device.

Compression ratio Ratio of total volume (piston at bottom of stroke) to unswept volume (piston at top of stroke) in an engine cylinder.

Condenser See 'Capacitor'.

Core plug Plug for blanking off a core or 'fettling' hole on an iron casting. A 'Welch' plug.

Crown wheel Large ring bevel gear, secured to differential housing in rear axle, transmitting drive from the bevel pinion on the propeller shaft to the rear wheel axles.

C spanner Spanner shaped like a letter C with a handle. Used on screw collars with slots instead of flats for turning.

Damper Modern term for shock absorber.

Depression Lowering of atmospheric pressure as, for example, in the inlet manifold or carburetter.

Dowel Close fitting pin, peg, tube or bolt for locating mating parts accurately.

Drive shaft Output shaft of gearbox transmitting torque to the propeller shaft. Sometimes 'third motion shaft'.

Dry liner Thin walled tube pressed into bored-out engine cylinder.

Dry sump Sump from which all oil collected is immediately scavenged and returned to a separate tank.

Dynamo See 'Generator'.

Electrode Terminal part of an electrical component such as the centre element of a sparking plug.

Electrolyte In car batteries, sulphuric acid diluted with distilled water.

End float Play or movement on a shaft in an axial direction; end play.

EP (Extreme pressure). As applied to lubricants, indicates special grades for heavily loaded bearing surfaces such as gear teeth in a gearbox or crown-wheel and pinion in a rear axle assembly.

Field coils Windings on polepieces of motors and generators.

Fullflow filter	Filter in which all the oil pumped around the engine passes for filtering. If the filter element becomes clogged, a bypass valve opens to circulate unfiltered oil.
Gear pump	Pump in which oil is circulated by two meshing gears in a close fitting casing. Oil is carried from one side around the outer periphery of both gears in the spaces between the teeth to the outlet at the other, the meshing teeth in the centre preventing passage back to the inlet.
Gearshaft	Shaft transmitting drive from clutch to layshaft in the gearbox. 'First motion' shaft.
Generator	A machine for generating direct current and incorporating a commutator and brushes. A dynamo.
Grommet	Close fitting ring of rubber or plastic around pipes or cables to protect them from abrasion in passage through bulkheads and to seal the opening against entry of dirt and water.
Grubscrew	Setscrew without a head, threaded full length, with slot for turning, usually for securing a pulley or collar to a shaft.
Gudgeon pin	Shaft connecting piston to the connecting rod; a 'wrist-pin' or 'piston-pin'.
Halfshaft	One of a pair transmitting drive from the differential gearing to the wheel hubs.
Helical	In spiral form. The teeth of helical gears are cut in a spiral at an angle to the side faces of the gearwheel.
Hot spot	Heated area assisting vapourization of fuel on its way to the cylinders. Usually provided by a close contact area between inlet and exhaust manifolds.
HT	High tension. The high voltage output produced by the ignition coil for the sparking plugs.
Hydrometer	Device for checking the specific gravity of battery electrolyte.
Hypoid gear	Form of bevel gear used in rear axle crown and bevel combinations in which the bevel pinion meshes with the crownwheel below its centre line, giving a lower propeller shaft line.
Idler	Device for passing on movement, e.g. a free-running gear between driving and driven gears; a lever transmitting track rod movement to a side rod in a steering gear.
Impeller	Rotating element of a water pump to produce flow.
Intermediate gear	In a gearbox, an idler gear introduced between layshaft and drive shaft to reverse motion.
Journals	Parts of a shaft in intimate contact with bearings.
Kingpin	Main vertical pin around which the front stub axle is turned to provide steering.
Layshaft	In a gearbox, the intermediate shaft, carrying the laygear, transmitting the drive from the gearshaft, or first motion shaft, to the drive shaft, or third motion shaft. The second motion shaft.
lb ft	Pound-feet, a measure of twist or torque; the product of radius and load. A pull of 10 lb at a radius of 1 ft is a torque of 10 lb ft.
Little-end	The small, or piston, end of a connecting rod.
l.s.	The leading shoe in a brake drum, has a tendency to wedge into the drum when applied, so increasing the braking effect.
LT	Low tension. The electrical output from the battery and generator.
Mandrel	Accurately machined bar or rod used for test or centring purposes.
Manifold	Pipe or duct with several branches. In car engines the duct between the cylinder ports and the carburetter or exhaust pipe.
Needle rollers	Bearing rollers whose length is many times their diameter.
Oil bath	Reservoir for lubricating parts by immersion. In air filters a separate oil supply for wetting a wire mesh element to hold the dust.
Overlap	Period during which inlet and exhaust valves are open together.
Pawl	Pivoted catch engaging the teeth of a ratchet to permit rotation in one direction only.
Peg spanner	Spanner with pegs or pins for insertion in holes or slots in a collar or cap for turning.
Pinion	The smaller of a pair of gears; a spur gear.
Piston type damper	Shock absorber in which damping is controlled by a piston working in a closed, oil-filled cylinder.
Preloading	Preset static pressure on ball or roller bearings not due to working loads.
Radial	Radiating from a centre, like the spokes of a wheel.
Radius rod	Pivoted arm confining movement to an arc of fixed radius.

Ratchet	Toothed wheel or rack capable of movement in one direction only. Movement in the other is prevented by a pawl.
Ring gear	Large diameter toothed ring secured to the outer periphery of a flywheel for engagement with the pinion of the starter motor.
Runout	Amount by which a rotating part is out of truth.
Semi-floating axle	Outer end of rear axle halfshaft carried on bearing inside the axle casing. Wheel hub is secured to the end of the halfshaft.
Servo	Hydraulic or pneumatic device for assisting or augmenting a force applied manually.
Setscrew	A screw threaded for the full length of the shank.
Shackle	Coupling link in the form of two parallel pins connected by side plates. Used to anchor one end of a leaf spring to take up length variation on deflection.
Shell bearing	Thin walled, steel shell lined with anti-friction metal. Usually semi-circular and used in pairs for main and big-end bearings.
Shock absorber	Device linked to front and rear suspensions to damp out vertical oscillation due to uneven road surfaces; a damper.
Socket head screw	Screw with hexagonal socket in head for an Allen key.
Solenoid	Coil of wire creating a magnetic field when electric current passes through it. Commonly applied to coil, complete with armature or core, for operating a mechanical device or contacts.
Spur gear	Gear with teeth cut axially across the periphery.
Stub axle	Short axle mounted at one end only.
Steering box	Gearbox at lower end of steering column, containing gearing for translating rotational steering wheel motion into lateral movement for swivelling the front wheels.
Sway bar	Bar connected between a fixed point on the chassis or body and an axle to limit sideways movement of the axle.
Tachometer	Instrument for the accurate measurement of rotational speed. Usually indicates revolutions per minute.

TDC	Top dead centre. The point of highest travel of a piston in its cylinder.
Thermostat	Device for regulating temperature. In cars, used to restrict the circulation of cooling water through the radiator until engine temperature has risen.
Threequarter floating axle	Outer end of rear axle halfshaft flanged and bolted to wheel hub which runs in bearing mounted on outside of axle casing. The axle shaft does not bear the vehicle weight.
Thrust bearing	—or washer. Bearings or washers for reducing friction through axial loading on rotating shafts or components.
Torque	Turning or twisting effort.
Track rod	Bar across the front underside of the vehicle coupling the steering arms and maintaining the front wheels in proper alignment.
Transducer	Electrical device for converting mechanical or thermal stress into an electrical signal for operating a warning lamp or indicator.
Transmitter	Electrical device for transmitting the state of a measuring device, such as a fuel gauge, to a suitably scaled indicator.
t.s.	Trailing shoe in a brake drum, has a tendency to break away from the drum when applied, so reducing the braking effect.
UJ	Universal joint. Coupling between shafts not in alignment permitting stress-free torque transmission.
UNF	Unified national fine screw thread.
Vacuum servo	Servo device, usually for brake operation, utilising the difference in pressure between atmospheric and that in the inlet manifold to augment the manually applied braking effort.
Venturi	Restriction or 'choke' in a tube, as in a carburetter, to produce a change in velocity and pressure.
Vernier	A pair of adjacent scales for determining very small measurements.
Welch plug	See 'Core plug'.
Wet liner	Removable cylinder barrel, sealed at both ends against surrounding coolant in a cylinder block but with coolant circulating around the centre section.
Wet sump	Detachable lower half of a crankcase in which the lubricant is allowed to drain and remain until re-circulated.

INDEX

THE AUTOBOOK SERIES OF WORKSHOP MANUALS

Make	Author	Title
AUSTIN		
A30 1951–1956	Ball	Austin A30, A35, A40 Autobook
A35 1956–1962	Ball	Austin A30, A35, A40 Autobook
A40 Farina 1957–1967	Ball	Austin A30, A35, A40 Autobook
A40 Cambridge 1954–1957	Ball	BMC Autobook Three
A50 Cambridge 1954–1957	Ball	BMC Autobook Three
A55 Cambridge Mk 1 1957–1958	Ball	BMC Autobook Three
A55 Cambridge Mk 2 1958–1961	Smith	BMC Autobook One
A60 Cambridge 1961–1969	Smith	BMC Autobook One
A99 1959–1961	Ball	BMC Autobook Four
A110 1961–1968	Ball	BMC Autobook Four
Mini 1959–1970	Ball	Mini 1959–70 Autobook
Mini Cooper 1961–1970	Ball	Mini Cooper 1961–70 Autobook
Mini Cooper S 1963–1970	Ball	Mini Cooper 1961–70 Autobook
1100 Mk 1 1963–1967	Ball	1100 Mk 1 1962–67 Autobook
1100 Mk 2 1968–1969	Ball	1100 Mk 2, 1300, America 1968–69 Autobook
1300 1968–1969	Ball	1100 Mk 2, 1300, America 1968–69 Autobook
America 1968–1969	Ball	1100 Mk 2, 1300, America 1968–69 Autobook
1800 Mk 1 1964–1968	Ball	1800 Autobook
1800 Mk 2 1968–1969	Ball	1800 Autobook
Maxi 1969	Ball	Austin Maxi 1969 Autobook
AUSTIN HEALEY		
100/6 1956–1959	Ball	Austin Healey 100/6, 3000 1956–68 Autobook
Sprite 1958–1969	Ball	Sprite, Midget 1958–69 Autobook
3000 Mk 1 1959–1961	Ball	Austin Healey 100/6, 3000 1956–68 Autobook
3000 Mk 2 1961–1964	Ball	Austin Healey 100/6, 3000 1956–68 Autobook
3000 Mk 3 1964–1968	Ball	Austin Healey 100/6, 3000 1956–68 Autobook
BEDFORD		
CA Mk 1 and 2 1961–1969	Ball	Vauxhall Victor 1, 2, FB 1957–64 Autobook
Beagle HA 1964–1966	Ball	Vauxhall Viva HA 1964–66 Autobook
BMW		
1600 1966–1969	Ball	BMW 1600 1966–69 Autobook
1600–2 1966–1969	Ball	BMW 1600 1966–69 Autobook
1600TI 1966–1969	Ball	BMW 1600 1966–69 Autobook
1800 1964–1968	Ball	BMW 1800 1964–68 Autobook
1800TI 1964–1968	Ball	BMW 1800 1964–68 Autobook
2000 1966–1969	Ball	BMW 2000, 2002 1966–69 Autobook
2000A 1966–1969	Ball	BMW 2000, 2002 1966–69 Autobook
2000TI 1966–1969	Ball	BMW 2000, 2002 1966–69 Autobook
2000CS 1967–1969	Ball	BMW 2000, 2002 1966–69 Autobook
2000CA 1967–1969	Ball	BMW 2000, 2002 1966–69 Autobook
2002 1968–1969	Ball	BMW 2000, 2002 1966–69 Autobook
COMMER		
Cob Series 1 1960	Ball	Hillman Minx 1 to 5 1956–65 Autobook
Cob Series 2 1960–1963	Ball	Hillman Minx 1 to 5 1956–65 Autobook
Cob Series 3 1963–1965	Ball	Hillman Minx 1 to 5 1956–65 Autobook
Imp Vans 1963–1969	Smith	Hillman Imp 1963–69 Autobook
DE DION BOUTON		
One-cylinder 1899–1907	Mercredy	De Dion Autobook One
Two-cylinder 1903–1907	Mercredy	De Dion Autobook One
Four-cylinder 1905–1907	Mercredy	De Dion Autobook One

Make				Author	Title

FIAT

Model				Author	Title
500 1957–1961	..	..	..	Ball	Fiat 500 1957–69 Autobook
500D 1960–1965	..	..	..	Ball	Fiat 500 1957–69 Autobook
500F 1965–1969	..	..	..	Ball	Fiat 500 1957–69 Autobook
600 633cc 1955–1961	..	..	..	Ball	Fiat 600, 600D 1955–69 Autobook
600D 766cc 1960–1969	..	..	..	Ball	Fiat 600, 600D 1955–69 Autobook
850 Sedan 1964–1969	..	..	..	Ball	Fiat 850 1964–69 Autobook
850 Coupé 1965–1969	..	..	..	Ball	Fiat 850 1964–69 Autobook
850 Roadster 1965–1969	..	..	..	Ball	Fiat 850 1964–69 Autobook
850 Family 1965–1969	..	..	..	Ball	Fiat 850 1964–69 Autobook
124 Saloon 1966–1969	..	..	..	Ball	Fiat 124 1966–69 Autobook

FORD

Model				Author	Title
Anglia 100E 1953–1959	..	..	..	Ball	Ford Anglia Prefect 100E Autobook
Anglia 105E 1959–1967	.	..	.	Smith	Ford Anglia 105E, Prefect 107E 1954–67 Autobook
Anglia Super 123E 1962–1967	..	..	.	Smith	Ford Anglia 105E, Prefect 107E 1954–67 Autobook
Capri 109E 1962	..	..	..	Smith	Ford Classic, Capri Autobook One
Capri 116E 1962–1964	..	..	..	Smith	Ford Classic, Capri Autobook One
Classic 109E 1961–1962	..	..	..	Smith	Ford Classic, Capri Autobook One
Classic 116E 1962–1963	..	..	..	Smith	Ford Classic, Capri Autobook One
Consul Mk 1 1950–1956	..	..	..	Ball	Ford Consul, Zephyr, Zodiac 1, 2 1950–62 Autobook
Consul Mk 2 1956–1962	..	..	..	Ball	Ford Consul, Zephyr, Zodiac 1, 2 1950–62 Autobook
Corsair V4 3004E 1965–1969	..	..	..	Smith	Ford Corsair V4 1965–69 Autobook
Corsair V4 GT 1965–1966	..	..	..	Smith	Ford Corsair V4 1965–69 Autobook
Corsair 2000, 2000E 1966–1969	..	..	..	Smith	Ford Corsair V4 1965–69 Autobook
Cortina 113E 1962–1966	..	..	..	Smith	Ford Cortina 1962–66 Autobook
Cortina Super 118E 1963–1966	..	..	..	Smith	Ford Cortina 1962–66 Autobook
Cortina Lotus 125E 1963–1966	..	..	..	Smith	Ford Cortina 1962–66 Autobook
Cortina GT 118E 1963–1966	..	..	..	Smith	Ford Cortina 1962–66 Autobook
Cortina 1300 1967–1969	..	..	..	Smith	Ford Cortina 1967–69 Autobook
Cortina 1500 1967–1969	..	..	..	Smith	Ford Cortina 1967–69 Autobook
Cortina 1600 (including Lotus) 1967–1969	..			Smith	Ford Cortina 1967–69 Autobook
Escort 100E 1955–1959	..	..	..	Ball	Ford Anglia Prefect 100E Autobook
Escort 1100 1967–1970	..	..	..	Ball	Ford Escort 1967–70 Autobook
Escort 1300 1967–1970	..	..	..	Ball	Ford Escort 1967–70 Autobook
Prefect 100E 1954–1959	..	..	..	Ball	Ford Anglia Prefect 100E Autobook
Prefect 107E 1959–61	..	..	..	Smith	Ford Anglia 105E, Prefect 107E 1954–67 Autobook
Popular 100E 1959–1962	..	..	..	Ball	Ford Anglia Prefect 100E Autobook
Squire 100E 1955–1959	..	..	..	Ball	Ford Anglia Prefect 100E Autobook
Zephyr Mk 1 1950–1956	..	..	..	Ball	Ford Consul, Zephyr, Zodiac 1, 2 1950–62 Autobook
Zephyr Mk 2 1956–1962	..	..	..	Ball	Ford Consul, Zephyr, Zodiac 1, 2 1950–62 Autobook
Zephyr 4 Mk 3 1962–1966	..	..	..	Ball	Ford Zephyr, Zodiac Mk 3 1962–66 Autobook
Zephyr 6 Mk 3 1962–1966	..	..	..	Ball	Ford Zephyr, Zodiac Mk 3 1962–66 Autobook
Zodiac Mk 3 1962–1966	..	..	..	Ball	Ford Zephyr, Zodiac Mk 3 1962–66 Autobook
Zodiac Mk 1 1953–1956	..	..	..	Ball	Ford Consul, Zephyr, Zodiac 1, 2 1950–62 Autobook
Zodiac Mk 2 1956–1962	..	..	..	Ball	Ford Consul, Zephyr, Zodiac 1, 2 1950–62 Autobook
Zephyr V4 2 litre 1966–1969	..	..	..	Ball	Ford Zephyr V4, V6, Zodiac 1966–69 Autobook
Zephyr V6 2.5 litre 1966–1969	..	..	..	Ball	Ford Zephyr V4, V6, Zodiac 1966–69 Autobook
Zodiac V6 3 litre 1966–1969	..	..	..	Ball	Ford Zephyr V4, V6, Zodiac 1966–69 Autobook
Capri 1300, 1300 GT 1968–1969	..	..	..	Ball	Ford Capri 1968–69 Autobook
Capri 1600, 1600 GT 1968–1969			..	Ball	Ford Capri 1968–69 Autobook

HILLMAN

Model				Author	Title
Hunter GT 1966–1970	..	..	..	Ball	Hillman Hunter 1966–70 Autobook
Minx Series 1 1956–57	..	..	..	Ball	Hillman Minx 1 to 5 1956–65 Autobook
Minx Series 2 1957–1958	..	..	..	Ball	Hillman Minx 1 to 5 1956–65 Autobook
Minx Series 3 1958–1959	..	..	..	Ball	Hillman Minx 1 to 5 1956–65 Autobook
Minx Series 3A 1959–1960	..	..	..	Ball	Hillman Minx 1 to 5 1956–65 Autobook
Minx Series 3B 1960–1961	..	..	..	Ball	Hillman Minx 1 to 5 1956–65 Autobook

O KAD

Make				Author	Title
Minx Series 3C 1961–1963	..	..	..	Ball	Hillman Minx 1 to 5 1956–65 Autobook
Minx Series 5 1963–1965	..	..	..	Ball	Hillman Minx 1 to 5 1956–65 Autobook
Minx Series 6 1955–1967	..	..	..	Ball	Hillman Minx 1965–67 Autobook
New Minx 1500, 1725 1966–1969	..	..		Ball	Hillman Minx 1966–69 Autobook
Imp 1963–1969	..	..	..	Smith	Hillman Imp 1963–69 Autobook
Husky Series 1 1958–1959	..	..		Ball	Hillman Minx 1 to 5 1956–65 Autobook
Husky Series 2 1960–1963	..	..		Ball	Hillman Minx 1 to 5 1956–65 Autobook
Husky Series 3 1963–1965	..	..		Ball	Hillman Minx 1 to 5 1956–65 Autobook
Super Minx Mk 1 1961–1962		..	..	Ball	Hillman Super Minx 1, 2, 3 1961–65 Autobook
Super Minx Mk 2 1962–1964		..	..	Ball	Hillman Super Minx 1, 2, 3 1961–65 Autobook
Super Minx Mk 3 1964–1965		..	..	Ball	Hillman Super Minx 1, 2, 3 1961–65 Autobook
Super Minx Mk 4 1965–1967		..	..	Ball	Hillman Minx 1965–67 Autobook

HUMBER

Sceptre Mk 2 1965–1967	..	..	..	Ball	Hillman Minx 1965–67 Autobook
Sceptre 1967–70	..	..	..	Ball	Hillman Hunter 1966–70 Autobook

JAGUAR

XK 120 1948–1954	..	..	..	Ball	Jaguar XK 120, 140, 150 Mk 7, 8, 9 1948–61 Autobook
XK 140 1954–1957	..	..	..	Ball	Jaguar XK 120, 140, 150 Mk 7, 8, 9 1948–61 Autobook
XK 150 1957–1961	..	..	..	Ball	Jaguar XK 120, 140, 150 Mk 7, 8, 9 1948–61 Autobook
XK 150S 1959–1961	..	..	..	Ball	Jaguar XK 120, 140, 150 Mk 7, 8, 9 1948–61 Autobook
Mk 7 1950–1954	..	..	..	Ball	Jaguar XK 120, 140, 150 Mk 7, 8, 9 1948–61 Autobook
Mk 7M 1954–1957	..	..	..	Ball	Jaguar XK 120, 140, 150 Mk 7, 8, 9 1948–61 Autobook
Mk 8 1956–1961	..	..	..	Ball	Jaguar XK 120, 140, 150 Mk 7, 8, 9 1948–61 Autobook
Mk 9 1958–1961	..	..	..	Ball	Jaguar XK 120, 140, 150 Mk 7, 8, 9 1948–61 Autobook
2.4 Mk 1 1955–1959	..	..	..	Ball	Jaguar 2.4, 3.4, 3.8 Mk 1, 2 1955–67 Autobook
2.4 Mk 2 1959–1967	..	..	..	Ball	Jaguar 2.4, 3.4, 3.8 Mk 1, 2 1955–67 Autobook
3.4 Mk 1 1957–1960	..	..	..	Ball	Jaguar 2.4, 3.4, 3.8 Mk 1, 2 1955–67 Autobook
3.4 Mk 2 1960–1967	..	..	..	Ball	Jaguar 2.4, 3.4, 3.8 Mk 1, 2 1955–67 Autobook
3.8 Mk 2 1959–1967	..	..	..	Ball	Jaguar 2.4, 3.4, 3.8 Mk 1, 2 1955–67 Autobook
240 1967–1969	..	..	..	Ball	Jaguar 2.4, 3.4, 3.8 Mk 1, 2 1955–67 Autobook
340 1967–1969	..	..	..	Ball	Jaguar 2.4, 3.4, 3.8 Mk 1, 2 1955–67 Autobook
E Type 3.8 1961–1965	..	..	..	Ball	Jaguar E Type 1961–69 Autobook
E Type 4.2 1964–1969	..	..	..	Ball	Jaguar E Type 1961–69 Autobook
E Type 4.2 2+2 1966–1969	..	..	..	Ball	Jaguar E Type 1961–69 Autobook
E Type 4.2 Series 2 1969	..	..	..	Ball	Jaguar E Type 1961–69 Autobook
S Type 3.4 1963–1968	..	..	..	Ball	Jaguar S Type and 420 1963–68 Autobook
S Type 3.8 1963–1968	..	..	..	Ball	Jaguar S Type and 420 1963–68 Autobook
420 1963–1968	..	..	..	Ball	Jaguar S Type and 420 1963–68 Autobook

JOWETT

Javelin PA 1947–1949	..	..	..	Mitchell	Jowett Javelin Jupiter 1947–53 Autobook
Javelin PB 1949–1950	..	..	..	Mitchell	Jowett Javelin Jupiter 1947–53 Autobook
Javelin PC 1950–1951	..	..	..	Mitchell	Jowett Javelin Jupiter 1947–53 Autobook
Javelin PD 1951–1952	..	..	..	Mitchell	Jowett Javelin Jupiter 1947–53 Autobook
Javelin PE 1952–1953	..	..	..	Mitchell	Jowett Javelin Jupiter 1947–53 Autobook
Jupiter Mk 1 SA 1949–1952	..	..	..	Mitchell	Jowett Javelin Jupiter 1947–53 Autobook
Jupiter Mk 1A SC 1952–1953	..	..		Mitchell	Jowett Javelin Jupiter 1947–53 Autobook

MG

TA 1936–1939	..	..	..	Ball	MG TA to TF 1936–55 Autobook
TB 1939	..	..	..	Ball	MG TA to TF 1936–55 Autobook
TC 1945–1949	..	..	..	Ball	MG TA to TF 1936–55 Autobook

Make					Author	Title
TD 1950–1953	..	..	..	..	Ball	MG TA to TF 1936–55 Autobook
TF 1953–1954	..	..	..	..	Ball	MG TA to TF 1936–55 Autobook
TF 1500 1954–1955	..	..	..	..	Ball	MG TA to TF 1936–55 Autobook
Midget 1961–1969	..	..	..	..	Ball	Sprite, Midget 1958–69 Autobook
Magnette ZA, ZB 1955–1959	..	..	..	..	Ball	BMC Autobook Three
Magnette 3, 4 1959–1968	..	..	..	..	Smith	BMC Autobook One
MGA 1500, 1600 1955–1962	..	..	..	..	Ball	MGA, MGB 1955–69 Autobook
MGA Twin Cam 1958–1960	..	..	..	..	Ball	MGA, MGB 1955–69 Autobook
MGB 1962–1969	..	..	..	..	Ball	MGA, MGB 1955–69 Autobook
1100 Mk 1 1962–1967	..	..	..	..	Ball	1100 Mk 1, 1962–67 Autobook
1100 Mk 2 1968	..	..	..	..	Ball	1100 Mk 2, 1300, America 1968–69 Autobook
1300 1968–1969	..	..	..	..	Ball	1100 Mk 2, 1300, America 1968–69 Autobook

MORGAN

Four-wheelers 1936–1969	..	..	..		Clarke	Morgan 1936–69 Autobook

MORRIS

Oxford 2, 3 1956–1959	..	..	..		Ball	BMC Autobook Three
Oxford 5, 6 1959–1969	..	..	..		Smith	BMC Autobook One
Minor Series 2 1952–1956	..	..	..		Ball	Morris Minor 1952–69 Autobook
Minor 1000 1957–1969	..	..	..		Ball	Morris Minor 1952–69 Autobook
Mini 1959–1970	..	..	..		Ball	Mini 1959–70 Autobook
Mini Cooper 1961–1970	..	..	..		Ball	Mini Cooper 1961–70 Autobook
Mini Cooper S 1963–1970	..	..	..		Ball	Mini Cooper 1961–70 Autobook
1100 Mk 1 1962–1967	..	..	..		Ball	1100 Mk 1 1962–67 Autobook
1100 Mk 2 1968–1969	..	..	..		Ball	1100 Mk 2, 1300, America 1968–69 Autobook
1300 1968–1969	..	..	..		Ball	1100 Mk 2, 1300, America 1968–69 Autobook
1800 Mk 1 1966–1968	..	..	..		Ball	1800 Autobook
1800 Mk 2 1968–1969	..	..	..		Ball	1800 Autobook

PEUGEOT

404 1960–1969	..	..	..	..	Ball	Peugeot 404 1960–69 Autobook

RENAULT

R8 956 cc 1962–1967	..	..	..		Ball	Renault R8, R10, 1100 1962–69 Autobook
R8 1108 cc 1966–1969	..	..	..		Ball	Renault R8, R10, 1100 1962–69 Autobook
1100 1108 cc 1964–1969	..	..	..		Ball	Renault R8, R10, 1100 1962–69 Autobook
R10 1108 cc 1967–1969	..	..	..		Ball	Renault R8, R10, 1100 1962–69 Autobook

RILEY

1.5 1957–1965	..	..	..	..	Ball	BMC Autobook Three
4/68 1959–1961	..	..	..	..	Smith	BMC Autobook One
4/72 1961–1969	..	..	..	..	Smith	BMC Autobook One
Elf 1961–1970	..	..	..	..	Ball	Mini 1959–70 Autobook
1100 Mk 1 1965–1967	..	..	..	..	Ball	1100 Mk 1, 1962–67 Autobook
1100 Mk 2 1968	..	..	..	..	Ball	1100 Mk 2 1300, America 1968–69 Autobook
1300 1968–1969	..	..	..	..	Ball	1100 Mk 2, 1300, America 1968–69 Autobook

ROVER

60 1953–1959	..	..	..	..	Ball	Rover 60–110 1953–64 Autobook
75 1954–1959	..	..	..	..	Ball	Rover 60–110 1953–64 Autobook
80 1959–1962	..	..	..	..	Ball	Rover 60–110 1953–64 Autobook
90 1954–1959	..	..	..	..	Ball	Rover 60–110 1953–64 Autobook
95 1962–1964	..	..	..	..	Ball	Rover 60–110 1953–64 Autobook
100 1959–1962	..	..	..	..	Ball	Rover 60–110 1953–64 Autobook
105R 1957–1958	..	..	..	..	Ball	Rover 60–110 1953–64 Autobook
105S 1957–1959	..	..	..	..	Ball	Rover 60–110 1953–64 Autobook
110 1962–1964	..	..	..	..	Ball	Rover 60–110 1953–64 Autobook
2000 SC 1963–1969	..	..	..	..	Ball	Rover 2000 1963–69 Autobook
2000 TC 1963–1969	..	..	..	..	Ball	Rover 2000 1963–69 Autobook

Make				Author	Title

3 litre Saloon Mk 1, 1A 1958–1962	..		..	Ball	Rover 3 litre 1958–67 Autobook
3 litre Saloon Mk 2, 3 1962–1967	..		..	Ball	Rover 3 litre 1958–67 Autobook
3 litre Coupé 1965–1967	..	..	..	Ball	Rover 3 litre 1958–67 Autobook
3500 1968–1970	..	..	..	Ball	Rover 3500, 3500S 1968–70 Autobook
3500S 1968–1970	..	..	..	Ball	Rover 3500, 3500S 1968–70 Autobook

SINGER

Chamois 1964–1969	..		..	Smith	Hillman Imp 1963–69 Autobook
Chamois Sport 1964–1969	..		..	Smith	Hillman Imp 1963–69 Autobook
Gazelle Series 2A to 5 1958–1965	..		..	Ball	Hillman Minx 1 to 5 1956–65 Autobook
Gazelle Series 6 1965–1967	..		..	Ball	Hillman Minx 1965–67 Autobook
New Gazelle 1500, 1725 1966–1969	..		..	Ball	Hillman Minx 1966–69 Autobook
Vogue Series 4 1965–1967	..		..	Ball	Hillman Minx 1965–67 Autobook
New Vogue 1966–1970	..		..	Ball	Hillman Hunter 1966–70 Autobook

SKODA

440, 445, 450 1957–1969	..	..	..	Skoda	Skoda Autobook One

SUNBEAM

Alpine Series 1 1959–1960	..	..	..	Ball	Sunbeam Rapier Alpine 1959–65 Autobook
Alpine Series 2 1960–1963	..	..	..	Ball	Sunbeam Rapier Alpine 1959–65 Autobook
Alpine Series 3 1963–1964	..	..	..	Ball	Sunbeam Rapier Alpine 1959–65 Autobook
Alpine Series 4 1964–1965	..	..	..	Ball	Sunbeam Rapier Alpine 1959–65 Autobook
Alpine Series 5 1965–1967	..	..	..	Ball	Hillman Minx 1965–67 Autobook
Alpine 1969–1970	..	..	..	Ball	Hillman Hunter 1966–70 Autobook
Rapier Series 3 1959–1961	..	..	..	Ball	Sunbeam Rapier Alpine 1959–65 Autobook
Rapier Series 3A 1961–1964	..	..	..	Ball	Sunbeam Rapier Alpine 1959–65 Autobook
Rapier Series 4 1963–1965	..	..	..	Ball	Sunbeam Rapier Alpine 1959–65 Autobook
Rapier Series 5 1965–1967	..	..	..	Ball	Hillman Minx 1965–67 Autobook
Rapier H.120 1967–1970	..	..	..	Ball	Hillman Hunter 1966–70 Autobook
Imp Sport 1963–1969	..	..	..	Smith	Hillman Imp 1963–69 Autobook
Stilletto 1967–1969	..	..	..	Smith	Hillman Imp 1963–69 Autobook

TRIUMPH

TR2 1952–1955	..	..	..	Ball	Triumph TR2, TR3, TR3A 1952–62 Autobook
TR3 1955–1962	..	..	..	Ball	Triumph TR2, TR3, TR3A 1952–62 Autobook
TR3A 1958–1962	..	..	..	Ball	Triumph TR2, TR3, TR3A 1952–62 Autobook
TR4 1961–1965	..	..	..	Ball	Triumph TR4, TR4A 1961–67 Autobook
TR4A 1965–1967	..	..	..	Ball	Triumph TR4, TR4A 1961–67 Autobook
TR5 1967–1969	..	..	..	Ball	Triumph TR5, TR250, TR6 1967–70 Autobook
TR6 1969–1970	..	..	..	Ball	Triumph TR5, TR250, TR6 1967–70 Autobook
TR250 1967–1969	..	..	..	Ball	Triumph TR5, TR250, TR6 1967–70 Autobook
1300 1965–1969	..	..	..	Ball	Triumph 1300 1965–69 Autobook
1300TC 1967–1969	..	..	..	Ball	Triumph 1300 1965–69 Autobook
2000 1963–1969	..	..	..	Ball	Triumph 2000 1963–69 Autobook
Herald 948 1959–1964	..	..	..	Smith	Triumph Herald 1959–69 Autobook
Herald 1200 1961–1969	..	..	..	Smith	Triumph Herald 1959–69 Autobook
Herald 12/50 1963–1967	..	..	..	Smith	Triumph Herald 1959–69 Autobook
Herald 13/60 1967–1969	..	..	..	Smith	Triumph Herald 1959–69 Autobook
Spitfire 1962–1969	..	..	..	Smith	Triumph Spitfire Vitesse 1962–69 Autobook
Vitesse 1600 and 2 litre 1962–1969	..		..	Smith	Triumph Spitfire Vitesse 1962–69 Autobook
GT6 2 litre 1966–1969	..	..	..	Smith	Triumph Spitfire Vitesse 1962–69 Autobook

VANDEN PLAS

3 litre 1959–1964	..	..	..	Ball	BMC Autobook Four
1100 Mk 1 1963–1967	..	..	..	Ball	1100 Mk 1 1962–67 Autobook
1100 Mk 2 1968	..	..	..	Ball	1100 Mk 2, 1300, America 1968–69 Autobook
1300 1968–1969	..	..	..	Ball	1100 Mk 2, 1300, America 1968–69 Autobook

Make	Author	Title

VAUXHALL

	Author	Title
Victor 1 1957–1959	Ball	Vauxhall Victor 1, 2, FB 1957–64 Autobook
Victor 2 1959–1961	Ball	Vauxhall Victor 1, 2, FB 1957–64 Autobook
Victor FB 1961–1964	Ball	Vauxhall Victor 1, 2, FB 1957–64 Autobook
VX 4/90 FBH 1961–1964	Ball	Vauxhall Victor 1, 2, FB 1957–64 Autobook
Victor FC 101 1964–1967	Ball	Vauxhall Victor 101 1964–67 Autobook
VX 4/90 FCH 1964–1967	Ball	Vauxhall Victor 101 1964–67 Autobook
Velox, Cresta PA 1957–1962	Ball	Vauxhall Velox Cresta 1957–69 Autobook
Velox, Cresta PB 1962–1965	Ball	Vauxhall Velox Cresta 1957–69 Autobook
Cresta PC 1965–1968	Ball	Vauxhall Velox Cresta 1957–69 Autobook
Viscount 1966–1969	Ball	Vauxhall Velox Cresta 1957–69 Autobook
Viva HA (including 90) 1964–1966	Ball	Vauxhall Viva HA 1964–66 Autobook
Viva HB (including 90 and SL90) 1966–1969	Ball	Vauxhall Viva HB 1966–69 Autobook
Victor FD 1599cc 1967–1969	Ball	Vauxhall Victor FD 1600, 2000 1967–69 Autobook
Victor FD 1975cc 1967–1969	Ball	Vauxhall Victor FD 1600, 2000 1967–69 Autobook

VOLKSWAGEN

	Author	Title
1200 Beetle 1954–1966	Ball	Volkswagen Beetle 1954–67 Autobook
1200 Karmann Ghia 1955–1965	Ball	Volkswagen Beetle 1954–67 Autobook
1200 Transporter 1954–1964	Ball	Volkswagen Transporter 1954–67 Autobook
1300 Beetle 1965–1967	Ball	Volkswagen Beetle 1954–67 Autobook
1300 Karmann Ghia 1965–1966	Ball	Volkswagen Beetle 1954–67 Autobook
1500 Beetle 1966–1967	Ball	Volkswagen Beetle 1954–67 Autobook
1500 Karmann Ghia 1966–1967	Ball	Volkswagen Beetle 1954–67 Autobook
1500 Transporter 1963–1967	Ball	Volkswagen Transporter 1954–67 Autobook

WOLSELEY

	Author	Title
1500 1959–1965	Ball	BMC Autobook Three
15/50 1956–1958	Ball	BMC Autobook Three
15/60 1958–1961	Smith	BMC Autobook One
16/60 1961–1969	Smith	BMC Autobook One
6/99 1959–1961	Ball	BMC Autobook Four
6/110 1961–1968	Ball	BMC Autobook Four
Hornet 1961–1970	Ball	Mini 1959–70 Autobook
1100 Mk 1 1965–1967	Ball	1100 Mk 1 1962–67 Autobook
1100 Mk 2 1968	Ball	1100 Mk 2, 1300, America 1968–69 Autobook
1300 1968–1969	Ball	1100 Mk 2, 1300, America 1968–69 Autobook